William Bacon Stevens

The Parables of the New Testament Practically Unfolded

William Bacon Stevens

The Parables of the New Testament Practically Unfolded

ISBN/EAN: 9783744793049

Printed in Europe, USA, Canada, Australia, Japan

Cover: Foto ©Lupo / pixelio.de

More available books at **www.hansebooks.com**

THE PARABLES

OF THE

NEW TESTAMENT

PRACTICALLY UNFOLDED.

BY

RT. REV. WM. BACON STEVENS, D.D., LL.D.,

LATE BISHOP OF PENNSYLVANIA.

WITH

PORTRAIT AND SKETCH OF THE AUTHOR.

MEMORIAL EDITION.

PHILADELPHIA:
BRADLEY & COMPANY,
66 NORTH FOURTH STREET.

PREFACE.

This work is designed to be, as its title indicates, a practical unfolding of the Parables of our Lord.

The author has not attempted to give the several explanations which various writers, in different ages, have made of these Parables, for that would require many volumes. Nor has he sought to store up in these pages the treasures of exegetical criticism which, under the minute labours of such men as Cocceius, Storr, Vitringa, Teelman, Ewald, Greswell, and Trench, have been accumulating since the days of Origen and Augustine. Neither has he inlaid his interpretations with those numerous gems of classical lore which tempt the scholar on every hand by the beautiful and pertinent illustrations which they furnish in support of the propriety and truthfulness of these Parables. Such a plan would have made the book more valuable to the student and the theologian, but it would have made it less acceptable to the popular mind, which it has been his special aim to reach, enlighten, and expand.

Waiving all these, he has kept steadily in view his original aim, and believing that there is a deep spiritual meaning in each one of these similitudes, which it becomes us as Christians to know and understand, he has sought to develop this with clearness and fidelity. If he shall be the means of alluring others to a more earnest study of these inimitable Parables, these "apples of gold in pictures of silver," and to a better understanding of their precepts and doctrine, he shall devoutly thank God, and feel that his labour has not been in vain in the Lord.

CONTENTS.

	PAGE
SKETCH OF THE AUTHOR'S LIFE	9
THE PARABLE	13
THE TEN VIRGINS	23
THE UNMERCIFUL SERVANT	37
THE RICH FOOL	55
POUNDS AND TALENTS	71
THE LOST SHEEP: THE LOST MONEY	91
THE PRODIGAL SON	107
THE UNJUST STEWARD	125
THE GOOD SAMARITAN	137
THE PHARISEE AND THE PUBLICAN	155
THE LABOURERS IN THE VINEYARD	177
THE BARREN FIG-TREE	193
THE UNJUST JUDGE: THE IMPORTUNATE FRIEND	207
THE WICKED HUSBANDMEN	227
THE SOWER	241

	PAGE
THE TARES	267
THE MUSTARD SEED	285
THE LEAVEN	297
THE HID TREASURE	307
THE PEARL	317
THE DRAW-NET	325
DIVES AND LAZARUS	339
THE MARRIAGE OF THE KING'S SON: THE GREAT SUPPER	361

SKETCH OF THE AUTHOR'S LIFE.

WILLIAM BACON STEVENS was born in Bath, Maine, on the 13th of July, 1815, and was the son of William and Rebecca Bacon Stevens. Both his parents were descended from ancestors who had distinguished themselves in Revolutionary times, and his father was an officer in the war of 1812. At the close of this war the family settled in Boston, and it was here that the earlier years of the future Bishop were passed.

Study soon became the great pleasure of life to the thoughtful and earnest lad, and he was sent to the Phillips Academy, at Andover, Mass., at which institution he seems to have over-crowded his powers, for his health failed signally, and he was compelled to go to Europe for rest and recuperation. The bent of his mind was scientific; and his was not the disposition to accept tradition blindly and without inquiry. He appears to have been at a loss at first to decide upon the particular line of effort to which he should devote himself, but at last settled down to the study of medicine, and entered Dartmouth College, graduating thence in his twenty-second year with the degree of M. D. The elder Stevens having died in 1825, the son was thrown to a great extent upon his own resources, and was forced to assume responsibilities of a riper age at a time when most boys are free from care. He however met these responsibilities with that bravery and self-confidence which distinguished him in later life; he shirked nothing and went earnestly to work to carve out success in his chosen calling.

It was not long after his graduation from Dartmouth that he went South, fixing his residence at Savannah, Georgia, where his abilities almost immediately made themselves felt. Not only did he establish a large and lucrative practice as a physician, but he was in rapid succession appointed to many important posts in public institutions.

There are indications that Dr. Stevens's mind had for some time been working more and more in the direction of theological inquiry, and ere long his interest led him to a point where the matter appealed to his conscience, and what had been but a field of interesting study became a path which he felt called upon to tread as the paramount duty of his life.

That he sacrificed much in turning away from the enviable position which his abilities had secured him as a physician must be self-evident to any one at all conversant with human nature. He stood at the head of his profession, and was on the rapid road to the attainment of a wide fame and probably large wealth.

Not only this, but his recognized literary qualifications had brought him into prominence in other directions. He had received the appointment of State Historian, and, as one of the organizers of the Georgia Historical Society, had been led into investigations which peculiarly fitted him to discharge the duties of that post. He had begun his "History of the State of Georgia," which is to-day a recognized, if not the highest, authority on the subject, and in many ways gave evidence of a versatility of intellect which promised a brilliant future. But to a man of his conscientiousness, the sentiment of duty must ever be paramount, and in spite of the remonstrances of many sincere friends, Dr. Stevens prepared himself for holy orders, studying under the supervision of the then Bishop of Georgia, the Right Reverend Stephen Elliott, D. D., by whom he was ordained deacon, February 24th, 1843, in Christ Church, Savannah.

Shortly after he went to the University of Georgia, at Athens, where he pursued his studies and was ordained to the priesthood, and in 1844 was elected to the chairs of Belles Lettres and Moral Philosophy in that university, and fulfilled these new duties with great success.

His election as a deputy to the General Convention of 1847, which met in the city of New York, was the event which, perhaps more than any other, shaped the course of his future life and indicated the channels in which his remarkable abilities and tireless energy were to display themselves. Attendance upon that assemblage brought him back to the North; it reintroduced him to the entirely different atmosphere which his long residence in the South had caused him almost to forget. The mental conditions to which he had, in early youth and manhood, accommodated himself were quite other than those which surrounded him in Savannah and at Athens, not necessarily better or higher, but different; the point of view was dissimilar; standards of thought were dissimilar. Dr. Stevens, who had become in a great degree Southern in his methods, now found the atmosphere of his youth congenial to him; and the rapid increase in the number of warm friends and acquaintances which his scholarly powers secured to him, acted as a strong incentive to him to make the North once more his home.

At this juncture, as though in accord with what seemed manifest destiny, Dr. Stevens received a call to the rectorship of Saint Andrew's Church, Philadelphia, to succeed the Rev. Thomas M. Clark (afterwards Bishop of Rhode Island), and, if he had felt any hesitation heretofore, this invitation appeared to be the weight which turned the scale in favor of a Northern residence. The call was accepted and he was instituted to the rectorship by Bishop Potter, August 1st, 1848.

Here his sermons commanded the rapt attention of the most cultured men and women; the polish and incisiveness of his style achieved a reputation which spread far and wide his fame as an orator and dialectician. He rose by sheer force of character and the exhibition of genius of a high order. For more than thirteen years he continued in this field of labor, adding during that period 550 communicants to the church.

He received two degrees in recognition of his worth, namely, from the University of Pennsylvania, that of D. D., and from Union College, Schenectady, that of LL. D.

But incessant devotion to his work again began to tell upon a physical constitution never too strong, and in the year 1857 he went abroad, travelling into Asia Minor, Egypt, and the Holy Land, whence he drew much of that material which was afterwards turned to account in his sermons, discourses and essays.

Not long after Dr. Stevens's return a vacancy was caused in the assistant bishopric of Pennsylvania by the death of Bishop Bowman, and after an exceedingly close election the choice of the diocese fell upon Dr. Stevens, who served as the assistant to Dr. Potter for four years, at which time he succeeded him as diocesan of the State, and entered upon duties of far-reaching and momentous importance.

No man could have assumed those duties with a more lively and prevailing sense of their magnitude. The same energy which we have seen in his other walks of life characterized Bishop Stevens in this wider field; but it was soon found too wide to render it physically possible for him to cover it adequately, and the necessity for a division of the diocese became every day more and more evident. This division was accomplished in 1865, when the Rev. Dr. Kerfoot was chosen Bishop of the diocese of Pittsburgh.

The new diocese of Pittsburgh covered about eighteen thousand square miles and had a population of nearly a million and a half, so that the relief to the Bishop was immediate and substantial. It was, however, found necessary to make a further subdivision, and in 1871 the diocese of Central Pennsylvania was erected, the Rev. Dr. Howe becoming its first Bishop. This Central diocese included all that portion of the State outside of the diocese of Pittsburgh, and not inclusive of Philadelphia, Chester, Delaware, Bucks and Montgomery counties—the latter constituting the Eastern diocese and remaining under the charge of Bishop Stevens.

Ill health now began to interfere with that vigorous discharge of duty which was one of the prominent virtues of the subject of this sketch. In 1868 he had been the victim of a second railroad disaster; the car in which he was travelling from Scranton, Pa., having been derailed and hurled down an embankment thirty feet, into the river below. The Bishop's injuries were so severe that for two months he was confined to his bed, and at the end of that time found his nerves so shattered that his physicians deemed a vacation abroad indispensable.

While abroad Bishop Stevens was in charge of the foreign congregations in communion with the Episcopal Church on the Continent, a position which he only resigned under pressure of increasing infirmity and manifold duties.

He officiated in 1876 at the Centennial Commemoration in Independence Square, Philadelphia, and in 1878 attended the Council of Anglican Bishops at Lambeth Palace, London, over which the Archbishop of Canterbury presided. Bishop Stevens preached the closing sermon of the Conference in Saint Paul's Cathedral, London, July 27th, 1878. He also preached in Westminster Abbey before the Society for Propagating the Gospel, at its one hundred and seventy-seventh anniversary, as well as in Canterbury Cathedral and the Royal Chapel, Savoy; the English prelates seeming desirous of showing him marked respect.

The diocese of Eastern Pennsylvania rose to the highest prosperity and efficiency under Bishop Stevens's administration, and he continued in the active conduct of its affairs until physical infirmities compelled the resignation of most of the active duties to the hands of Bishop Whitaker, who had been elected Assistant Bishop.

For some weeks previous to his death Bishop Stevens had been slowly and surely failing, being sustained only by the wonderful vitality of his constitution; but the end came very peacefully on Saturday morning, June 11th, 1887.

The funeral took place on Wednesday, the 15th, at the Church of the Holy Trinity, Philadelphia, a large body of clergy and laity attending. The services were of the most impressive character. The interment was at the Church of Saint James the Less, at the Falls of Schuylkill.

Bishops Stevens's bibliography includes his discourses before the Georgia Historical Society; a "History of Georgia, from its Discovery by Europeans to the Adoption of its Constitution in 1797;" "*Parables of the New Testament Practically Unfolded;*" "Consolation, the Bow in the Cloud;" "Home Service;" "The Lord's Day, its Obligations and Blessings;" "Past and Present of Saint Andrew's;" besides a number of discourses, essays, sermons, etc., all marked with the power and persuasiveness of their author's personality.

Bishop Stevens was twice married, his first wife being Miss Coppee, of South Carolina, and his second Miss Conyngham, daughter of Judge Conyngham, of Wilkes-Barre. The children by the first marriage were one son, Wm. C. Stevens, now of Chicago; and two daughters, one of whom is the widow of Professor E. C. Mitchell, of Philadelphia, and the other was married to Rev. H. C. Mayer and died some years ago.

The children by the second wife, namely, John and Anna M., are now living.

F. H. W.

TO THE

RIGHT REVEREND STEPHEN ELLIOTT, JR., D. D.,

BISHOP OF THE DIOCESE OF GEORGIA.

My Dear Bishop—

The memory of many years of sweet Christian intercourse; the ties of official relation as parishioner, vestryman, pupil, and presbyter; the sacred associations connected with the laying on of your hands in the rite of Confirmation, and in admission to the Diaconate and the Priesthood, constitute such a claim upon my grateful regard, that I dedicate to you this humble volume, the first fruits of my expository labours. I offer it as a small expression of the love which I bear to you personally, and of the admiration which I entertain for your noble qualities, nobly exercised in the noblest of all human offices.

That your future course may be "as the shining light that shineth more and more unto the perfect day," is the fervent wish of

Your affectionate and grateful friend,

WM. BACON STEVENS.

THE PARABLE.

THE presentation of moral truth in the form of Parables is one of the most ancient as well as one of the most interesting forms of literature.

Parables are found far back in the earliest ages of the world; they exist in most of the cultivated languages of the East; they are used by the poet, the historian, and the philosopher; they are listened to with delight by all classes of people, and, as Jerome has well said, are among the favourite vehicles for the conveyance of moral truth throughout the Oriental world.

Many of these ancient parables are happily couched, and possess both point and beauty. Many of them are picturesque and forcible to a high degree; but a careful study of all merely human parables, from whatever source gathered and by whomsoever uttered, will soon show how superior to them all, in every point, are the Parables of our Lord and Saviour Jesus Christ.

To these Parables we shall confine ourselves, not only because they embody every parabolic excellence, but also, and chiefly, because they present to us by means of a series of exquisitely wrought pictures, the great truths which lie at the foundation of man's salvation from sin, and his final condition beyond the grave.

We have a personal interest in these Parables. There is not one from which we may not gather a personal lesson: for, though addressed to men who lived eighteen centuries ago, yet so analogous are our spiritual wants to theirs, so similar our relations to God, and so applicable to all the phases of humanity, and all the changes of time, with a divinely perpetuated and self-adapted vitality, that they are just as important to the Church now as when first uttered; for they embody truths that cannot die—they illustrate principles that must ever operate on society—they afford directions that are ever needed, and they minister reproof and comfort with as much freshness and pungency to-day as when first uttered by our blessed Lord The study of the Parables, therefore, cannot fail to prove deeply interesting. They are so many portraits of the duties and principles of the Christian religion, and they hang around the four walls of the Gospels of Matthew, Mark, Luke, and John, as pictures drawn by a heavenly artist to embody heavenly truth; and as, in recommending to a young student of sculpture, the statue of Apollo Belvidere as the most perfect specimen of art, the Abbe Winkelman adds, "Go and study it; and if you see no great beauty in it to captivate you, go again; and if you still discover none, go again and again: go until you feel it, for be assured it is there." So we say to the student of the Parables, "go and study these parables, and if you see not their beauty at first, go again and again, gaze at them, ponder upon them, pray over them, until you feel them, then will they impress their lineaments upon your own soul, and be the model of your daily walk and conversation.

The word Parable means a similitude taken from natural things in order to instruct us in things spiritual. It has been defined as a "fictitious narrative, invented for the purpose of conveying truth in a less offensive or more engaging form, than that of direct assertion."

In this respect, the Parable is not unlike the Fable, yet they are essentially distinct. The genuine Fable does not move at all in the field of actual existence. It allows irrational and inanimate things from the kingdom of nature to think, act, speak, and suffer. The Parable derives its material only from within the range of possibility and truth, and from events and scenes that have their likeness in the occurrences of every day life.

"The Parable is constructed to set forth a truth spiritual and heavenly: this the Fable, with all its value, does not do; it is essentially of the earth, and never lifts itself above the earth. It never has a higher aim than to inculcate maxims of prudential morality, industry, caution, foresight; and these it will sometimes recommend even at the expense of the higher self-forgetting virtues."

The Parable also is essentially different from the Allegory. The Allegory is a figurative sentence or discourse, in which the principal subject is described by another subject resembling it in its properties and circumstances.

That exquisite passage in the eightieth Psalm, where

David portrays Israel as a vine which God brought out of Egypt; and that more precious declaration of our Lord in the 15th chapter of St. John, where, alluding to the same natural object, he says, "I am the true vine, and my Father is the husbandman," &c., are specimens of the Allegory, which carries its own interpretation along with it, while the Parable must be interpreted by its author, or by its resemblance to the truths with which it is placed side by side.

Several instances occur in the Bible where the Parable is spoken of as synonymous with the Proverb. The Proverb is a short, condensed sentence, full of pith, and barbed with a distinctive point; the Parable is elaborate, figurative, fictitious, and its meaning lies parallel with the whole current of its narrative.

"Physician, heal thyself" is termed by Luke a Parable: it is in rhetorical strictness a Proverb. The same may be said of other passages of the New Testament. "To sum up all, then, the Parable differs from the fable, moving as it does in a spiritual world, and never transgressing the actual order of things natural,—from the mythus, there being in the latter an unconscious blending of the deeper meaning with the outward symbol, the two remaining separate and separable in the parable,—from the proverb, inasmuch as it is longer carried out, and not merely accidentally and occasionally, but necessarily figurative,—from the allegory, comparing as it does one thing with another, at the same time preserving them apart as an inner and an outer, not transferring, as does the allegory, the properties and qualities and relations of one to the other."

In using Parables as the media of instruction, our blessed Lord conformed to ancient usage and to the constitution of the human mind, which is so much more influenced by the senses than by abstract ideas. Parabolic writing i. naturally adapted to engage attention, is easily comprehended, is suited alike to the lowest and to the loftiest capacity, leaves strong impressions on the mind, gives great force to truth by strikingly personifying it, and enables one to unfold doctrines distasteful to the natural heart by images which attract the mental eye, which convey the truth directly to the soul, before passion and prejudice have time to array themselves against its reception.

This was peculiarly the case in reference to the doctrines which Christ promulged. The Jewish mind was not prepared for their reception—certain truths, such as the bringing in of the Gentiles, the dispersion of the Jews, the abrogation of the temple service, the atonement and death of Christ, the resurrection and ascension, the final judgment, could only be gradually unfolded, and must first be taught in Parables, for had our Lord spoken plainly, the multitude would not so easily have listened to his words; but being insensibly drawn by the happy incidents, the touches of history, the beautiful illustration, to hear his discourses, they were taught many doctrines and truths to which their hearts would have offered malignant resistance had they been conveyed in any other form.

The perfection of the Parables of Christ is evident to

the most casual observer. They are perfect and inimitable models, "apples of gold in baskets of silver."

There is nothing superfluous, nothing meretricious; each is a picture to the mind's eye, complete in all its lights and shades, and perfect in its groupings and design.

With reference to the Parables, we may say what Luther does of the Bible at large, that "it is a garden of God, with many a lovely tree laden with lordly fruit; and that, often as he had shaken the boughs and received the delicious fruit into his bosom, yet had he ever found new fruit when he had searched and shaken them anew."

Admirably, then, did our Lord adapt his instructions to the mental and moral necessities of his hearers; and we might appeal to his Parables alone, in proof of the divinity of his mission.

The fables and allegories of the heathen world, were interwoven with their fictitious history, with their debasing mythologies, with their poetic extravagancies, and were designed to support that idolatry and polytheism which it was the object of the gospel to destroy. The moral instruction, if any was intended, must be dug out from the rubbish of poetical images and superstitious conceits. A very slight comparison of the abstruse allegories of Plato, the monstrous fables of the Jewish Talmud or the Asiatic Vishnu, with the Parables of the gospel, will suffice to show, that while delicacy, wit, virtue, truth, are continually violated in the former; purity, elegance, pathos, point, and sublime power are found in the latter. The former, like the ignes fatui, are born in the foul fens and marshes of man's depraved nature, and are earthly, sensual, devilish; the latter, like the guiding pillar of fire in the camp of the Israelites, is heavenly, spiritual, and divine.

But a quality which distinguishes them above all other parables, is the universality of their application, and the perfect, real value of their instruction. In their original delivery, they were wisely adapted to the people and the time at which, and for whom, they were spoken. Yet they are equally valuable now, and in all parts of the world, "for doctrine, for reproof, for correction, for instruction in righteousness." They never weary the mind, never become distasteful to the soul, never grow old and obsolete, never lose their force or beauty; but will ever be read with delight, ever be studied with interest, and ever be esteemed the most precious as well as most beautiful and instructive passages of God's Holy Word.

The Ten Virgins

THE TEN VIRGINS.

"THEN shall the kingdom of heaven be likened unto ten virgins, which took their lamps, and went forth to meet the bridegroom. And five of them were wise, and five were foolish. They that were foolish took their lamps, and took no oil with them; but the wise took oil in their vessels with their lamps. While the bridegroom tarried, they all slumbered and slept. And at midnight there was a cry made, Behold the bridegroom cometh; go ye out to meet him. Then all those virgins arose, and trimmed their lamps. And the foolish said unto the wise, Give us of your oil; for our lamps are gone out. But the wise answered, saying, Not so; lest there be not enough for us and you: but go ye rather to them that sell, and buy for yourselves. And while they went to buy, the bridegroom came; and they that were ready went in with him to the marriage: and the door was shut. Afterward came also the other virgins, saying, Lord, Lord, open to us. But he answered and said, Verily I say unto you, I know you not. Watch therefore; for ye know neither the day nor the hour wherein the Son of man cometh."

MATT. XXV. 1-13.

THE simple diction, the attractive similitudes, and the solemn moral of this parable, invest it with peculiar interest. Many ancient and modern writers have attempted to compose like allegories, but in elegance, fitness, and didactic force, they fall far below this parable of our Lord. Witness, for example, the following by Rabbi Jochanan ben Zaccai, who lived in the century before Christ: "A certain king invited his servants to a feast, but did not fix any time for them to come. Those of them who were wary and prudent adorned themselves and sat at the gate of the king's house, but those of them that were fools went and did their work, and said, Is there any work without trouble?

"On a sudden the king inquired after his servants; the wise went in before him as they were adorned, but the fools went in before him as they were, filthy and soiled.

"The king rejoiced at meeting the wise, but was angry at meeting the foolish, and ordered that those who had adorned themselves for the feast should sit and eat, and those who had not adorned themselves should stand."

This, however, as well as other parables in the Talmuds, lack many of the essential points which distinguish those recorded in the Gospel.

We are here introduced into the stirring and picturesque scenes of an oriental marriage.

The nuptial ceremony in the East is always one of display and often magnificence, is full of excitement, and marked by many peculiar customs, an understanding of which is necessary to a full appreciation of this beautiful parable.

These marriage festivals lasted sometimes several days, but the period of greatest public interest was that when the bridegroom conducted his bride from her parent's house to her future home. This was usually done at night, when the parties, accompanied by their respective friends, joined in glad procession, and the scene, lit up by countless torches, and enlivened by choral songs or instrumental music, was peculiarly exciting and delightful. The custom still pre vails in Asiatic countries, and we have been present at an Eastern wedding, where the ceremonies observed corresponded very much to those here described. We well remember the moving lamps glittering like so many fireflies in the darkness; the strains of music varying in volume, in measure, in expression, yet mostly jubilant; the advancing procession, the shout of those stationed at the bridegroom's house, as the head of the nuptial column came in sight, "behold the bridegroom cometh!" and the expressions of joy and hilarity which lighted up every countenance and animated every heart, and while beholding this scene we felt, as we had never before done, the force and fidelity as well as emphasis of the Parable of the Ten Virgins.

The design of this parable is to enforce Christian watchfulness; and nothing could more aptly illustrate its necessity than the felicitous similitude here employed.

By "the kingdom of heaven" is meant the state of things under the gospel dispensation; by the "virgins," the members of Christ's church, the professors of his religion, who should be like virgins in the purity and innocence of their lives and conversation.

The number ten was doubtless mentioned because it was a favourite one among the Jews. According to the Mishna, a congregation consisted of ten persons, and less than that number did not make one; and whenever there were ten persons in a place they were obliged to build a synagogue. With less than ten men they did not divide the Shema, i. e. "Hear, O Israel," &c., nor did the messenger of the congregation go before the ark to pray, nor did the priest lift up the hands to bless the people, &c., &c. The Lamps represent the profession of godliness, the Bridegroom is Christ, his Spouse the Church.

The words rendered respectively "wise" and "foolish," mean, the former: sensible, prudent, having sagacity and discernment; and the latter: dull, sluggish and slow, evidencing the lack of those very qualities which make up the character of the wise; and the wisdom and folly of each five was seen in the fact mentioned by our Lord, "That they that were foolish took their lamps and took no oil with them; but the wise took oil in their vessels with their lamps."

The obscure ideas which this passage conveys to an English reader is made clear by a recurrence to Eastern customs. Rabbi Jarchi says that it was the custom in the land of Ishmael to bring the bride from her father's house to her husband's in the night, and to carry before her about ten staves. Upon the top of each staff was the form of a brazen dish, and in the midst of it pieces of garments, oil, and pitch, which they set on fire: holding these in one hand, they carry in the other a vessel full of oil, with which they replenish from time to time their else useless lamps.

The having or not having "Oil in their vessels with their lamps," is the hinge upon which turns the whole moral of the parable.

Many and very diverse have been the interpretations given of this emblem; and many a controversial battle has been fought upon this narrow verse.

Looking only at the animus of the parable, and the circumstances under which it was uttered, we feel warranted in saying, that while the "lamps" represent the outward profession of religion, the "oil in their vessels with their lamps," signifies the grace of God in the heart, by which only true religion can be nurtured and sustained; for wherever the spirit of Christ is not, there, of course, is an absence of that oil of grace by which the professor can become "a burning and a shining light."

Taking then the wise and foolish virgins as exponents respectively of true and false professors of religion, let us notice first the points of resemblance between them. They were both virgins in name and character, outwardly unimpeachable and chaste in conduct. They were both attendant on the bridegroom, had received and obeyed the external calling which enrolled them as his attendants. They were both invited to the marriage-feast, and had held out before them the bliss of that festive occasion, when they should sit down with the bridegroom at the nuptial supper. They both had lamps, the outward signs and evidences of being attendant on the bridegroom, the symbols of a professing faith. They both, while the bridegroom tarried, slumbered and slept; relapsed from a watchful into a careless, nodding, sleeping condition. They both arose at the midnight cry, "Go ye out to meet him," and "trimmed their lamps," to comply with the summons.

So with regard to true and false professors. They are all nominal Christians, visible and outward attendants on the bridegroom Christ. They have all the lamp of a holy profession, and maintain the same general character for virgin purity; they are strict in the performance of all moral duties, constant in their attendance on the house of God, give, perhaps liberally, for the support of the Gospel, manifest much zeal for Christ, and bear towards men the form and visage of true devotion. These are some of the points wherein the true and the false professor agree; they travel thus far in the same visible path, and the eye of the world cannot, up to this point, detect any difference. But to the eye of Him who seeth in secret, there is a marked and eternal dissimilarity; for, secondly, the points of dissimilarity, though not so numerous as those of resemblance, are very distinct and significant. The wise virgins had taken oil in their vessels with their lamps, but the foolish virgins neglected this precaution, and when the first flame of enthusiasm or mental fervour was burnt out, they had no supply of grace to sustain the light of life.

They differed also in the fact that, while, at the midnight cry, the lamps of the wise virgins were still burning, and only needed "trimming," the lamps of the foolish had altogether "gone out." Consequently, while the one class was prepared to go out to meet the bridegroom, the other was embarrassed and unprepared. The midnight hour was no time wherein to buy the needed oil; and, though they attempted to repair their indiscretion, it was too late. The wise virgins, joining the procession with trimmed and burning lamps, passed on in the bridegroom's train, and "the door was shut."

The broad difference thus indicated still exists between the sincere Christian and the hypocrite.

The lamps of the false professor often go out in this life, when they who have begun in the spirit end in the flesh, and they break out perhaps into open apostacy. How often, in the language of Job, is "the candle of the wicked" thus "put out," for they have not, with the lamp of profession, a heart filled with the oil of grace. This oil of grace, lodged in the heart, is the sole replenisher of the lamp of profession. Each Christian's heart must be like the bowl of the golden candlestick which Zechariah saw in vision in the Sanctuary, wherein was kept the oil—pure—costly—elaborately prepared, which, through golden pipes, "fed the seven lamps on the top thereof." Every lamp of the Christian profession must draw its oil through these golden pipes of the Sanctuary, and from this golden bowl, filled with the oil of God's spirit. That life of outward devotion, of external profession, which is not daily fed by the indwelling grace of the Holy Ghost, is a foolish virgin's lamp. It will do while they slumber and sleep, but will fill them with sore dismay when the cry shall be made at midnight: "Behold the Bridegroom cometh; go ye out to meet him!" when they shall discover—alas! too late—that they have "no oil in their vessels with their lamps."

Such being the points of similarity and dissimilarity between the wise and foolish virgins, we turn to examine the respective results in the case of each.

The wise virgins, though sleeping when the midnight cry was heard, "arose, and trimmed their lamps," and were soon in a condition to go out and meet the bridegroom. Joining the nuptial procession, they moved along to the bridegroom's house, and " went in with him to the marriage." The others, like the wise virgins, arose and trimmed their lamps, but having no oil wherewith to replenish them, sought to borrow some of their sister virgins, and failing in this, " went to buy" some of those that sold. While thus engaged, the bridegroom came; the procession moved on; the wise virgins passed in to the feast; and when afterward the other virgins came, they found the streets dark and deserted, and when they reached the bridegroom's house, " the door was shut." In vain they cried, " Lord, Lord, open to us!" His reply was, " I know you not." It was dark; he could not see their faces, and he might perhaps have thought that it was part of a marauding band, thus feigning the character and the voices of his chosen attendants, and seeking to enter his house, and break up the festal scene.

In like manner will the false professors fail to gain admittance to the marriage-supper of the Lamb in Heaven. Lacking the oil of grace, they will not be able to join with the bridegroom's train; and when in despair they besiege the ear of God with the cry, " Lord, Lord, open unto us," they will find the door shut, and will hear the voice of the Heavenly Bridegroom saying from within, " I know you not." There is no entreaty that will then avail—the virgin chasteness of an outward morality; the lamp of a once bright profession; the companionship of the wise virgins; will each be worthless. What is needed at that midnight hour, and to gain an entrance through that open door to the marriage-feast, is, the burning lamp fed with the oil of grace, and shining out in the holy faith and pious works of one made "wise" by the renewing of the Holy Ghost.

The Lord Jesus gives us the moral of this parable in the words, "Watch, therefore, for ye know neither the day nor the hour wherein the Son of Man cometh."

Watchfulness is an essential requisite of Christian character; and this watchfulness must be exercised in reference to things within and things without. We must watch the affections of the heart, their character, their direction, their force; we must watch the operations of our minds, their motions, thought, imaginations; we must watch the outgoing desires of our soul, their aim, their tendency, their exciting cause; we must watch also our outward temptations, the snares spread for our feet, the wiles of the adversary, and the manifold arts and transformations whereby he lays in wait to deceive.

If it be true in politics, where we have but human enemies to contend with, that the price of liberty "is eternal vigilance;" much more in religion, where we wrestle not against "flesh and blood, but against principalities, against powers, against the rulers of the darkness of this world," is it true that the price of eternal life is unrelaxing watchfulness.

The unwatching, will soon be a conquered Christian.

The Christian's lamp needs daily replenishing from the fountain of all light. The oil of grace needs daily renewal; it must be daily sought for at the mercy seat; for, if the

Holy Spirit's beams are quenched, there is no relighting of his lamp, and no going in to the marriage.

Especially is there a necessity for this constant preparation to meet the Bridegroom, in view of the uncertainty of the time when He will appear.

That "He will come and will not tarry," is a revealed and certain truth: but when He will come; the week, the day, the hour; we know not. How He will come, suddenly or slowly, at home or abroad, with lingering disease or unforeseen accident, we know not; hence the necessity of being always prepared, of having our lamps always "trimmed," and of having "oil in our vessels with our lamps," that when the summons comes we may be prepared to obey it, and go in unto the marriage supper of the Lamb in heaven.

There are, then, in the visible church, such persons as correspond in character to the "foolish virgins;" and it becomes us then to mark well the points wherein they are deficient, and seek, where only it can be found, at the throne of grace, for that wisdom which is liberally given of God, that fear of the Lord which is the beginning of wisdom, and by which we are made "wise" unto everlasting life.

There is, then, such a thing, as an oilless lamp. Many such are carried by the professed attendants of the Bridegroom, Christ; and it behooves us to see to it that there is oil in our vessels, the oil of grace, as without it we have but "a name to live and are dead."

There is, then, to be heard a midnight cry. "Behold

the Bridegroom cometh, go ye out to meet Him!" and we must see to it that we arise and trim our lamps, that Death surprise us not in our slumber, and find us unprepared for the summons that must soon ring upon our ears.

There will be found, at last, by every possessor of a lamp which has "gone out," an unopened door and a rebuking Saviour; and it is of the utmost importance that we should diligently seek every needed preparation, so that we may go in with the Bridegroom to the marriage supper, and not come at the last, after fruitless effort to buy the oil of grace at human shambles, amidst the unillumined darkness of the midnight of death, to that unopened door, only to hear from within, in response to our knocks, and our cry "Lord, Lord, open unto us," the stern rebuff, "Verily I say unto you, I know you not."

That we may, therefore, avoid the doom of the foolish virgins, and secure the position of the wise, let us give all diligence to our Lord's injunction, "Watch, therefore, for ye know neither the day nor the hour when the Son of Man cometh."

The Unmerciful Servant.

THE UNMERCIFUL SERVANT.

"Therefore is the kingdom of heaven likened unto a certain king, which would take account of his servants. And when he had begun to reckon, one was brought unto him, which owed him ten thousand talents. But forasmuch as he had not to pay, his lord commanded him to be sold, and his wife, and children, and all that he had, and payment to be made. The servant therefore fell down, and worshipped him, saying, Lord, have patience with me, and I will pay thee all. Then the lord of that servant was moved with compassion, and loosed him, and forgave him the debt. But the same servant went out, and found one of his fellow servants, which owed him a hundred pence: and he laid hands on him, and took him by the throat, saying, Pay me that thou owest. And his fellow servant fell down at his feet, and besought him, saying, Have patience with me, and I will pay thee all. And he would not: but went and cast him into prison, till he should pay the debt. So when his fellow servants saw what was done, they were very sorry, and came and told unto their lord all that was done. Then his lord, after that he had called him, said unto him, O thou wicked servant, I forgave thee all that debt, because thou desiredst me: shouldest not thou also have had compassion on thy fellow servant, even as I had pity on thee? And his lord was wroth, and delivered him to the tormentors, till he should pay all that was due unto him. So likewise shall my heavenly Father do also unto you, if ye from your hearts forgive not every one his brother their trespasses." MATT. XVIII. 23–35.

THIS parable, which Bishop Porteus says "is one of the most interesting and affecting that is to be found either in Scripture or in any of the most admired writers of antiquity," was drawn from our Saviour by the inquiry of St. Peter—"Lord, how oft shall my brother sin against me, and I forgive him?"

In a conversation with his disciples, just before, our Lord had directed what course to pursue in reference to trespasses, and in what way to seek redress of our grievances. The subject arrested the attention of Peter. The duties enjoined and the precepts delivered by Christ, were new, striking, important. Peter was anxious for more information, and for some specific rule. He knew, doubtless, that the rabbinical law of forgiveness said, that "three offences were to be remitted, but not the fourth," and putting what, perhaps, he supposed an extreme case, he asks if he shall forgive his brother "until seven times?" thus doubling the number which the Talmud required him to pardon. To this question Christ promptly answers, "I say not unto thee until seven times, but until seventy times seven;" thus inculcating a breadth of forgiveness widely removed from the narrow law of the Rabbins on the one hand, or the supposed liberality of Peter on the other.

But our Lord did not design to affix any definite limit to the number of offences which it was our duty to forgive. Seven, as is well known, was, among the Hebrews, a number representing perfection, and therefore is frequently used in the Scriptures to denote frequency, fullness, multitude; so that, to forgive "seven times" means to forgive many times, but to forgive "seventy times seven" expresses the full and perfect forgiveness which should be manifested towards all offenders.

Here, then, was the utterance of a great and heaven-born principle—the unlimited forgiveness of injuries! and to illustrate this principle on a scale commensurate with its real greatness, our Lord related the parable of "The Unmerciful Servant."

In this parable "a certain king" is represented as taking "account of his servants," or fiscal ministers, to whom were committed the farming and collecting of his royal revenues. He had scarcely "begun to reckon," before his attention was drawn to one who "owed him ten thousand talents." When he "was brought unto him," it was found that he had not wherewith to pay, being hopelessly bankrupt. He was evidently a tributary prince or treasurer, in whose custody were placed the revenues of the realm, and who had abused the confidence of the king by appropriating to himself "ten thousand talents." This amount, even taking the talent at its lowest value, was more than equal to the enormous sum of fifteen millions of dollars, and evinces, at once, the elevated dignity to which this servant of the king was raised, and the boldness of the peculation which he attempted on the royal exchequer.

Confessing his inability to pay, the king, termed here "his lord," because, in those countries, all subjects, from the lowest to the highest, were the virtually owned servants of the monarch, "commanded him to be sold, and his wife, and children, and all that he had, and payment to be made." This severe penalty for insolvency was one often used in the East, as is testified to by sacred and profane writers; and, even in the Roman law, wife and children being part of the father's possessions, were sold with him into slavery when he could not pay his debts.

As soon, however, as he learns the order of his king, and

knowing the miserable servitude into which it will plunge him—an abasement the more galling because of the height from which he fell—he falls down, and, in oriental fashion, "worships him"—prostrating himself upon his face before him—"saying, Lord, have patience with me, and I will pay thee all." Touched with the abject misery of the suppliant, and feeling in his own heart the relentings of compassion, the king orders his fettered prisoner to be loosed; revoked the sentence which consigned him to the auction-mart of the slave; restored to him his wife, his children, his goods; and "forgave him the debt."

What a sense of relief must that wretched criminal have experienced as the word "forgive" fell upon his ear! What a change in his condition—from a prostrate, condemned beggar, ordered out for sale, with his wife and children, to freedom, wealth, and happiness! Yet his subsequent conduct proved how unworthy he was of this royal clemency; for, as the sacred narrative leads us to infer, he had scarcely gone out from the presence of his king, relieved of his onerous debt, when he met "one of his fellow servants," who "owed him a hundred pence," or about fifteen dollars; and, instead of being softened by the mercy which he had experienced, he lays violent hands on him, and "took him by the throat, saying, Pay me that thou owest." The action of prostration, the plea for patience, and the promise eventually to pay all, which he had just made to his king, is now made by his fellow servant to himself; there is an identity of act and language, in order to give greater force to the unforgiving nature of this imperious creditor. Though that abasement and plea found mercy *for* him, it obtains no mercy *from* him. One would have supposed, that touching that tender chord would have procured at once a compassionate response; that the hundred pence would at once have been forgiven, in view of the ten thousand talents remitted by his lord. But no! Avarice is deaf, and cannot hear; blind, and cannot see; heartless, and cannot feel. It has no bowels of mercy, no finely strung sympathies; it is relentless in its grasp, cruel in its aims; and the horse-leech cry of its insatiate appetite is "give! give!"

To get gain, it will steal from the treasuries of kings, or grind the face of the poor; it will wrench open the clenched hand of penury for its uttermost farthing, and wring from the widowed mother the pittance which gives her children their daily bread. Of all such oppressors God declares, "they have swallowed down riches, and shall vomit them up again; he shall suck the poison of asps; the viper's tongue shall slay him; that which he laboured for he shall restore, according to his substance shall the restitution be, and he shall not rejoice therein. In the fulness of his sufficiency he shall be in straits; every hand of the wicked shall come upon him." And this is but part of that remarkable portraiture of a wicked, grasping, avaricious man, drawn at such full length in the book of Job.

Refusing to listen to the cry of his fellow servant, the heartless creditor "went and cast him into prison until he should pay the debt." This conduct was soon reported to the king, who, indignant at his course, ordered him into his presence, and, addressing him in stern and angry words, said, "Oh, thou wicked servant, I forgave thee all that debt because thou desiredst me; shouldst not thou also have had compassion on thy fellow servant, even as I had pity on thee?" Well might the king be "wroth;" and, with a justice which commended itself to every observer, he revoked his cancellation of the debt, and "delivered him to the tormentors, until he should pay all that was due unto him." He merited his doom by his avarice, and he brought it upon himself by his extortion.

Having thus shown the injustice of this man's proceeding, and the iniquity of an unforgiving spirit, Christ draws the moral—"So likewise shall my Heavenly Father do also unto you, if ye from your hearts forgive not every one his brother their trespasses."

The design then of the parable is to teach us forgiveness of injuries, and the Christian grounds of it. The doctrine of heathen philosophers on the subject of forgiveness of injuries, was altogether vague and unsatisfactory. Some, indeed, as Plato, Maximus Tyrius, Epictetus, and Marcus Antoninus, commend clemency; but others, of equal name and learning, as Aristotle, Cicero, Democritus, held revenge to be a duty, and forgiveness of injuries to be a narrow-minded weakness. Cicero, in his "Offices," gives it as the character of a good man, "that he does good to those whom it is in his power to serve, and hurts no man unless he be provoked by an injury." Many modern infidels have followed in the track of ancient moralists. Bayle declares that the precept prohibiting revenge "is contrary to the law of nature," and Tindal goes so far as to make the doctrine of forgiving injuries an objection to the Gospel. It was important, therefore, that there should be some divine and immutable legislation on this subject, so that the world would know the truth, and have before it a certain guide. This great want the Lord Jesus supplied, not only by the delivery of this parable, but in various other passages, in a manner at once clear, full, and authoritative.

Let us examine, then, the basis on which this doctrine rests, and the arguments by which it is sustained. The foundation of this virtue is the revealed fact, that God has announced himself as a sin-pardoning God. Had there been no forgiveness in the Divine mind, there could have been none in the human, for while the vices of men are self-begotten, their virtues are in every instance copies in miniature of some of God's perfections. Hence the whole superstructure of forgiveness of injuries, and of loving our enemies, is built upon those unfoldings of the Divine character, which represent Him as a God, pardoning iniquity and showing mercy to the unrighteous. It was necessary that this trait should first be seen in Him, that He should pattern it forth in His own acts, and illustrate its workings in His own dealings with the sinful and the rebellious; for how should we know what it was, or how it was to be exercised, had we not previously beheld it in operation; or how could we have been commanded to exercise a virtue which God had not himself manifested in nature or revelation? But He has not thus required of us a moral impossibility. How He has forgiven, is admirably set forth in this parable; and the relations between ourselves, as debtors, and God, as a merciful creditor, are there strikingly illustrated.

We are debtors to God in sums beyond our ability to pay; we owe him love, obedience, faith, and the duties of a Christian life; we owe him our minds, our souls, our bodies; and when He calls us before Him to take an account of us, He finds us in arrears to the full extent of the Law, which we have not obeyed, and of the salvation which we have rejected, so that as he "who offendeth in one point of the Law, is guilty of all;" and as he who is not with Christ, "is against him," it follows that we are moral insolvents, owing more than ten thousand talents of service, yet unable to pay down the first instalment of spiritual duty. He has called upon us to "bring all the tithes into the store-house," tithes of Christian offerings and devotion,—and we have brought none. He has given us talents, with the injunction, "occupy till I come"—and we have gracelessly "wrapped them in a napkin," or buried them in the earth. He has called to us, "give an account of thy stewardship"—and we have stood before him, speechless bankrupts.

Could we fully obey God's law, we should then fully pay all our moral indebtedness to Him, for, in the words of the Prophet, "what doth the Lord require of thee but to do justly, and to love mercy, and to walk humbly with thy God?" He who keeps God's law does all this; hence he who keeps the law does all that God requires, and cannot therefore become a debtor.

But, as each act of disobedience, each failure in duty, each moment's continuance in a state of rebellion, is a debt, a perpetually accumulating debt, not one item of which can we, of ourselves, pay, and which, aggregated, are faintly represented by the ten thousand talents of the parable, so do we find ourselves in the condition of this servant, brought into the presence of our Lord, with a perfectly uncancellable debt, threatening us with its impending woe. If we cannot balance our accounts with God, He will, He must, if He is true to Himself and just in His moral government, require us to make up our delinquencies, "even to the uttermost farthing;" and, as we cannot pay all that is due unto Him, so must He visit our defaulting souls with the punishment due to such great transgressors.

This punishment is everlasting ruin, to be sold, not as the Jewish law directed, for six years only, but for ever; and thus made the slaves of the Prince of Darkness, with no year of release at hand, no jubilee of emancipation in prospect. The language of the Bible in reference to every unrenewed man is, that "he is sold under sin," that he is "a servant of iniquity;" for, "know ye not," says the Apostle, "that, to whom ye yield yourselves servants to obey, his servants ye are whom ye obey, whether of sin unto death, or of righteousness unto holiness?" In this condition of bankruptcy and servitude lay the whole human race; and had God, like an inexorable creditor, refused to forgive us our debt, we should, even now, be under the hand of tormentors, and yet without any hope of paying what was due unto him.

But this was not like God. He was a God of mercy, as well as justice; and in His counsels purposed to "deliver from curse and damnation those whom He hath chosen in Christ out of mankind, and to bring them by Christ to everlasting salvation, as vessels made to honour." To this end Christ became incarnate of the Virgin Mary—"God manifest in the flesh"—taking upon him the sinner's nature; standing in the sinner's place; and "by the one oblation of himself, once offered, made a full, perfect, and sufficient sacrifice, oblation, and satisfaction for the sins of the whole world;" so that now forgiveness of sin is proclaimed to mankind, a forgiveness which is bestowed freely, and without price, upon all who believe in the Lord Jesus Christ, and who make him the alone hope of their salvation. The greatness of this act of forgiveness we can never know this side the eternal world, because we can never, here, fully measure the malignity of the sins which we have committed, and the dreadfulness of the curse which has been remitted, and the blessedness of state to which, through this forgiveness of sins, we are to be introduced. These elements, which enter into a consideration of the munificence of God in pardoning our debts, are but faintly understood here; but in the world to come, where we shall see sin in its full deformity, and the curse in its direful reality, and the bliss of heaven in its unspeakable glory, then shall we know somewhat of the infinite grace and mercy which God manifested when he was "moved with compassion" toward us, and "loosed" us from the bondage of death, and "forgave us the debt." Its consideration will fill us with ever-increasing praise and wonder; its greatness will loom up more and more clearly; the mercy of God will develop its riches with a perpetually growing glory; and, as the great cycles of eternity turn upon the axles of love, we shall still discover new grace, new grandeur, new cause of thanksgiving that there was with God forgiveness of sin, that the ten thousand talents of man's indebtedness to His holy law have been remitted, and guilty mortals were now, through the payment of this debt by our Divine Substitute and Surety, made "kings and priests unto God."

It is this forgiveness, divine in its nature, eternal in its duration, world-wide in its compass, and unchangeable in its operation, which is the basis on which rests the superstructure of what we term the virtue of forgiving the trespasses of our fellow men.

The arguments by which we enforce and sustain this virtue have great force and authority, and may be reduced to two general heads, viz., those which are derived from our relations to God, and those which spring from our relation to our fellow men.

Beginning with this lower argument, we find a forgiving spirit is that by which we most secure the love and favour of our fellow men. We are all erring creatures; we daily offend in word or deed, designedly or undesignedly, against those around us; and as, if each of our offences was severely judged and rigidly condemned, we should be for ever miserable, and the sweet amenities of life would be altogether lost, so must we be ever ready to forgive others; for he who makes haste to take his fellow servant by the throat, with the inexorable demand, " pay me that thou owest," will be most likely to meet with the same rough treatment himself. The uncommiserating, unforgiving man is generally uncommiserated and unforgiven. There is always a fearful reaction to the outgoings of hatred and revenge. There is a return tide which washes back upon the heart the evils that flowed from it; and it often rolls in upon the soul with aggravated power.

Surely we are too frail ourselves to act rigidly towards the frailties of our fellows. We too much need forgiveness to be ourselves unforgiving; and the cultivation or manifestation of a relentless spirit is sure to bring down upon us the unpitying vengeance of those among whom we dwell. So that policy, pride, self-love, personal comfort, social position, and other even selfish motives, combine to press upon us this important yet too much neglected duty; for the experience of the world confirms the truth uttered by St. James, "He shall have judgment without mercy that hath showed no mercy."

Rising to those higher motives derived from our relations to God, we find that the forgiveness of injuries done to others, is one of the conditions of our salvation. This truth is clearly established by God's Holy Word. In the sermon on the mount, our Lord declares, "If ye forgive men their trespasses, your Heavenly Father will also forgive you; but if ye forgive not men their trespasses, neither will your Father forgive your trespasses." On another occasion he instructed His disciples, "When ye stand praying, forgive if ye have aught against any, that your Father also which is in heaven may forgive you your trespasses; but if ye do not forgive, neither will your Father which is in heaven forgive your trespasses;" and on yet another occasion he exhorted them, saying, "Forgive, and ye shall be forgiven; for with what measure ye mete it shall be measured to you again." Were anything more necessary to establish this point, it is found in the last verse of this parable, where punishments condign and ignominious are threatened if we do not "from our hearts" forgive every "one his brother their trespasses." These passages, every one of which fell from the lips of Christ himself, prove demonstrably that one of the conditions on which we receive salvation is forgiveness of others in the injuries which they have done to our persons, our names, and our estates; and that this forgiveness must be not of the lips, not in professions merely, but "from the heart;" and will be judged of by Him "who searcheth the hearts and trieth the reins of the children of men." And as we cannot begin the Christian life without taking this initial step, so neither when once taken, can we continue it under any other condition. There can be no sanctification in the heart that is filled with strife and anger. The Holy Ghost is a spirit of peace, of love, of unity, and He cannot tabernacle with discord and anger; and whatever then drives away the Sanctifier, or neutralizes His influence, hinders our sanctification; and, consequently, we can never, so long as He is absent from the heart, "be made meet for the inheritance of the saints in light." Let no one who harbours an unforgiving spirit pretend to say, I am a Christian. St. John has denounced such as liars; for, says this "beloved disciple," "if he love not his brother whom he hath seen, how can he love God whom he hath not seen?"

In looking at this subject in the light of our relations to God, we further discover that an unforgiving spirit not only will destroy the grace of God within us, but will turn our prayers into invocations of wrath. Our daily prayer is, "forgive us our debts or trespasses, *as* we forgive our debtors, or those who trespass against us," *i. e.*, we pray that God would forgive us, just in proportion as we forgive others. If we forgive others wholly, we pray that we may be wholly forgiven; if we forgive but little, we pray that we may be forgiven little; if we forgive none, we pray that we may not be forgiven. What a fearful prayer! To go upon our knees, to clasp our hands and close our eyes, to bow our heads, and then, in the solemn tones of prayer, ask God never to forgive us our sins! never to blot them from the book of His remembrance! but as we cherish with emotions of hatred the trespasses of our fellow mortals against us, so we beg God to cherish the remembrance of our transgressions, and to nurse up His wrath against us until the judgment hour! He surely is unworthy to receive of God forgiveness of his ten thousand talent debt, who is unwilling to pass over the hundred pence trespass of his fellow servant! "And think not," says Archbishop Leighton, "to satisfy God with superficial forgiveness and reconcilements, saying I will forgive, but will not forget," &c. Would we be content of such pardon of God? to have only a present forbearance of revenge, so that He should not quarrel with us, but no further friendship with him; that he should either use strangeness with us and not speak to us, or only for fashion's sake; and yet such are many of our reconcilements of our brethren. God's way of forgiveness is both thorough and hearty, both to forgive and to forget; His language is, "I will forgive their iniquity, and I will remember their sin no more." And if thine be not so, thou hast no portion in His, for you only ask God to "forgive you as you forgive others."

Lastly, there is laid upon us a Divine injunction to the performance of this duty. In addition to the directions of our Lord, already quoted, there are very many other texts enforcing the same truth. St. Paul's sentiments may be condensed in his direction "owe no man anything, but to love one another," "be ye kind one to another, tender-hearted, forgiving one another, even as God for Christ's sake hath forgiven you." St. James's views are expressed in the words, "He shall have judgment without mercy that hath showed no mercy." St. Peter's earnest exhortation is, "above all things have fervent charity among yourselves;" and St. John declares, "he that loveth not his brother abideth in death." And when to these apostolic testimonies you add the great law that comprehends within itself all the duties of the second table, "Thou shalt love thy neighbour as thyself;" and the grand exemplification of this rule in the example of our Lord and Saviour Jesus Christ, whose steps we are to follow, whose mind we are to possess, whose spirit we are to copy;—what more cogent motives could be found to press upon us this holy and forgiving spirit with which God is so well pleased?

As Christians then—as followers of the meek and forgiving Jesus—as those who hope that the immense debt of their sins has been forgiven by God, let us go out into the world and act towards our fellow men as God has acted towards us; for "it is the glory of a man to pass by a transgression; but to forgive, as we are forgiven of God, is Divine."

The Rich Fool.

THE RICH FOOL.

"AND he spake a parable unto them, saying, The ground of a certain rich man brought forth plentifully: And he thought within himself, saying, What shall I do, because I have no room where to bestow my fruits? And he said, This will I do: I will pull down my barns, and build greater; and there will I bestow all my fruits and my goods. And I will say to my soul, Soul, thou hast much goods laid up for many years; take thine ease, eat, drink, and be merry. But God said unto him, Thou fool, this night thy soul shall be required of thee: then whose shall those things be, which thou hast provided? So is he that layeth up treasure for himself, and is not rich toward God." ST. LUKE, XII. 16-21.

A STRIKING feature in the parables of Jesus Christ is their adaptation to the immediate circumstances in connexion with which they were delivered.

They are not fetched from afar—detached and isolated allegories. They are not strained and forced into positions to which they are not adapted; but they fall in most naturally with the subject of His discourse, and are mortised and tenoned so aptly to the occasion, that we can scarcely see the joint by which they are framed together.

The parable of the Rich Fool furnishes an instance of this felicitous illustration.

In the midst of a discourse to his disciples, one of the company, impatient of spiritual truth, and anxious only for worldly benefit, said unto Him, "Master, speak to my brother, that he may divide the inheritance with me," but Jesus, aware of the jealousy of the Jews, should he exercise any judicial functions, "said unto him, Man, who made me a judge or a divider over you?"

Whether this was a real cause, wherein a wronged brother desired one like our Lord, whom he considered a just umpire, to arbitrate between them, or whether, like the question of the Herodians about the tribute-money, or the efforts of the Scribes and Pharisees to extort from him a judgment concerning the woman professedly taken in adultery, a mere feint to entrap him in his words, and, by causing him to exercise civil jurisdiction, furnish a ground of complaint against him, as a traitor or usurper, we know not. He was not entrapped, but, disclaiming all civil authority, and persisting in that of the Teacher, He warns him whose heart is so set upon a worldly inheritance—"Take heed, and beware of covetousness; for a man's life consisteth not in the abundance of things which he possesseth.'

This great truth—that the real interests of life, the soul's life, lie outside our worldly possessions—a truth so opposed to the usual doctrines and feelings of the worldling, He enforces by a short but forcible parable, wherein covetousness, in its relations to God and man, time and eternity, is comprehensively portrayed.

Having delivered this parable and sealed it upon the mind by an aphoristic moral, Jesus resumes his discourse to his disciples, and leaves the offended brother to ponder the solemn truths which he had heard.

The first thing presented to us in this parable is the fact, that the riches of this man were honestly acquired. It was the legitimate produce of his fields. "The ground of a certain rich man brought forth plentifully." His wealth was not wrung from penury, extorted by oppression, or amassed by fraudulent trade. It was not the result of cupidity and avarice, seeking out every avenue to gain and every method of accumulation, but the product of honest industry, crowned with the Divine blessing, "which maketh the earth to bring forth abundantly and the clouds to drop fatness."

It was highly important to the success of this parable, that the riches of this man should be of this honest sort, for, had they been ill-gotten gains, the rebuke, in the minds of most persons, would have rested upon the manner in which he acquired riches, rather than in the trusting to riches itself, however honestly obtained.

With the increase of his wealth, however, there is found no opening of his heart. The liberality of God to him calls out no liberality from him towards his fellow men; but, intent only upon hoarding up what he has, "he thought within himself, 'what shall I do, because I have no room where to bestow my fruits?'"

"He thought within himself!" how expressive of the internal working of covetousness, that dares not utter itself in words, but that plots its plans in the recesses of the heart, away from the sight of men, but not away from the eyes of God.

Having revolved the matter on wholly selfish principles,

never once thinking that he was God's steward to disburse those riches, rather than his banker to hoard them; he comes to a resolve " to pull down his barns, and build greater," saying, " and there will I bestow all my fruits and my goods." Beautifully does Ambrose allude to his perplexity about "having no room where to bestow his fruits." " No room !" " Thou *hast* barns—the bosoms of the needy; the houses of the widows; the mouths of orphans."

To relieve the poor and the destitute did not, however, enter into his calculations; self-aggrandizement was his end and aim, as is evident by the address which he makes to his soul in view of the increase of his riches: " Soul, thou hast much goods laid up for many years: take thine ease, eat, drink, and be merry." He felt himself placed by his actual abundance, beyond the caprice of fortune, and not thinking of the uncertainty of life, he settles down in the comfortable assurance, that henceforth his life will be one of enjoyment, with no cares to perplex, no toil to fatigue, no poverty to cramp, no fear to paralyze the desires and affections of his heart.

To human eyes, how bright and beautiful his prospect! The future lay spread out before him enamelled with light; visions of joy danced in jocund rounds before his eyes; no thought had he of sorrow; no care for the morrow; no concern for eternity. He had entrenched his heart about with gold; adversities surely could not make a breach there! He had arranged all his schemes of life; death surely would not interrupt his long-cherished plans! He had just reached the point where most of all desired to live; the grave surely would not yawn beneath him at such a time! It never seems to have occurred to him that God, and not himself, was the disposer of his wealth, his happiness, his life. Absorbed in the things of time, his crops, his fields, his barns, he totally forgot his soul, or had no other idea of it than that of a gross and sensual substance that could be filled and satisfied with the grovelling things of earth. He was a materialist in doctrine, and a sensualist in practice.

But in this state of peace, plenty, and pleasure, his thoughts stretching out into the future, and his plans maturing to perfection, he is suddenly aroused by the voice of God, saying unto him, "Thou fool, this night thy soul shall be required of thee: then whose shall those things be which thou hast provided?" What a startling annunciation this! the curfew bell of the soul, extinguishing every light of hope and of joy, leaving it in the blackness of darkness for ever! He was a "fool" to imagine that the soul needed no preparation for an exchange of worlds,—for none he made or thought of. He was a "fool" for supposing that his soul would be satisfied with wealth or pleasures of this world. He was a "fool" for believing that life had no other purpose than self-gratification, no other ends than sensual delights. He was a "fool" in thinking that his riches were his own, to hoard them in barns, rather than intrusted to him as a steward to disburse to the Lord's poor, and for the Lord's service.

Alas! how quickly do his dreams of pleasure, and schemes of greatness, and hopes of life, vanish at the awful voice of God. Barns, stores, fruits, pleasures are scattered by that dread annunciation, "This night thy soul shall be required of thee!" Instead of building for him a barn, they must dig a grave; instead of having "much goods laid up for many years," he had nothing laid up for eternity; instead of his soul taking ease and being merry, he must lie down in everlasting sorrow, saying "to corruption, thou art my father; to the worm, thou art my mother and my sister." So great is the change, so sudden the surprise, so mighty the wreck of wealth when God calls the sinner to his bar.

It was a saying of some of the Jewish doctors, that the angel Gabriel drew out the souls of the righteous by a gentle kiss upon their mouths: but not thus gentle was the death of the rich fool; for in the language of Theophylact, "terrible angels, like pitiless exactors of tribute, required of him, as a disobedient debtor, his soul." His departure was like that described by Job: "The rich man shall lie down, but he shall not be gathered: he openeth his eyes and he is not; terrors take hold on him as waters, a tempest stealeth him away in the night, and as a storm hurleth him out of his place; for God shall cast upon him and not spare; he would fain flee out of his hand."

Of the rich man thus driven away in his wickedness, Jesus well asks, "Then whose shall those things be which thou hast provided?" He gathered, but another shall scatter; he laid up in store, but another shall lay out in waste, and what he provided for himself shall be used by others: in the words of the Psalmist, "He heapeth up riches, and knoweth not who shall gather them."

Having thus interested them in the parable, our Lord draws out the moral in a short but comprehensive sentence. "So is every one that layeth up treasure for himself, and is not rich towards God." "So,"—there is emphasis in this word, as it throws us back upon certain results, brought out in the rich man's case, which will find perhaps their parallel in the results of all who like him, "lay up treasure for themselves, and are not rich towards God." "So," in the suddenness with which they shall be called away from their barns and wealth. "So," in the scattering at their death of the riches, so carefully gathered in their life. "So," in the requirements which will be made of their stewardship at the bar of God. "So," in the folly of their course in setting their hearts solely upon things present and earthly. "So," in the final ruin and misery which await all such rich fools beyond the grave.

But what is meant by "laying up treasure for himself?" The great pursuit of life, with most men, is the acquisition of wealth, as in the possession of it they expect to find their chief good and happiness. That money is the great idol of mankind, is evident to the most superficial observer. It is true that the children of this world have "Lords many and gods many," but to Mammon is paid the chief homage of their hearts, and minds, and strength. Other idols have strong and powerful attractions, but their altars are deserted when Mammon beckons them away. The softest blandishments of pleasure, the most stirring scenes of ambition, the attractive pursuits of learning, yield to his superior claims. All, of every rank and condition, are gathered together to the dedication of "the image of gold," which the Prince of this world hath set up in the plains of earth. For money, life is perilled, health sacrificed, and youth blighted in the bud. For money, peace is discarded, home abandoned, and friends deserted. There is nothing men will not do to get money; to acquire it they will break every law of God, and every edict of man. They will stifle conscience, hoodwink reason, quench the Holy Spirit, and barter every hope of heaven. Such is the universal passion, as demoralizing to man as it is hateful to God.

Leaving this general truth, and descending to particulars, the man who layeth up treasures for himself is one who regards his own interests alone. The eminently selfish man; such an one strives for riches, because riches beget honour. Want is always obsequious to wealth; penury always pays homage to plenty. He strives for riches, because riches bring pleasure. With wealth he can gratify his senses, his appetites, his passions. He can with it build lordly mansions, set up a stately equipage, array himself in costly garments, and fare sumptuously every day. He strives for riches, because riches create influence and friends. "The rich man," says Solomon, "hath many friends;" and again, "the rich man's wealth is his strong city." A moneyed man is always an influential man; he is always surrounded by those who call themselves friends, though in reality fawning sycophants, human parasites. If born in poverty, his ambition is to rank among the rich;

if born to fortune, he seeks to excel his ancestral wealth. If he spring from ignominy, he wishes to throw a mantle of gold over his mother's shame; if the scion of rank, he longs to quarter the arms of mammon on the heraldic shield of a noble lineage. Is he ignorant? wealth can atone for stupidity; is he learned? wealth can ennoble knowledge, for "the crown of the wise is their riches."

Thus does the man, who layeth up riches for himself, manifest, at all times (though it is often covered up from public view by an outward benevolence, which, after all, is concentrated egotism), a grasping avarice, a clenching covetousness, a blunted conscience, a contracted, indurated heart. Self is the centre, self the radii, self the circumference of his plans.

But he who layeth up riches for himself is one who regards this world alone. All the aims of such a man are bounded by the horizon of earth. He looks not beyond the earthly and sensual gratification which riches bestow, and he thinks not and cares not for another state of being. He counts upon life as extending many years; he boldly lays down plans which stretch far into the future; he toils on as if there was no death to interrupt his labours, as if life's tide would never ebb, as if earth had for him no grave. The world fills his eye, engrosses his mind, absorbs his affections, and consumes his strength. Oh, the short-sightedness and narrow-mindedness of the rich man! Well did did David pray, "deliver my soul from men of the world, who have their portion in this life!" Well might our Lord declare, "It is easier for a camel to go through the eye of a needle, than for a rich man to enter into the kingdom of Heaven!" Well may God say of such, "Thou fool!" for when he shall be brought down to the grave, it shall be said, "Lo, this is the man that made not God his strength, but trusted in the abundance of his riches; therefore shall his riches, like canker, eat into his soul for ever." This is an outline sketch of one "who layeth up riches for himself;" and if it appears so selfish and grovelling to us, how abhorrent must it be to Him, who, looking beyond the outside coverings, searcheth the reins and trieth the hearts of the children of men!

But what is involved in the idea of being rich towards God?

This implies two things: 1. Such a using of riches as shall result to the glory of God. How this can be done is indicated in the 33d verse of this chapter—"Sell that ye have and give alms; provide yourselves bags which wax not old, a treasure in the heavens that faileth not;" and by the 20th verse of the 6th chapter of St. Matthew—"Lay up for yourselves treasures in heaven, where neither moth nor rust doth corrupt, and where thieves do not break through nor steal."

Riches are used to the glory of God, and thus become, in a figurative sense, "treasures in heaven," when the possessors of them regard themselves as stewards of God's bounty, and expend what they have in the extension of Christ's kingdom on earth.

It must be confessed that much of the so-called benevolence of the day is nothing but refined selfishness, or egoustical philanthropy. Many give largely to a charitable object, because they know that a trumpet will be sounded before their alms, and it will " be seen of men." This is not true Christian benevolence, which, regarding ourselves as " bought with a price," and nothing that we have as our own, uses all in subordination to the one sacred principle of " doing all to the glory of God." The noblest use, then, to which wealth can be put, is to use it in carrying on those ordinances of grace and institutions of religion which are linked with Christ's glory and man's salvation.

As these ordinances and institutions are extended, souls are saved, and every soul saved is a treasure laid up in heaven; and as these means of grace are, in their earthly operations, sustained by money, so do we, through these benefactions, fulfil our Lord's injunction, and " lay up for ourselves treasures in heaven," beyond the reach of thief, of rust, and of moth.

2. The expression, being rich towards God, implies a being rich in respect to God or Divine blessings. Under this phase of the subject, the riches do not consist in silver and gold, and goods, and fields, and barns, and plenty, but in that wealth of soul which is given by " the God and Father of our Lord Jesus Christ, who hath blessed us with all spiritual blessings in heavenly places in Christ, in whom we have redemption through His blood, the forgiveness of sins according to the riches of His grace." He only is truly rich who has " put on Christ;" "for in Him dwelleth all the fulness of the Godhead bodily;" for of such Christians the Apostle says, " all are yours, and ye are Christ's, and Christ

is God's." He, therefore, who is so living by faith in the Son of God as to be daily advancing in godliness of heart, is, through the power of the Holy Ghost, laying up in heaven treasures of love, joy, hope, peace—those soul-riches which will endure unto everlasting life. When called from earth, instead of being like the rich man, wrenched away from all his goods, wherein he trusted and delighted, he will pass to the full possession and enjoyment of that eternal, all-glorious, and undefiled inheritance which Christ hath reserved for him in heaven. He has sent his treasures before him, and death will bring him to his possessions again. These two classes comprise all members of the human family. Under one or other of these heads may each living being be ranked. To which do you belong? Are you one of those laying up riches for yourselves? endeavouring to satisfy your immortal soul with the husks of earth? who live only for the world? who concentrate all their interests in time? who virtually ignore the soul, and heaven, and God? And do you not for such conduct deserve to be called a fool? This is God's epithet—the deliberate judgment of infinite knowledge and wisdom; and it will be confirmed bye and bye by the accordant verdict of the universe. And what will you do when He whom you have thus far set at nought shall say, "This night thy soul shall be required of thee!"

To all such let me urge at once a radical change of conduct. Be no longer one of those who lay up treasures for themselves, but join yourselves to those who are rich towards God. Use your substance in such a manner as shall best prove your love, and gratitude, and reverence for God, and best advance the glory of His name and the salvation of souls; and especially seek those spiritual riches which alone are to be found in Christ Jesus. The riches of faith, of hope, of love, of joy and peace in the Holy Ghost; "durable riches," which will ever increase in value, and ever impart bliss, when the world, with its treasures of gold and silver and precious stones, shall be burned up. Let thy possessions be laid up in "everlasting habitations," not stored up on a world devoted to destruction.

Pounds and Talents.

POUNDS AND TALENTS.

"The kingdom of heaven is as a man travelling into a far country, who called his own servants, and delivered unto them his goods. And unto one he gave five talents, to another two, and to another one; to every man according to his several ability; and straightway took his journey. Then he that had received the five talents went and traded with the same, and made them other five talents. And likewise he that had received two, he also gained other two. But he that had received one went and digged in the earth, and hid his lord's money. After a long time the lord of those servants cometh, and reckoneth with them. And so he that had received five talents came and brought other five talents, saying, Lord, thou deliveredst unto me five talents: behold, I have gained besides them five talents more. His lord said unto him, Well done, thou good and faithful servant; thou hast been faithful over a few things, I will make thee ruler over many things: enter thou into the joy of thy lord. He also that had received two talents came and said, Lord, thou deliveredst unto me two talents: behold, I have gained two other talents besides them. His lord said unto them, Well done, good and faithful servant; thou hast been faithful over a few things, I will make thee ruler over many things: enter thou into the joy of thy lord. Then he which had received the one talent came and said, Lord, I knew thee that thou art a hard man, reaping where thou hast not sown, and gathering where thou hast not strewed: And I was afraid, and went and hid thy talent in the earth: lo, there thou hast that is thine His lord answered and said unto him, Thou wicked and slothful servant, thou knewest that I reap where I sowed not, and gather where I have not strewed: Thou oughtest therefore to have put my money to the exchangers, and then at my coming I should have received mine own with usury. Take therefore the talent from him, and give it unto him which hath ten talents. For unto every one that hath shall be given, and he shall have abundance: but from him that hath not, shall be taken away even that which he hath. And cast ye the unprofitable servant into outer darkness: there shall be weeping and gnashing of teeth."

MATT. xxv. 14–30.

"A certain nobleman went into a far country to receive for himself a kingdom, and to return. And he called his ten servants, and delivered them ten pounds, and said unto them, Occupy till I come. But his citizens hated him, and sent a message after him, saying, We will not have this man to reign over us. And it came to pass, that, when he was returned, having received the kingdom, then he commanded these servants to be called unto him to whom he had given the money, that he might know how much every man had gained by trading. Then came the first, saying, Lord, thy pound hath gained ten pounds. And he said unto him, Well, thou good servant: because thou hast been faithful in a very little, have thou authority over ten cities. And the second came, saying, Lord, thy pound hath gained five pounds. And he said likewise to him, Be thou also over five cities. And another came, saying, Lord, behold, here is thy pound, which I have kept laid up in a napkin: For I feared thee, because thou art an austere man; thou takest up that thou layedst not down, and reapest that thou didst not sow. And he saith unto him, Out of thine own mouth will I judge thee, thou wicked servant. Thou knewest that I was an austere man, taking up that I laid not down, and reaping that I did not sow: Wherefore then gavest not thou my money into the bank, that at my coming I might have required mine own with usury? And he said unto them that stood by, Take from him the pound, and give it to him that hath ten pounds. (And they said unto him, Lord, he hath ten pounds.) For I say unto you, That unto every one which hath shall be given; and from him that hath not, even that he hath shall be taken away from him. But those mine enemies, which would not that I should reign over them, bring hither, and slay them before me."

LUKE, XIX. 12–27.

THESE parables are similar, without being identical. They were delivered on different occasions, and for different purposes; but though they have some points of divergence, they have many of convergence, and are sufficiently alike in parabolical structure and practical design to be treated under one head, as enforcing the one great truth pertaining to the trusts confided to us by God: "Occupy till I come!"

In the parable of the Pounds, spoken in the house of Zaccheus, and recorded by St. Luke, where it is said, "A certain nobleman went into a far country, to receive for himself a kingdom, and to return;" and of whom it is subsequently added, " but his citizens hated him, and sent a message after him, saying, " we will not have this man to reign over us;" there is evidently an historical allusion to the political condition of Judea under the Roman power.

Judea had been conquered by the Romans, under Pompey, 63 B. C., and though it was still governed in part by native princes, yet they ruled as deputies of Rome, and under its protectorate. Those, therefore, who, by hereditary succession or interest, thought they had any title to the government of the Jewish provinces, sought of course to confirm their claim by an appeal to the Emperor or Senate of the imperial city. Thus Herod the Great hastened to Rome, to obtain the kingdom of Judea from Antony, which having received, he was solemnly proclaimed King of the Jews. By the last will and testament of this monarch, his son Archelaus was constituted ruler of Judea, Samaria, and Idumea, yet could not enter upon his Ethnarchship until his dignity was confirmed by Augustus. Accordingly he went to Rome, literally " into a far country, to receive for himself a kingdom;" but the Jews, knowing his purpose, sent thither fifty ambassadors, to entreat Augustus that Archelaus might not be made their king, and were so far successful that, though Augustus confirmed him in his government as Ethnarch, he would not invest him with the regal name and dignity. The allusion of our Lord, therefore, to this well-known historical fact, gave deepesignificance to the parable, and made the people more attentive to the truths which it was intended to convey.

But, while it had this historical basis, it had also a prophetic aspect; for that "nobleman" was Christ, "heir of all things," "the first-born of every creature;" that "travelling into a far country," the coming down of the Lord Jesus from heaven to earth; that "kingdom" which he came "to receive," was the Church; that "calling his own servants, and delivering unto them his goods," the selection of His Apostles and ministers, and the committing to them the "gifts" and "graces" which are the spiritual "pounds" and "talents" of the Church; that "taking his journey," in the one case, and that "return," in the other, His ascension into Heaven; that "hatred" of "his citizens," and their sending "a message after him, saying, We will not have this man to reign over us," the secret enmity and open opposition of the human heart against the spiritual reign of Jesus Christ.

In both of these parables we find that certain moneys were given to certain servants. The first bestows "talents:" giving to one "five talents," or about six thousand dollars; "to another two," or nearly twenty-four hundred dollars; "to another, one," or twelve hundred dollars. The second gives to each of ten persons a pound (mina), equivalent to twenty dollars. In the first parable, our Lord was addressing His Apostles only, to whom had been specially intrusted large gifts, for the planting, erecting, teaching, governing of the Church; well expressed by the term "talents," as distinguished from those lower, yet still important gifts, which pertain to private Christians, and which, when Jesus addressed His "disciples," He called by the humbler designation of "pounds." In both instances, however, the pounds and the talents were given to be improved and augmented, by such an occupancy or use as would increase the amount originally bestowed, and bring in large profits to the holder.

Years roll on; the several servants pursue different courses with their talents and pounds; until, "after a long time," as St. Matthew expresses it, "the lord of those servants cometh and reckoneth with them;" or, as St. Luke says, the returned nobleman "commanded these servants to be called unto him to whom he had given the money, that he might know how much each man had gained by trading."

On presenting themselves before their respective lords, it is found, that some improve their means more than others. He to whom five talents had been given had "traded with the same, and made them other five talents;" "likewise he that had received two, he also had gained other two;" one of those to whom one pound had been delivered came, "saying, Lord, thy pound hath gained ten pounds;" and another reported, "Lord, thy pound hath gained five pounds." In the case of the recipient of the talents, there was simply a duplicating of the original sum received, evincing diligence and fidelity in the trust committed to them; but in the case of the pounds, the increase was vastly greater; instead of being twofold, it was, in one instance, tenfold, and in another, fivefold; and this, too, with less original capital, thereby showing a greater zeal in the lord's service, and deeper wisdom in business plans than those to whom had been committed the more valuable talents; and as our Lord uttered no words without meaning, may not this be designed to show us, by a delicate yet truthful allusion, that not those alone who receive even two or five talents, the higher denomination of God's gifts, shall be rewarded with kingly munificence; but that those who rightly employ even the humbler trust of a single pound, may, by faithful effort, so improve the little, as to become a ruler over ten cities or over five cities; far outstripping, in real increase of grace and fruit, those to whom had been intrusted higher gifts and larger portions. It is not those who have "talents," costly though they be, and minister as they may in the high places of the Church, admired, honoured, blessed, who will prove themselves the most active accumulators of the Divine blessing, or receive the most flattering plaudits; on the contrary, some humbler Christian, scarcely known even in the Church to which he belongs, some diligent cultivator of his single "pound," may, through prayer and faith and zeal, bring in from his small portion a larger revenue of glory to God and blessedness for souls, than the more richly endowed and more conspicuous possessor of his Lord's bounty.

The rewards bestowed upon these profitable servants, varied with their several degrees of fidelity. The possessor of five talents, whose industry had "gained besides them five talents more," receives the approbation of his lord, and the assurance that he would make him "ruler over many things." The diligent improver of two talents obtains the same commendation, with the promise that as he "had been faithful over a few things," he would make him "ruler over many things;" while both received the invitation "enter thou into the joy of thy lord;" implying, according to Oriental usage, that the lord had celebrated his return by a sumptuous feast, to which these his servants had been invited, and by this invitation and participation of the feast, received manumission, and thus as "freedmen" were designated to rule over others. The indefiniteness which attaches to the rewards in the parable of the talents, does not obtain in that of the pounds. Here all is distinct: for he whose pound had gained ten pounds, and he whose pound had multiplied to five, were severally made rulers over ten and five cities; in evident allusion to the custom formerly prevalent in the East, of assigning the government or revenues of a certain number of cities as rewards to meritorious officers, as Artaxerxes assigned several cities to Themistocles for his services in the cause of Persia; of which cities, Myus was to supply him with viands, Magnesia with bread, Lampsacus with wines.

The disproportion between fidelity in the use of a single pound of Hebrew money, and the reward consequent thereon, of being made a ruler over five or ten cities, cannot fail to arrest attention; and yet how beautifully does this apparent disproportion illustrate a marked feature of the Divine economy, whereby God rewards not deeds, but motives; not results, but principles. So here the principles of faithful zeal to the humblest trust is requited by transferring that lowly labourer to a broader field of action, where this principle, so fully tested in small matters, has now scope for noble and efficient development. And a blessed thought it is, that we are not rewarded so much for the outward and visible ministrations of duty, as for the inward and spiritual principles which guide our souls, which principles indeed are not of our own getting, but are implanted in us by the Holy Ghost. Hence it follows that the humblest servant of God may attain to heights in glory, and reaches of power, far above what may be accorded to the more seemingly active and fruitful professor, because of the different principles which were the motive power in each.

In both parables, however, we find one instance of misimprovement of the money bestowed. The recipient of "one talent," after wrongfully accusing his lord as "an hard man," tells him, "I was afraid, and went and hid thy talent in the earth;" and one of the receivers of the pound brings it back, saying, "Behold, here is thy pound, which I have kept laid up in a napkin;" at the same time laying grievous things to his charge. Their lord answers in both cases—if you knew that I was an austere or hard man, "taking up that I laid not down, and reaping that I did not sow," you should have put my money "into the bank," or "to the exchangers," and then at my coming I should have received mine own with usury. By pursuing such a course you would have lost nothing, even though I was such an one as you represent me to be; while my money, instead of lying idle, would have been gathering the usual per centum of interest from those whose business it was to exchange the different coins of Eastern currency for the shekel of the temple; and who thus, upon their little tables or counters, carried on a profitable trade with "the strangers, Jews, and proselytes," who resorted to Jerusalem for business or devotion. Unable to answer a word in extenuation of such neglect, they are both deprived of the sum originally placed in their keeping, and cast as "unprofitable servants" into outer darkness, or as enemies of their lord brought and slain before him. Such was the deserved end of those who could impugn the honesty, clemency, and goodness of their respective masters, as well as abuse, by not rightly employing, the trusts committed to their care. The bearing of these parables is very plain, and the truths they teach are very important.

God has committed to us certain interests which pertain to man as a moral and accountable being—*the present and future interests of the soul.* These, like the ten pounds to the ten servants, are committed alike to all. But, though God has given a soul and a conscience, and the light of nature, to every child of Adam, and for the occupancy of which trust each will be called into judgment at the great day, yet do we also learn, by the parable of the Talents, that, over and above these interests, which are common to all, there are special deposits of ability and grace made to some individuals, which bring them under heavier responsibility and demand of them peculiar fidelity and zeal.

6

Among these may be mentioned, First, superior mental endowments. The varieties of mind are as great as the varieties of features and temperament; and while some persons evidence so low a rationality, as to seem but one link removed from a high order of instinct, others exhibit powers of intellect so gigantic, so noble, so elevated above the mass of minds, as to compel the homage of the world. Whenever God has bestowed these superior endowments, it has always been with the injunction, "Occupy till I come." He did not bestow them merely to subserve individual aggrandisement, that the possessor might leave behind him the impress of his genius stamped upon the laws, literature, science, or institutions of the world; but to cultivate them to their utmost capacity, and put them to their highest efforts in advancing the glory of God and the salvation of souls. Not that all minds should occupy themselves solely on religious topics; not that all such mighty men of thought should preach the Gospel; but that the ultimate aim and tendency of all mental efforts, on whatever subject they may be occupied, should be "to glorify our Father which is in Heaven."

We assert, without the fear of contradiction, that there is no department of solid learning which does not, if rightly cultivated, lead the mind directly or indirectly to God, and none which cannot directly or indirectly be made to augment his glory. All the lines of knowledge centre in God; and the circle of sciences, as it is called, is but the earthly circumference of that wisdom which radiates from the Omniscient Mind: the more diligently, therefore, we follow up any one of these radii to its centre, the nearer do we get to God. Yet the vast majority of great minded men cast off God and restrain prayer, and, in the selfish pursuit of personal honour, and the embalmment of fame, employ their powers rather against, than for, God; rather to the dishonour than the honour of their Creator. It is lamentable to observe, even with superficial eye, the enormous waste and misapplication of the human mind. See intellects of the highest order bending almost angelic energies to the purpose of ministering to the amusement, the pride, the sensuality, the taste, the pomp of this fallen world. There has, for example, been more waste of mental strength in striving after the batons and ribbons and titles of military glory, than would suffice to convert the world to Christ. The intellect which has been lavished upon the drama, from the days of Thespis and Æschylus to the present time, in writing and acting plays, would, if concentrated on the advancement of Divine truth, have made the earth " a dwelling-place of righteousness."

What a glorious spectacle would earth present, could we behold all its noble intellects bowing, like the wise men from the East, at the feet of Jesus, and presenting unto him " the gold, frankincense, and myrrh" of their sanctified minds! for every mind, no matter how tall, how strong, how rich, which is not consecrated to Jesus, is morally lost, and can never fulfil the purposes of its creation. An intellect, unbaptized by the blood of Christ, and unsanctified by the Holy Ghost, is an immortal curse: the curse may not come in this life, but it will fasten upon it beyond the grave.

Ever keep in view the solemn fact, that God has given you minds to educate for eternity, and to be expended in his glory; that he has enjoined upon you, "Occupy till I come;" and that you can only fulfil the injunction by cultivating all your powers as under His eye, and for the bringing in of His kingdom.

As among the talents or pounds committed to our care, we mention, Secondly, superior means of personal, social, or civil influence. These may arise from birth, education, fortune, standing in society, or personal endowments. Through the operation of one or more of these you come to be regarded with more respect or attention; your opinions are more esteemed; your views are sought for, your wishes consulted; and you find yourself wielding an influence more or less potent upon the circle around you. Whatever enables you then to mould or guide the opinions and actions of your fellow men, is a talent, a pound committed to you, with the injunction of the Divine Giver, "Occupy till I come;" and hence you are bound to make your influence healthful in all its operations, and beneficial wherever exerted.

God demands that this influence should be on His side, that all the advantages which He has conferred upon you should be used in His service, and not be selfishly employed in seeking personal or family aggrandizement and distinction. It is a lamentable fact that most of the influence which goes out from the educated, wealthy, and high-born classes, is baneful and debasing. They are the leaders in all sinful fashions and worldly schemes,—but very rarely are they found doing the work of the Lord. Yet what a change would pass over society, if those who stand at the head springs of social life and civil affairs, directed their aim to the spiritual welfare of the souls of men, and put forth their influence under the guidance and baptism of the Holy Ghost! This is what God requires; this is the purpose for which He conferred these advantages, and for their proper use and occupancy He will at the last day make rigid inquisition.

Thirdly: Wealth is another of the talents committed to the occupancy of some. As "we brought nothing into the world, and can carry nothing out of it," it is evident that what pecuniary means we have are the gift of God; and hence, we are exhorted in the Bible—"thou shalt remember the Lord thy God, for it is he that giveth thee power to get wealth." The property which we call ours we hold only as tenants at will; God is the proprietor of all; we are but the stewards of His bounty, solemnly responsible to Him for the disbursement of that wealth, be it more or less If now we squander it on our own persons or lusts or pleasures; if we withhold it from Christ, and refuse to use the Master's means for the Master's work; if when self calls we pour it out freely, but when God calls we dole it out with reluctance, are we not sinning against our own souls and a holy God? There is much force in the word "occupy;" it means, literally, to trade, to negotiate, as in commerce or business; and so we are to trade or carry on a spiritual commerce with the wealth which God has given us. We are to put it out to the Exchangers, those benevolent treasuries where we exchange dollars for Bibles, tracts, missionaries, Sunday-schools. We are to make investments in the Bank of Christian Enterprise, that we may gain the usury, the dividends of grace and love which He imparts to all who spend and are spent in His service. We are to trade with our wealth in such wise, that we may lay up treasures in heaven; for every investment of worldly means, made in the cause of Christ, and for His sake, will repay us, not only a large percentage of happiness here, but be honoured by our Lord with special grants of favour in the world to come.

We might indicate many other talents committed to our trust; but time allows of but one more specification, and that is, our religious privileges. Greater gifts than these no man can receive. The pardon of God; the sacrifice of Christ; the renewing of the Holy Ghost; the revelation of the Divine will; the ministry of reconciliation; the Church of the living God; the ordinances of grace! Can we adequately comprehend the value of talents like these? In the possession of them we are peculiarly distinguished; "the lines have fallen to us in pleasant places, and we have a goodly heritage." But for what purpose were these given? Have we sought the offered pardon? have we been washed in the sacrificial blood of the Redeemer? have we been sanctified by the Spirit of Holiness? have we made God's Word a light to our feet and a lamp to our path? have we been led by this ministry to "the Lamb of God, who taketh away the sins of the world?" have we united ourselves to this mystical body of Christ? have we been nourished and strengthened by the sacraments of Christ's institution? have we, in fine, so spiritually traded with these "unspeakable gifts," as, thereby, to make rich increase in grace and godliness? Are we diligently "occupying" them until we are called to "enter into the joy of our Lord?"

But the final award is before us, and let us briefly mark its results.

Those who have traded with their pounds and talents, and duplicated or multiplied them, are commended with the plaudit, "Well done, good and faithful servants;" are bidden to enter into the joy of their Lord, and are appointed to rule in the heavenly kingdom. They are made to sit "in heavenly places in Christ Jesus;" they "are called unto the marriage-supper of the Lamb;" they "judge angels;" they are crowned and anointed "as kings and priests unto God." On the other hand, those who contemned their Lord, and wrapped their pound up "in a napkin," or buried their talent "in the earth," are "cast into outer darkness," and are visited with the pains and eternal woe of the second death; and the one great thought which, like a red-hot share, shall plough its furrows in their inmost souls, is, that they had talents committed to their trust; they had pounds, with which to trade; but, by their own obstinacy and sinfulness, have wilfully put themselves into that place of torment, "where their worm dieth not, and their fire is not quenched;" and, lest any should think that, because they have moderate or common abilities, and are not among the gifted, the wealthy, the influential, therefore they will not be condemned, our Saviour has brought out very distinctly the fact that the misapplication of small abilities will meet with condign punishment. Say not, "Since so little is committed to my charge, that it matters not how I administer that little. What signifies the little, whether it be done or left undone?" for God requires as much fidelity and zeal in those to whom little is given, as in those to whom much is bestowed. The misimprovement of one talent, the hiding away of a one-pound ability, will call out the judgment of God. Remember, also, that, in both cases of delinquency, the servants did not waste or destroy the money given them: *they only suffered it to lie idle and unimproved.* This was their sin; and the simple misimprovement of even one-pound abilities, the suffering to lie idle and unaccumulating but a single talent, is a crime so great in the sight of God, who has intrusted us with these for the promotion of our salvation, and the advancement of His glory, that He will punish it with casting such spiritual idlers, such moral sluggards, into outer darkness, "where there is weeping and wailing and gnashing of teeth."

Every motive that can influence human conduct urges us to be faithful to the abilities and endowments which God has given us. The love that we should feel for the Giver, the value of the trusts committed to our care, the short time in which we are permitted to occupy them, the prolific increase which the right use of our pounds and talents will produce, the certainty of our Lord's return to inquire "how much every man had gained by trading," the fearful doom which awaits the neglecter and idler even of the smallest trust, and the magnificent rewards of glory, of praise, of authority, of sovereignty, which are promised to the diligent and the faithful, conspire to press upon us the duty of rightly occupying our several talents, until, gaining for our Lord a revenue of glory here by their spiritual increase, He will say to each of us, at the last, " well done, good and faithful servant, enter thou into the joy of thy Lord."

The Lost Sheep: The Lost Money.

THE LOST SHEEP: THE LOST MONEY.

"WHAT man of you, having a hundred sheep, if he lose one of them, doth not leave the ninety and nine in the wilderness, and go after that which is lost, until he find it? And when he hath found it, he layeth it on his shoulders, rejoicing. And when he cometh home, he calleth together his friends and neighbours, saying unto them, Rejoice with me; for I have found my sheep which was lost. I say unto you, That likewise joy shall be in heaven over one sinner that repenteth, more than over ninety and nine just persons, which need no repentance.

"Either what woman, having ten pieces of silver, if she lose one piece, doth not light a candle, and sweep the house, and seek diligently till she find it? And when she hath found it, she calleth her friends and her neighbours together, saying, Rejoice with me; for I have found the piece which I had lost. Likewise, I say unto you, There is joy in the presence of the angels of God over one sinner that repenteth." LUKE XV. 3–10.

THE three parables recorded in the fifteenth chapter of St. Luke, were spoken by our Lord in order to rebuke the murmuring of the Scribes and Pharisees, whose great complaint was, "This man receiveth sinners, and eateth with them."

It seems that multitudes of the publicans and sinners had drawn near to Christ "to hear Him." These classes, hated as vile extortioners, and profligate livers, were regarded as beyond the pale of mercy, and outside the sympathies and courtesies of social life. The learned Scribe, swollen with the traditions of the elders, and proud of the distinction which his legal knowledge secured, affected to despise the vulgar tax-gatherer, and the outcast sinner; the phylacteried Pharisee, with his long prayers, and ostentatious alms, and minute ritualism, and self-created holiness, disdained the exactors of tribute, and the notoriously unclean, and would have felt that his fringed garments were soiled by a touch of such transgressors: and though their curiosity was stimulated to the utmost to hear the Lord, yet they complained that they had to listen to His teachings in company with the publicans and the profligate, saying in disparagement of the Saviour, "This man receiveth sinners, and eateth with them."

This murmuring of the Pharisees and Scribes elicited from our Lord three parables, designed to illustrate the seeking love and receiving grace of God, and to vindicate his course in thus receiving sinners and eating with them. As the Saviour of men, it was important that we should know the grounds and methods of His procedure, when He undertook the restoration of our race; and these He condescends to set forth, not by laboured argument, not by philosophical analysis, but by parables, illustrating to the humblest, as well as the highest, the purposes and dealings of God toward His rebellious children.

It is wonderful, when we think of it, what weighty, sublime, and eternal truths are embedded in the simple parables of Jesus. While the sages of the world wrapped up their enigmatical propositions and mysterious sayings in the integuments of philosophy, or the embroidered robes of rhetoric; while the doctrines of human ethics were couched in language high above the comprehension of the vulgar; our Lord proclaimed His truths with clearness and fulness, and His language and illustrations, so far from covering up His thoughts, were rather like the veil of the atmosphere, enveloping all things indeed, yet the medium of a clear and perfect vision. It is easy enough to take a pigmy thought, and make it walk on high on the stilts of bombast and hyperbole. It is common enough to see a little thin idea that would not burden an infant's brain, puffed out with gaseous words, until it looms up and floats away in aerostatic nothingness; but it is evidence of a mind of Divine compass and power, to condense the infinite and eternal truths of the Godhead, in its schemes for man's redemption, into words so few, and illustrations so simple, that the ignorant, the degraded, the little child even, can perceive and understand them.

In both the parables of the Lost Sheep and the Lost Piece of Money, Christ takes common and almost every-day occurrences to illustrate why He received sinners and ate with them: illustrations which, while glorious as the unfoldings of Divine love, are yet exquisite in their very homeliness and simplicity. A man losing a sheep from his flock, a woman losing a piece of money from her scrip, are familiar and every-day occurrences; yet, in the hands of the Saviour, they are made to stand out as the exponents of the great principles of the Divine economy in the salvation of mankind.

The shepherd missed one sheep from his flock; and, accustomed as the Eastern shepherds are to know the countenance of each, and even to call each sheep by name, this loss would soon be discovered; and when known, the faithful man would at once seek to reclaim the wanderer. Leaving the rest of the flock in the wilderness, not, indeed, in the sandy, howling wastes, but in the uninhabited yet grassy and pastoral plains or valleys, where they would have herbage and shelter, the shepherd goes out to seek and save that which was lost. He goes into the mountains; he exposes himself to perils; he endures fatigue; he experiences great anxiety; but does not give up the search "until he find it." And then, instead of beating the wayward sheep, or rudely driving it before him, or roughly upbraiding it for wandering, the shepherd takes the long-lost one in his arms, lays it on his shoulders, saves it from the weariness of travel and the accidents to which it might be exposed; and thus, bearing his precious burden, "cometh home," and "calleth together his friends and neighbours, saying unto them, Rejoice with me, for I have found my sheep which was lost."

But as, among his auditors, there were doubtless those who would better understand a different simile, our Lord condescends to take a very humble figure, and says, "Either what woman, having ten drachmas, if she lose one piece, doth not light a candle"—because the oriental houses have few openings or windows, and the extra candle-light would be needed—" and sweep the house"—not merely look through it, removing the furniture to make the search more thorough, but sweeping its floors, sweeping it by the light of the candle; and to the cleansing of the broom she adds the diligent search of the eye, and leaves no place unexplored "until she find it?"

In the recovery both of the lost sheep and the lost coin, we find peculiar evidences of joy and peculiar language to express it.

The returning shepherd, as he comes within sight of his flock, which he had left, now quietly browsing on the plain or folded for the night, calls out to the dwellers in the tent, "Rejoice with me, for I have found my sheep which was lost;" and, as they came out to meet the shepherd, weary and faint with his tedious search, and see the wandering sheep safe upon his shoulders, they respond loudly to his call, and mingle together their pastoral rejoicings.

And when the poor woman, for we are led to infer that she was such, finds her lost drachma, she gathers her female friends to tell them of her success, and calls upon those who once sympathized with her loss—"Rejoice with me, for I have found the piece which I had lost."

In what a graphic manner do these two parables set forth the seeking love of Jesus to our lost and sinful race! We are wanderers from God; "all we, like sheep, have gone astray, we have turned every one to his own way," and had lost ourselves upon the dark mountains of sin and unbelief. The innocence which was once ours, and the companionship of angels which we were once privileged to enjoy, were voluntarily renounced; and, forsaking the green pastures and still waters of the Lord's providing, we have strayed away from the Good Shepherd into the rugged paths and dangerous defiles of sin and woe. Originally made in the likeness of

God, and once bearing in our souls the image and superscription of our King, we have now lapsed from our rightful owner, and fallen away into the dust and earthiness of a deep moral debasement. But Christ, infinite in His love and mercy, did not leave us thus lost and wandering. He sought us out; He addressed Himself to the work of our recovery; He girded Himself about with the vestment of humanity; He came to this sin-cursed earth, and wandered up and down in its highways and hedges, enduring the malice of enemies, the rebukes of the proud, the suspicions of friends, mockings and buffetings and countless sorrows, until, arrested as a malefactor, condemned as a blasphemer, crucified as a slave, the Good Shepherd had given his life for His sheep, and, that they might be saved, bowed His head and died. "He was wounded for our transgressions, He was bruised for our iniquities, the chastisement of our peace was upon Him, and with His stripes we are healed." In a most emphatic manner did Christ "go after the sheep that was lost until He find it." The love that prompted the search was an infinite love; its well-spring was in the beginning; it had flowed from all eternity, and its fulness and richness are best illustrated in the costliness of its sacrifice and the value of its atonement. It was not the lost sheep seeking out the Shepherd, and making efforts to get back to the fold; there was in us no desire to return; we loved our sins and we revelled in them; and man even slew the Lord of life and glory, because he sought to redeem him from his sins. It was like the diseased and loathsome patient, killing the physician because he would rescue him from his sickness, and give him health and soundness instead of rottenness and pain.

What Christ did as our Good Shepherd, to seek and save us, may be learned in the wonderful record of His life,— for the thirty-three years of His earthly pilgrimage, were so many years of toil, anguish, endurance, and search after the wanderers from God. No dangers daunted Him, no fatigue exhausted Him, no obloquy turned Him aside, no assaults of enemies caused Him to desist. He plunged into the deepest thickets of sin; He entered the most forbidding morasses of life; He exposed himself in the most dangerous and darksome valleys of humanity, without regard to His own comfort, and at the sacrifice of His own blood, that He might find His lost sheep, and laying them on His shoulders return with them to His Father's fold rejoicing, seeing in their recovery "the travail of His soul," and being "satisfied."

These parables were designed by our Lord to illustrate the great concern which He felt for souls. The value of the soul is well known to the Lord Jesus. We do not know it, because our arithmetic is finite, and it has no factors to express the worth of an immortal spirit; we judge of everything by worldly standards, by what it can give us, or what it can do for us, as beings of time and earth; consequently, that which enables us to rank high, to amass wealth, to secure praise, to dwell at ease, to live in pleasure, is that which most absorbs our thoughts and engages the powers of our being. Hence, the soul, in its eternal interests, is overlooked, or regarded as a disagreeable something, ever standing in the way of our pleasure and advancement, which we would gladly be rid of if we could. The Blessed Saviour, having created the soul, having endowed it with its wondrous powers, having given it immortality as its birthright, knows its worth; and when He saw us wandering into bye and forbidden paths, He knew the greatness of the loss which would ensue, and hence manifested such Divine concern to secure its recovery and salvation. He was happy in the glories which he had with the Father before the world was; He was blessed in the worship of the Angelic Host who ministered before Him; but all this availed not; His eye saw, His heart loved our race, even though it was fallen and alien;" and " not willing that any should perish," He came down to deliver from eternal ruin all who should believe on Him, and receive Him as the Saviour of their souls. There was deep concern in heaven for the soul of man. God felt it, and so felt it as to give His only begotten Son, that " whosoever believeth on Him might not perish, but have everlasting life;" and when it so moved the mind of Jehovah, how ought our minds to be under deepest concern for their recovery! Did the shepherd leave the ninety and nine unwandering ones, and go out into the mountains to seek and save one wanderer? So the Lord of Glory left the innumerable company of unsinning angels, that He might go forth to find the lost sheep, man; so did He light the candle of revelation, and with the besom of a holy law, sweep the floor of this earthly house of our tabernacle, until he found the piece which was lost, relaxing no effort which Divinity could devise or execute, to recover the wanderer, and search out the lost; for "He delighteth not in the death of a sinner, but rather that he should turn from his wickedness and live."

The parable of the Lost Sheep also teaches us the tender care and compassion of our Lord towards the recovered wanderers. What could illustrate this more than the shepherd's act of laying the lost sheep, when he found it, "on his shoulders," and so bearing it home? When Christ finds the wandering sinner, He does not roughly upbraid him, He does not drive him harshly before Him, but throws around him His loving arms, takes him to His bosom, lays him on His shoulder, where no harm can reach him, protects him by His hands, and pledges the mightiness of His own power to return the wanderer to the fold of God.

And with what joy is the sinner welcomed! It is faintly shadowed forth in the rejoicings made by the friends and neighbours of the shepherd and the woman at the recovery of the lost sheep and the lost silver. It is more emphatically declared, in the words of the Saviour, after the parable of the Lost Sheep—"Likewise joy shall be in Heaven over one sinner that repenteth, more than over ninety and nine just persons which need no repentance;" and in almost similar words after the parable of the Lost Piece of Silver—"Likewise I say unto you, there is joy in the presence of the angels of God over one sinner that repenteth."

In this twice-uttered declaration Jesus enunciates the truth, that there is an interest and a sympathy felt for man by the angels in heaven; a truth confirmed by several other passages of Scripture, wherein they are not only represented as "ministering spirits sent forth to minister to the heirs of salvation," but as desiring to look into the mysteries of man's redemption.

There is something very sublime in the thought that angels take an interest in the moral affairs of this earth. Were our world the only orb which Divine power had framed and peopled, and poised in the else solitary field of space, there would be something of condescension in such holy beings, dwelling in the presence of God, stooping to interest their mighty minds and spotless souls in the spiritual affairs of men.

But when we are compelled to believe, however humbling to human pride, that the earth which we inhabit is so small as to appear but a sparkling point to some, and not visible at all to other planets, even of our own solar system; while myriads of suns, with attendant families of worlds, spangle the floor of heaven, and mock the powers of the most potent telescope; then the condescension of the heavenly host becomes more marked and significant, and seems to indicate that there must have been some special display of God's glory on this little earth, to which other greater and brighter worlds were strangers; and hence they concentrate upon this spot a more intense gaze, and feel for us a more vivid interest. The solution of this interest is found in the fact that, for all we know, this earth is the spot where was seen the highest display of God's moral glory, and where was waged the great battle of God's supremacy, in which sin and death were conquered, and grace and salvation won

We know not that any other world revolted from God; we infer, indeed, from the transactions which took place here, that all other portions of His universe adhered to the holiness of their original creation; and if, as we justly suppose, this earth alone broke out in rebellion, and threw off its allegiance to Jehovah, we can well understand how, for a time, the fact of such an outbreak would be heralded throughout the skies, and how the questions—shall rebel man be punished? can rebel man be saved? would for a season occupy the thoughts and fix the deepest interest in the heavenly host. In such a case, the littleness of the terrestrial spot was nothing—the greatness of the principle at stake was everything. The smallness of the world was lost sight of in the magnitude of the issue, even as the intrinsic worthlessness of Pharsalia, and Agincourt, and Waterloo, and Yorktown, is lost in the immense issues which were decided in battle on those fields of blood. The great principle that was here to be established, and the mighty wonder that was here to be disclosed, was the principle that "God could be just and yet the justifier of him that believeth on Jesus;" and the awful mystery of a "God manifest in the flesh, seen of angels, believed on in the world," and redeeming that world by "humbling Himself unto death, even the death of the cross." Hence angels gathered around this single wandering world; hence they watched the dealings of God with its sinful inhabitants; and hence we find them, in all ages of the world, mingling their services to carry on the scheme of grace in its various manifestations — Patriarchal, Levitical, and

Christian. Angels came to Abraham, and Lot, and Jacob, and Moses. Angels appeared to David, to Elijah, to Daniel, to Ezekiel. Angels foretold the birth of Christ to Zecharias, to Mary, to Joseph, to the Bethlehem shepherds. Angels ministered to Christ on the mount of temptation, in the garden of Gethsemane, at the rock-hewn sepulchre, and announced to the women who had gone thither to anoint the Saviour, "He is risen; He is not here; come see the place where the Lord lay." And angels shall attend Him in His second advent to judge the world, for St. Matthew says, "When the Son of man shall come in His glory, and all His holy angels with Him, then shall He sit upon the throne of His glory."

All these angelic appearances are connected with the incarnation of Jesus Christ. The incarnation of Christ is the greatest moral epoch in the universe of God; and as this incarnation was "for us men and our salvation," hence it would necessarily be a matter of profound interest to angelic beings, whose service was in the presence of God, to watch the results of that great mystery, and to rejoice, as each new convert to Christ gave proof of the power, and wisdom, and grace of God in planning out such a perfect and complete salvation. They rejoice that God's grace, and Christ's blood, and the Spirit's power, have not been bestowed in vain. They rejoice that another soul is "snatched as a brand from the burning," and has become "an heir of God and a joint heir with Christ to an inheritance" in heaven; and though supremely happy themselves, though dwelling in the presence of God, "in whose presence is fulness of joy, and at whose right hand are pleasures for ever more," yet such is the depth of their interest in Christ, who is their Divine Head, such the outgoing of their affection to Him in all His mediatorial work, that they find it a source of ecstatic joy to follow out the wondrous exhibitions of His redeeming love, as it flows down to the individual heart, and new creates the soul in righteousness and true holiness. Warranted by the repeated words of Jesus, we can imagine the angels—forgetful, as it were, for a time, of the "just who need no repentance," those who have already been renewed by the Holy Ghost—bending all the force and anxiety of their celestial interest upon one poor sinner, watching his wandering steps as he strays away further and further, now almost stumbling with fear, as his feet tread nearer and nearer to the slippery edge of ruin, and now all excitement, as, arrested by the call of mercy, he listens, turns, retraces his steps, is found by the Good Shepherd, is laid upon His shoulder; and as the once lost one is brought back to the fold, we can conceive that there would rise from that heavenly host, from every rank and order, till the wave of their mighty gratulation would reach the Eternal Throne, the ecstatic exclamation, "He is found! he is saved! one sinner more redeemed! one saint more for glory!"

The Prodigal Son.

THE PRODIGAL SON.

"A certain man had two sons; and the younger of them said to his father, Father, give me the portion of goods that falleth to me. And he divided unto them his living. And not many days after, the younger son gathered all together, and took his journey into a far country, and there wasted his substance with riotous living. And when he had spent all, there arose a mighty famine in that land; and he began to be in want. And he went and joined himself to a citizen of that country, and he sent him into his fields to feed swine. And he would fain have filled his belly with the husks that the swine did eat: and no man gave unto him. And when he came to himself, he said, How many hired servants of my father's have bread enough, and to spare, and I perish with hunger! I will arise and go to my father, and will say unto him, Father, I have sinned against Heaven, and before thee, and am no more worthy to be called thy son: make me as one of thy hired servants. And he arose, and came to his father. But when he was yet a great way off, his father saw him, and had compassion, and ran, and fell on his neck, and kissed him. And the son said unto him, Father, I have sinned against Heaven, and in thy sight, and am no more worthy to be called thy son. But the father said to his servants, Bring forth the best robe, and put it on him; and put a ring on his hand, and shoes on his feet: and bring hither the fatted calf, and kill it; and let us eat, and be merry: for this my son was dead, and is alive again; he was lost, and is found. And they began to be merry. Now his elder son was in the field: and as he came and drew nigh to the house, he heard music and dancing. And he called one of the servants, and asked what these things meant. And he said unto him, Thy brother is come; and thy father hath killed the fatted calf, because he hath received him safe and sound. And he was angry, and would not go in: therefore came his father out, and entreated him. And he answering, said to his father, Lo, these many years do I serve thee, neither transgressed I at any time thy commandment; and yet thou never gavest me a kid, that I might make merry with my friends: but as soon as this thy son was come, which hath devoured thy living with harlots, thou hast killed for him the fatted calf. And he said unto him, Son, thou art ever with me, and all that I have is thine. It was meet that we should make merry, and be glad: for this thy brother was dead, and is alive again; and was lost, and is found."   LUKE XV. 11–32.

THE parables of The Lost Sheep, The Lost Piece of Silver, and The Prodigal Son, were spoken by our Lord on one occasion and for one general purpose.

The occasion, as we have already seen, was the carping of the Scribes and Pharisees at the gracious reception which sinners received from Jesus; and the general purpose was, to illustrate the seeking love and pardoning mercy of God toward the wandering, the lost, and the prodigal.

Our Lord had already, to a great extent, vindicated his procedure in receiving sinners, by showing, through the two preceding parables, that it was natural that he should feel a deep interest in those who, having wandered, had now been reclaimed, having been lost, were now found. But many, probably, of his hearers were fathers, who, un-influenced, it may be, by similitudes drawn from pastoral or domestic life, might yet be deeply touched by an appeal to parental emotions, the natural outgushings of a heart for the sons of their affection. Nothing, then, could be more relevant, both to the audience which he addressed, and the truth which he wished to enforce, than the touching incidents related in the parable of the Prodigal Son.

We picture to ourselves the venerable father, blessed with an abundance of this world's goods, and happy in possessing two sons, to whom he looked for comfort in his advancing years.

But discontent has already begun its work upon the

younger son; and, after long nursing his unhappy feelings, and long manifesting an increasing bitterness of spirit, he seizes upon some trifling excuse, and, in an exacting and unfeeling way, demands, "Father, give me the portion of goods that falleth to me." He wishes to get it into his own hands, to spend it as he pleases, without either parental advice or control.

Hitherto, the two sons had shared their father's house, table, bounty, love; but, on occasion of the peremptory demand of the younger, the father, in the words of the parable, "divided unto them his living."

Waiting "not many days," only long enough to convert his "portion of goods" into ready money, he turned his back upon his father and his boyhood's home, and "took his journey into a far country;" where no parental control would restrain him in his course of sin; where, master of himself and of his means, he could do "whatsoever he listed."

In this "far country," mingling with the dissolute and abandoned, he soon wastes "his substance in riotous living." Deserted by his parasitic friends, who attached themselves to him only so long as they could draw out the sap and strength of his pecuniary substance, he found himself "in want," with "a famine" pressing upon him, and not a friend to lean upon for even a temporary support. In this starving, desolate, ruined condition, he seeks, as a last resort, for some menial employment, by which he can at least satisfy his hunger, and secure a temporary home. He let himself out for hire to "a citizen of that country," and is sent by him "into his fields to feed swine"—the meanest of all employment, one abhorred by the Jews as unclean, and so contemned by the Egyptians, that swineherds were the only persons excluded from their temples.

But the depth of his misery was not yet reached, for such were the cravings of hunger, and such the miserable portion of food allotted him, in this time of famine, that he would fain have eaten the husks or pods of the carob tree, used only as fodder for beasts, but "no man gave unto him." Wretched object! stripped of his money, shrunken with hunger, turned out as a swineherd into the fields, a beggar and a stranger in a far-off land, with the glad remembrances of a former and happy life, making more vivid and sorrowful his present wretchedness; there he lay, the younger son of a liberal and bountiful father, loathsome, degraded, wretched: a melancholy picture of self-begotten misery and woe.

How long he remained thus is not stated. The next intimation we have of him is, that "he came to himself," as if all this time he had not been himself, had been acting as a crazy man, and had now only just awoke from his demented condition, and looked at himself in a true light. He compares himself not with his former condition and circumstances, when, as a son, he sat at his father's table, and lodged in his father's mansion, and was waited on by his father's servants; so low is he debased in his own eyes, that he does not raise himself to the height of this comparison, which, on first thought, we might suppose would be the very one that would be uppermost in his mind; but he himself humbly compares himself to his father's menials, and as his thoughts wander afar off from the swine and the husks around him, to his distant boyhood's home, they bring up before him the plenty which fills his father's house: the very "hired servants" of which have "bread enough and to spare," while he, the son, whom those full-fed servants once obeyed, now "perishes with hunger." The thought stings him to the quick, and he resolves, under the influence of the deep emotion, "I will arise, and go to my father;" no longer will I sit down here in these distant fields, watching these loathsome beasts, but remembering the love and care of my father, and the plenty that fills his barns and board, to him I will go; yet not as a son; this relationship I have forfeited by my base desertion; but as a servant, and not as a servant only, but as a confessing, humbled penitent, for I will "say unto him, Father, I have sinned against Heaven and before thee, and am no more worthy to be called thy son; make me as one of thy hired servants."

His resolve was followed by action. He "came to his father;" and we can almost picture out his appearance and feelings as he reaches his native fields, and comes within sight of his father's house. Wan and weary with his journey, faint with hunger, emaciated with long fasting and walking, his face furrowed by the ploughshare of care, and his brow corrugated by the turbulence of mental anguish, clad in the tattered and besmeared garments of a swineherd, and leaning heavily upon his staff, he stands on the brow of the first hill from which he can catch a glimpse of his once happy home, and as it meets his eyes they fill with tears, and his heart is too full for utterance. The terrible contrast between his present and his past condition; the fearful wastings of life, health, strength, money, which a few months have made; the pictures of childish happiness enjoyed there, intermingling with the deep shadows which darkened his life in the land he had just left; must have crowded thickly upon his mind, and made his weak frame tremble as these emotions wrestled within him.

The father spies the returning prodigal even "when a great way off;" feels in his heart the wellings up of compassion towards his son, and not waiting to see what was the temper and condition of that son, he "runs to meet him," "falls upon his neck" with joy, and "kisses him" with parental affection. The son, overpowered by this display, begins his premeditated speech; "Father, I have sinned against Heaven in thy sight, and am no more worthy to be called thy son." The father stopped to hear no more; the sentence, "Make me as one of thy hired servants," was arrested on his lips by the father's orders to the servants, "Bring forth the best robe and put it on him, and put a ring on his hand, and shoes on his feet; and bring hither the fatted calf, and kill it, and let us eat and be merry: for this my son was dead, and is alive again; he was lost, and is found." Thus by these four signs, the freeman's robe, the patrician's ring, the sandals of honour, and the feast of gladness, did the father manifest the highest regard for his son, and confer on him the highest honours of his house.

What a contrast between the morning and evening of

that day! The morning swineherd, the way-worn beggar, the hunger-pinched prodigal, is now, at eventide, the robed and ringed and sandalled son, the restored wanderer, the feasted guest, the joy of his father's heart and home.

While thus merry, father and younger son together, "the elder son," who, when the meeting took place, "was in the field" superintending his labourers, "drew nigh to the house," and was astonished to hear sounds "of music and dancing;" inquiring of "one of the servants" "what these things meant?" he was told the story of the prodigal's return. Instead, however, of rejoicing at the coming back of his erring brother, and going in and congratulating his father, and joining in the festive scene, he becomes "angry, and would not go in." The kind father, hearing of his feelings, goes out to him, and aims to soften down his wrath; but the surly brother rebuffs him by relating his long-continued goodness, and hints even at unrewarded services; while his dissolute brother no sooner returns from disgrace and beggary and crime, than there is "killed for him the fatted calf." The ill-natured attack of the elder brother, both upon his father and the prodigal, is met by the gentle yet forcible reply of the father, "Son, thou art ever with me, and all that I have is thine; it was meet that we should make merry and be glad, for this thy brother was dead, and is alive again; he was lost, and is found."

Such is the exquisitely beautiful parable of the Prodigal Son, which Trench calls "the pearl and crown of all the parables of the Scripture;" and of which Lavater says, "Had Christ only come to earth for the purpose of delivering this parable, on that account alone should all mortal and immortal beings have concurred in bending the knee before Him."

In considering the moral of this parable, we find that it resolves itself into four stages, viz., the prodigal's departure, his degradation, his return, and his reception. In each of these courses of action there is furnished a complete type of the human heart; and in the reception which the returning wanderer meets with, there is set out the free and pardoning love of a great and holy God.

The prodigal began his departure by the exacting request, "Give me the portion of goods that falleth to me." The desire to throw off the reins of God's government and to be independent of Him, is the root sin of all sins. It was this which cast down the rebel angels; which entrapped Adam into disobedience, and by which death was brought into the world and all our woe. As soon as the heart begins to be conscious of its relations and duties to God it grows restive, and commences its efforts at departure. The sinner selfishly craves "his portion of goods" from God, as if God was bound to divide unto him his living; and where there is this perversity of mind, God often permits men to make the experiment which they desire. He gives them "their portion in this life;" appears to bless them, and crown their lives with mercies: so far, however, from being satisfied, they collect the energies of mind and body, their influence and their resources, and having "gathered all together" with them, they commence their career of apostacy and crime. This career is a rapidly downward and an increasingly wicked one; for when the soul has once so compacted its energies as to cast off its filial duty to God and the checks of his Fatherly control, there is nothing to impede its onward course, for all the breaks of human resolves are powerless upon the rushing wheels of passion-driven man. The soul that has departed from God has commenced a series of sins which will ever augment in size, and increase in power, and deepen in guilt throughout eternity.

This departure from God is a wilful one. It is not God the Father thrusting the son out of his house, and exiling him to a "far country," but the son voluntarily breaking away from the Father, and recklessly plunging into ruin, preferring the "far country" to his father's house. That "far country" is this fallen world. We are here at a great moral distance from our Father's Home. We here waste the powers of mind and body in riotous living, in doing those things which God forbids and our consciences disapprove, and the pangs of spiritual want soon seize upon us. For in this far off land there is a famine in all those things that the soul most needs; and the world, so far from satisfying our spiritual cravings, like a hard master, sends us, immortal beings as we are, to the vilest of employments and the meanest of food. It is markedly emphatic of the debasing influence of the world, that our Lord should select such a loathsome and, by the Levitical law, almost accursed employment as a swineherd, as an illustration of the depths of misery to which it would reduce us, having first caused us to "waste our substance in riotous living." And as all those drudging occupations to which men bind out their souls for hire, are, in comparison to those employments of holiness in which they should be engaged, as brutish as the swineherd's, so also is the food which the world offers to the starving spirit but husks—worthless, unsatisfying. The soul can never thrive upon such bestial diet, and it famishes for something real, true, holy; something suitable to its wants here and its destinies hereafter.

As soon as the grace of God visits such a soul, it becomes at once conscious of its wants. There is a waking up to its needs, an opening of the eye to its miseries, a disenchanting of the spell which has so long perverted the judgment; and the poor debased sinner begins to feel his wretchedness, his degradation, his perishing condition. The sin of his departure from God comes into clear view; his guilt in his subsequent course stands out in its true light; the woe of his present position darkens over him, like a lowering cloud charged with the arrowy lightnings of an angry God; and the future lies before him, a yawning, bottomless gulf of woe, to the brink of which he feels that he is speedily hasting. This is the hour when the Holy Spirit begins his work of conviction, holding up the sins of his life in the light of God's countenance, and causing him to mourn with a godly sorrow that needeth not to be repented of. He shows him that he is "wretched, and miserable, and poor, and blind, and naked;" and having convinced him of his undone condition, points him to his Father's house, stirs up within him a desire to return, and strengthens him to resolve, "I will arise and go to my Father."

Not, however, until driven from every "refuge of lies," does the sinner desire to return. His proud heart rebels against going back to God, from whom he so vauntingly departed. The doctrine of free grace ill comports with his boasted self-righteousness and independence. If he could, by any works of penance, hew out for himself a salvation, so that the merit of it should be all his own, and of which he could say, "my power and the might of my hand hath gotten me this victory," he would gladly do it; and he makes a great variety of attempts to obtain peace of mind before he turns with a simple faith to "Behold the Lamb of God, which taketh away the sin of the world." Then it is that the sinner "comes to himself;" up to this period he is beside himself." He calls good evil, and bitter sweet; his moral sense is perverted; his mind acts without due control; he yields himself as a servant to sin; he "loves darkness rather than light;" he runs greedily in the way of sin; he seeks supremely his own selfish ends; is under the governance of merely worldly influences; shuts his eyes to the future, and madly rushes on to eternal ruin. Now, however, this delusion is being broken up: he begins to look at things in their just relation: reason recovers its ascendancy, and reflection busies itself with his past life. Now he thinks on God, his Father, and what he has left in his Father's house, and the rich provision there made for the souls of His servants, and the fulness of bread therein for all who will resort thither. He begins his repentance by a resolve to break off his present course of life—for there is no repentance where there is a continuance in sin

—saying, "I will arise;" I will sit no longer in these distant fields, in this brutish servility. "I will arise," and renouncing my employment, will "go to my Father." And this indicates the second essential element of true repentance, which is a turning to God; for when the Holy Ghost produces in the soul that godly sorrow for sin which is the result of his convicting power, then there results a repentance which manifests itself in a turning away from sin, and a turning unto God, with full purpose of heart to serve Him in sincerity and truth.

The resolve to return is accompanied by a penitent confession, "Father, I have sinned against Heaven and before thee." Under the enlightening influences of the Spirit, the sinner is taught to behold his iniquities in a new point of view. Hitherto he has regarded sin only as it has affected his worldly interests and standing. Its heinousness has been measured by the discomforts of mind or body to which it has subjected him; now, however, the mere earthly aspect of sin is overtopped by its appearance in the light of God's countenance. He sees it to be that abominable thing which God hateth; and as the holy character of God rises into view, he beholds more clearly the baseness of his iniquity; and so filled is he with a sense of his vileness in God's sight, that he exclaims with David, "Against thee only have I sinned." The idea that he "has sinned against heaven," against the laws, the love, the mercy, the long-suffering, the holiness of the God of Heaven, is the absorbing idea of the repenting sinner. He never thought before of sin as it appears in the view of

God, and of Christ, and of the Holy Ghost; and he is amazed at its grossness and baseness, and exclaims, "Behold, I am vile;" "I abhor myself, and repent in dust and ashes."

For humility necessarily follows true repentance and confession. It is impossible for the soul to say, "Father, I have sinned against Heaven," without that conscious worthlessness on account of guilt so humbling the soul as also to call out the further exclamation, "I am no more worthy to be called thy son; make me as one of thy hired servants." To occupy the lowest place in the Church militant or Church triumphant is far too good for the now abased penitent. To be a "doorkeeper," "a hired servant," is all to which the prostrate, sin-stricken soul dares aspire; and he feels that, to be "least in the kingdom of God" is higher honour than to be the greatest in the kingdoms of men. And well may the soul be humble when it contemplates the number, malignity, and constancy of its sins of thought and word and deed, secret and open, of omission and commission, on the one hand; and the character of God—holy, supreme, eternal, infinite—against whom it has sinned, on the other. In the presence of such mountain-like sins, and before such an ineffably glorious God, what position can the penitent take, but that of deepest humility and abasement; putting his hand upon his mouth, and his mouth in the dust, crying, "unclean, unclean," "God be merciful to me a sinner."

From the depths of penitent humility, rises the most vigorous Christian action. He will love Christ the most, who has seen most of the plague of his own heart, and been made to feel most keenly the bitings of the "famine," and the worthlessness of the "husks" in that "far country" of sin, wherein he was in bondage; and he will work for Christ the most energetically who loves most ardently, for there is no motive power to action so strong, so enduring, so elevating as the constraining love of Christ. Hence the prompt carrying into effect of the resolve, "I will arise and go to my Father." He arises, departs, leaves all behind him, and bends his eager steps towards his Father's house. He does not allow any doubts as to his Father's readiness to receive him to disturb his mind; he does not stop to make himself more respectable, more externally worthy; he does not hesitate and say, "If my Father wants me or loves me, it is easy enough for him to send out his hired servants and find me, and bring me home. In the confidence of a faith in his Father's readiness to receive and willingness to forgive, which is based on the immutable promise of God, he goes to that Father; for, over the gateway that leads to His mercy-seat is inscribed in bold letters, "Him that cometh unto me I will in no wise cast out."

As soon as there is this putting forth of the hand of faith, and laying hold on Christ as the hope set before us in the Gospel, there is a sensible appreciation of the fact that our Father, while we "were yet a great way off," has seen us, has had compassion on us, has come out to meet us, and has, with more than oriental manifestations of His love, taken us to His bosom and led us to His earthly courts. Beautifully as the touches of this exquisite parable illustrate the tenderness of an earthly parent, they come far short of expressing the infinite, the divine, the eternal love of God for us miserable sinners, or the wonderful displays of His compassion when He gave His well-beloved and only-begotten Son " to die—the just for the unjust—that we might be reconciled to God." Oh, impenitent man! only obey the motions of the Holy Ghost, and leave your swine-like lusts, your worldly husks, your servitude to sin, and arise and go to your Father; you will soon see that Father hasting towards you; His Divine love moving Him to truest compassion, and causing Him to meet you while "yet a great way off;" for the language of this loving Father is, as Hosea tells us, "How shall I give thee up, Ephraim? How shall I deliver thee, Israel? How shall I make thee as Admah? How shall I set thee as Zeboim? Mine heart is turned within me; my repentings are kindled together."

The rich provision which God makes for the repenting sinner illustrates still further his abounding love. The prodigal comes in the rags of his degradation, and is, by the ministering hand of faith, clothed in the robe, "the best robe," of Christ's perfect righteousness, so that he exclaims with Isaiah, "I will greatly rejoice in the Lord; my soul shall be joyful in my God; for He hath clothed me with the garments of salvation. He hath covered me with the robe of righteousness."

The hand which squandered his Father's gifts, and doled out husks to the swine, is now adorned with a ring, the covenant ring of a new and everlasting alliance, the " token and pledge" of a union which the Lord will bless.

He comes, with feet lacerated and wearied with the roughness and greatness of the sinner's way, and receives the shoes of the " preparation of the Gospel of peace," by which he is enabled to tread with confidence in the path of duty, and run with fleetness in the way of God's commandments. He comes, hungry and famished, and God spreads for him in His house the Gospel feast, "a feast of fat things, a feast of wines on the lees, of fat things full of marrow, of wines on the lees well refined." And this eucharistic feast, at which the truly penitent and believing soul feeds by faith on the body and blood of Calvary's Sacrifice, and is nourished and strengthened thereby, is but the antepast of that more glorious reunion when, with Abraham, and Isaac, and Jacob, " he shall sit down to the marriage-supper of the Lamb in Heaven."

He comes in sorrow and humility, feeling that he is unworthy to be called a son, and desiring to take a low place, even as " a hired servant," and he is received with every demonstration of joy; the church on earth rejoices, and welcomes him with music and thanksgiving; Christ rejoices, for He then sees of the travail of his soul, and is satisfied; and "there is joy in the presence of the angels of God," for this their earthly " brother was dead, and is alive again; was lost, and is found."

The Unjust Steward.

THE UNJUST STEWARD.

"And he said also unto his disciples, There was a certain rich man, which had a steward; and the same was accused unto him that he had wasted his goods. And he called him, and said unto him, How is it that I hear this of thee? give an account of thy stewardship; for thou mayest be no longer steward. Then the steward said within himself, What shall I do? for my lord taketh away from me the stewardship: I cannot dig; to beg I am ashamed. I am resolved what to do, that, when I am put out of the stewardship, they may receive me into their houses. So he called every one of his lord's debtors unto him, and said unto the first, How much owest thou unto my lord? And he said, A hundred measures of oil. And he said unto him, Take thy bill, and sit down quickly, and write fifty. Then said he to another, And how much owest thou? And he said, A hundred measures of wheat. And he said unto him, Take thy bill, and write fourscore. And the lord commended the unjust steward, because he had done wisely: for the children of this world are in their generation wiser than the children of light. And I say unto you, Make to yourselves friends of the mammon of unrighteousness; that, when ye fail, they may receive you into everlasting habitations." LUKE XVI. 1–9.

COMMENTATORS, while they have done much to explain the parables, have also done much to obscure them. They have sometimes created more obstacles than they have removed, and, by their multifarious explanations and hypercritical emendations, have involved passages in perplexity, which before were clear and simple.

It is the duty of the biblical scholar to study when to let the subject plead its own cause, and when to play the able advocate for its rendering or its doctrine, but never to overlay the words of God with human explanations, however ornate or beautiful. The Apollo of Praxiteles needs no cloak of gold from the hand of Demetrius.

These remarks apply with some force to the parable under consideration, which some of the ancient fathers looked upon as the most difficult and obscure of all; and one learned divine (Cajetan) has gone so far as to declare that it is not only difficult but impossible to give its true meaning.

The error under which most of the expositors of this passage have laboured has been that of attempting to fit an interpretation to every circumstance and incident of the parable, instead of attempting to seize upon and elucidate its main scope and design. "A parable, and the moral accommodation of it, are not," as one well observes, "like two planes, which touch one another in every part, but like a globe upon a plane, which only touches in one point."

Though this may not be true of all the parables, it is certainly very near the truth as it respects this, for the one point of contact here between the parable and the moral accommodation of it to men, is the word "wisely:" the incident in the first part of the parable being designed to show that the steward acted "wisely," or with temporal prudence and foresight, in making provision for the future; and the latter part of it, or application, being intended to urge upon us in reference to our soul's future, a spiritual wisdom, corresponding in its prudence and foresight to this wise acting in the things of earth.

"Wisely," then, seems to be the key word of the parable, opening before us "the two-leaved gates" of the similitude and the application. Let us examine the similitude or parable first, and then the moral or application. In applying the term "wisely" (or "prudently," as Wiclif more properly renders the original) to the unjust steward, it signifies merely temporal wisdom, sagacity, discernment, foresight to perceive danger, and wit to provide for it, according to the best classical usage of the word as found in the writings of Aristotle, Xenophon, Plato, and Euripides. In this strictly worldly sense the unjust steward acted "wisely," in making full provision for the future.

When accusation was made against him that he had "wasted" his master's goods, and he was called upon to answer to the charge by giving an account of his stewardship, he was at a loss how to proceed, and asks the anxious question, "What shall I do?" The charges against him he knew to be true; dismissal from office must inevitably follow an examination of his rent-rolls and accounts; how therefore to acquire a livelihood when discharged from his present lucrative station, perplexed his mind. Unaccustomed to labour, he could not work; puffed up with pride, he could not beg; and between his inability to do the one and his unwillingness to do the other, he had but a poor prospect for the future.

He soon settles the matter by adding iniquity to iniquity, and completing a long course of dishonesty by open fraud. He makes his resolve, comforts himself with the assurance that it will secure him a home, and then proceeds to carry his plan into operation.

He immediately summons his lord's debtors or tenants, looks over the various amounts which they had obligated themselves to pay for their lands or dwellings, rentals which, to this day, in Eastern countries, are mostly paid in the produce of the land, as corn, oil, wheat, wine. Finding that the first to whom he spoke was bound for "a hundred measures," or about a thousand gallons of olive oil (a valuable article of oriental commerce), he tells him to take his "bill" or lease, erase the hundred, and "sit down quickly and write fifty," thus, cancelling at a stroke one-half his debt.

He then calls a second, and learning from his answer that he was to pay "an hundred measures of wheat," or over 1400 bushels, he directed him to strike off one-fifth, and thus make his obligation but "fourscore." Two, only, are mentioned, but the tenor of the narrative implies that there were other debtors, and that the like reduction was made in all their contracts; and this the steward could easily do, because he was the one through whom the estates were rented, the one to whom the revenue was paid; and as these "bills" or obligations were in the handwriting of the renters, countersigned and witnessed by the steward, hence, it was very easy so to collude with the debtors as to produce the changes in the lease of each which are specified in the parable. The result of this was, that he placed each under an obligation to himself, varying, probably, with the ability of each to meet that obligation, and thus made sure of a welcome among these "debtors" when his lord should discharge him from his stewardship.

He reasoned upon the general law of reciprocity, and, though he was faithless to his master, he believed these obliged debtors would be faithful to him.

For this act of worldly wisdom the lord (not Jesus) or master of the steward was forced to commend him, for, though he saw the crime, he could not but praise the foresight and sagacity by which he secured to himself both friends and home.

Much unnecessary obloquy has been thrown upon our blessed Lord, by attributing the commendation of the unjust steward to Him, rather than to the master or lord of the steward. From the time of the emperor Julian, who made this an occasion of vilifying the character of Christ, down to the neological interpreters of the present day, it has been made an instrument, either of attacking the character of Christ, or of giving Divine support to knavery and fraud; and though some excellent commentators, as Henry and Whitby, favour the idea that the commendation proceeded from Jesus, yet the peculiar construction of the original Greek words, as well as the propriety of the thing itself, renders it certain that the "lord" indicated was the steward's master, and not Jesus Christ. It was, then, the same "lord" mentioned in the third verse, "for my lord taketh away my stewardship;" and the same "lord" mentioned in the fifth verse, "How much owest thou unto my Lord?" who, in the eighth verse, "commended the unjust steward, because he had done wisely."

At this word 'wisely,' the parable proper ends. And now, with a sort of parenthetical remark, that "the children of this world are in their generation wiser than the children of light," Christ enforces the true moral of the parable in the emphatic words, "And I say unto you, make to yourselves friends of the mammon of unrighteousness, that when ye fail they may receive you into everlasting habitations." In which application to His disciples, "yourselves" answers to the "steward" of the parable; the "friends" to the "Lord's debtors;" "when ye fail," to the removal of the steward from his office; and "the reception into everlasting habitations" is antithetical of the temporary lodgings into which the steward was received by his earthly friends, when "put out of the stewardship;" and all turns upon the word "wisely," which is the hinge of the parable.

This we learn from looking into the parable itself. Why was it uttered? To teach us to waste goods intrusted to us? to teach us to cheat and defraud our employers? to show us how to make our fellow-men accomplices in our crimes? to commend injustice? Certainly not. So that we are shut up to the word wisely as the true pith of the parable, or else must discard it as teaching nothing worthy to be learned.

What, then, in reference to the wise actings of this steward, would our Lord have us imitate? What are the real lessons which this parable was designed to teach? That we should use our riches with a wise reference to our soul's future existence, and, regarding them as treasures given us in trust, and ourselves as stewards, amenable to our Divine

Lord, so spend this "mammon of unrighteousness" in the cause of God, the extension of the Church, and the relief of human misery, as that we do by a figure of speech "make friends" thereby; "friends" who, when we "fail," or "die," shall, as it were, receive us "into everlasting habitations." "We shall find friends there," says Luther, "for the good deeds we have done, the kindness and beneficence we have shown to the poor; these shall not only be witnesses of our brotherly and Christian behaviour, but shall also be commended and recompensed. Then one shall come and say, 'Lord, here is a person who gave me a coat, a little money, a piece of bread, a cup of water in the time of need.' Yea, as Christ tells us in the 25th chapter of Matthew, He, Himself, shall come forth and testify before His Heavenly Father, angels, and saints what we have done for Him, and how we have thereby approved our faith." Luther also adds this important remark—"it is not works which gain heaven for us, but Christ freely grants eternal life to those who believe, and give evidence of their faith in works of love and the right employment of their earthly goods."

Riches, termed here "the mammon of unrighteousness," or the false, fleeting, uncertain riches of earth, in the abstract have neither moral good nor evil. They are, so long as unused, passive and innocuous: it is riches in motion which gives them a definite character; and here they move under two laws, and in two directions, the law of selfishness and the law of love: the direction towards God, and whatever tends to advance His glory, and the direction towards earth, and whatever abets its lusts and pleasures.

As, then, we cannot live in the world without making use of mammon after some sort, so must we use it as to make friends by it, not consuming it upon our lusts, not squandering it in frivolous schemes and pursuits, not hoarding it up for family aggrandisement; for then it truly becomes unrighteous mammon, one of the most powerful instruments of vice and wickedness; then truly, as the heathen poet writes, is "gold more destructive than the sword;" and becomes, as an Apostle declares, " the root of all evil." But we must appropriate it to works of mercy, feeding the hungry, relieving the poor, assisting the afflicted, ministering to the heirs of salvation, extending the gospel of Christ; thus putting it out to interest in God's service, so that in the end we shall receive unfading riches for filthy lucre, with the usury of grace here and glory in heaven.

This is the way to "provide ourselves bags which wax not old;" "a treasure in the heavens that faileth not," where no thief steals, no moth frets, no rust corrodes. Into these habitations all will be received when discharged from earth, who have that faith which, working by love, brings forth the fruits of righteousness and true holiness. The steward was received into the wooden tenements or clay-built cottages of his lord's debtors, and by earthly and mortal friends. The friends have long since departed, the dwellings have long since crumbled away; but "the friends" which the right users of mammon make, are in heaven, and the "habitations" into which they will welcome us are "everlasting;" for the inheritance of the Christian is "incorruptible, undefiled, and passeth not away."

Let us imitate then the foresight of the unjust steward in making provision for the future, by acting wisely for the eternal interests of our souls; let us imitate the alacrity and promptness of the unjust steward, who lost not a moment in view of his speedy discharge to secure friends and homes, by being as prompt and eager in the prospect of our failing life to gain the favour of Him who is "a friend, that sticketh closer than a brother," and a mansion among the "everlasting habitations;" "for we know," says St. Paul, "that if our earthly house of this tabernacle were dissolved, we have a building of God, a house not made with hands, eternal in the heavens." And finally, let us remember, that it behoves "the children of light" to be as wise, as cautious, as circumspect, as far-seeing, as prompt in devising, and as liberal in executing every good plan for the salvation of souls, and the glory of God, as "the children of this world are in their generation."

Yet how seldom is this the case! How very far the spirit of Christian enterprise falls below the level of worldly enterprise! We need then, as "children of light," to go to the "Father of lights" for that illumination which will enable us to act with more judgment, tact, zeal, and forecast in our spiritual concerns, beseeching Him that He would strengthen us "with the Holy Ghost, the Comforter, and daily increase in us thy manifold gifts of grace, the spirit of wisdom and understanding, the spirit of counsel and ghostly strength, the spirit of knowledge and true godliness, and fill us, O Lord, with the spirit of thy holy fear, now and for ever."

The Good Samaritan.

THE GOOD SAMARITAN.

"A certain man went down from Jerusalem to Jericho, and fell among thieves, which stripped him of his raiment and wounded him, and departed, leaving him half dead. And by chance there came down a certain priest that way; and when he saw him he passed by on the other side. And likewise a Levite, when he was at the place, came and looked on him, and passed by on the other side. But a certain Samaritan, as he journeyed, came where he was: and when he saw him, he had compassion on him, and went to him and bound up his wounds, pouring in oil and wine, and set him on his own beast, and brought him to an inn, and took care of him. And on the morrow, when he departed, he took out two pence, and gave them to the host, and said unto him, Take care of him: and whatsoever thou spendest more, when I come again, I will repay thee. Which now of these three, thinkest thou, was neighbour unto him that fell among the thieves? And he said, He that showed mercy on him. Then said Jesus unto him, Go, and do thou likewise." LUKE x. 30–37.

THE law of benevolence never received a more beautiful illustration than in the parable of the Good Samaritan. The tact with which it was introduced, and the judicious selection of its circumstances, are only equalled by the felicity of its similitude and the force of its appeal.

For the purpose of putting to the proof Christ's knowledge and wisdom, a lawyer, on one occasion, asked Him the momentous question—" Master, what shall I do to inherit eternal life?" As one conversant with the law, our Lord referred him back to the law, and asked him what that said upon the subject. He immediately returned the prompt reply, "Thou shalt love the Lord thy God with all thy heart, and with all thy soul, and with all thy strength, and with all thy mind; and thy neighbour as thyself." Jesus replied, "Thou hast answered right; this do, and thou shalt live." But the lawyer was not prepared to fulfil the broad provisions of this law, and hence, in order to justify any remissness, or to excuse the performance of his duty under the plea of ignorance, he says to Jesus, "And who is my neighbour?" for the Pharisees, to which sect the lawyers mostly belonged, acknowledged none as neighbours but those of their own faith and nation.

Instead of giving a categorical reply, our Lord brings before him the case of a man, who, on his journey from Jerusalem to Jericho, about fifteen miles to the south-west, on the river Jordan, fell among the thieves which infested the lurking places of that wilderness road. These bandits not merely robbed the traveller of his money, but "stripped him of his raiment, and wounded him, and departed, leaving him half dead."

While thus lying weltering in his blood, "there came down a certain priest that way," for thousands of priests and Levites dwelt at Jericho, and passed to and fro as they went up to Jerusalem to minister before the Lord, or returned from the Temple, having finished their course of service.

This priest saw the wounded man, but, instead of pausing to alleviate his suffering, and thus fulfilling, only in a higher degree, the Levitical law which declared, "Thou shalt not see thy brother's ass or his ox fall down by the way, and hide thyself from them; thou shalt surely help him to lift them up again;" "he passed by on the other side."

Soon a Levite came to the place, and, moved by a curiosity that had in it no element of compassion, "came and looked on him;" saw his helpless state; and yet, unmoved by the sight, he also "passed by on the other side."

But that which the wounded man's own countrymen refused to do, the nation's enemy, a Samaritan, did; for "a certain Samaritan, as he journeyed, came where he was; and when he saw him, he had compassion."

This compassion was no mere barren emotion, but active and practical. He went to him where he lay in his blood; he washed his bruises with wine, the styptic qualities of which were well known; and allayed the pain of the wounds with the soothing oil of Samaria; carefully binding up his wounds, and preparing him for removal from his painful position. Nor did his compassion end here. He set the miserable man "on his own beast;" and, walking by his side to support him in his seat and to guide the ass, he "brought him to an inn," and there tarried with him all night, ministering those attentions which the traveller so much needed, over and above those which he had received at the wayside.

On the morrow, before he left to go on his journey, he paid the host of the inn in advance, for the care of the sick man,—giving him two denarii, or twenty-eight cents of our money: a sum quite insufficient, according to modern expenditures, but at that time equal to the full pay of a labourer for two days, and therefore ample for the wants of the sick man until the Samaritan could return again. Having committed him to the care of the innkeeper, with the promise, "whatsoever thou spendest more, when I come again, I will repay thee," the compassionate Samaritan departed.

Spreading out this scene before the eyes of the lawyer, our Lord puts to him the question, "Which now of these three, thinkest thou, was neighbour unto him that fell among thieves?" The lawyer replied, "He that showed mercy on him;" a correct judgment, and one which settled at once the great principle of moral relationship between man and man.

It was not possible for our Lord to take stronger antagonistic elements whereby to illustrate the fusing power of neighbourly affection, than the Jew and the Samaritan. There existed between the two people a national hatred of the most implacable kind. The Samaritans had built on Mount Gerizim a temple, in opposition to the one at Jerusalem; they had established a priesthood in rivalry of the Aaronic order; they rejected all of the Sacred Scriptures but the five books of Moses; they paid no heed to the tradition of the elders, which the Jews so tenaciously held; and though, according to the glosses of the Pharisees, the Jews might buy of the Samaritans, they were not to borrow anything of them, were not to receive them into their houses, were not to accept from them any kindness, and were bound under an anathema not to eat or drink with them. Thus, as the woman of Sychar truly said to Jesus as he sat at Jacob's well, "the Jews have no dealings with the Samaritans:" and thus also, when the enemies of our Lord wished to stigmatize Him with the most contemptuous epithet, they termed him "a Samaritan that had a devil."

When, therefore, Jesus selected, as the representative of that love which he would inculcate, the deeds of a despised Samaritan, and when he compelled Jewish lips to utter praises to the compassion and kindness of this "alien and stranger to the commonwealth of Israel," he gave expression in the most forcible form possible, to the broad, binding, universal nature of that second table of the Law, which Himself had summed up in the command, "Thou shalt love thy neighbour as thyself."

Those who, like Origen in the early ages of the Church, search for a hidden and mysterious sense under the plain and literal text, interpret this parable in reference to the fall and recovery of man. Such is the explanation made by Luther and Melancthon, in former days; by the Baptist commentator Gill, by the learned Jones of Nayland, and by the recent work of Trench, to say nothing of minor and uninfluential authorities. These writers differ about many of the details of the parable, but their general views may be thus expressed: The "certain man" is "Adam as he is the head and representative of his race;" the going "down from Jerusalem to Jericho" is emblematical of his going out from Paradise into a world of thorns and briars; his falling "among thieves" indicates the malignant powers of hell, who assail the sinner and rob him of his heavenly birthright; his being stripped "of his raiment," marks his despoliation of the robe of original innocence; his "wounded" state shows the work of sin upon man, which makes him, "from the crown of his head to the sole of his foot, to be full of wounds, and bruises, and putrifying sores, which have neither been healed, neither bound up, neither mollified with ointment;" their "leaving him half dead" exemplifies the fact that Adam did not die in body the day in which he sinned, but that having pronounced against him the sentence of death, he may in truth have been declared "half dead." By the Priest and Levite is meant the Patriarchal (as in that age each head of the family was priest in his own house) and the Levitical dispensation, which, of themselves, could do nothing to recover lost man, "for it was not possible that the blood of bulls and of goats should take away sin." "But what the law could not do, in that it was weak through the flesh," was at length effected by Him whom the Jews called " a Samaritan," even Jesus Christ. The journey which He took was that of His incarnation, by which He "travelled in the greatness of His strength" from heaven to earth, and coming in the capacity of a Great Physician, He had oil and wine; the wine of His own cleansing and purifying blood, and the oil of His own anointing grace, which healeth all our infirmities. He is said to set him on His own beast, because of man's own inability to move of himself in the direction of his salvation; His being brought to an inn represents his admission to the visible Church; the ministry is "the host;" the Old and New Testaments " are the two pence" which this "Host" is to expound and administer as being steward of the manifold grace of God.

Such is the drift of these ingenious interpretations. They are very prettily wrought up, and, to some extent, perhaps, profitable; but such fancies will not admit of a close scrutiny, and lead us away from the real intent of our Lord when he spoke the parable. There may very often be parallels and coincidences between these beautiful similitudes and certain other truths of Scripture history, or doctrines of revelation, but these must not lead us astray from the plain design of the parable, which, in nearly every instance, can be ascertained by carefully studying its context and its bearing.

The plain import of this parable seems to be to teach us the necessity of actively obeying the second great command, "Thou shalt love thy neighbour as thyself," as an essential prerequisite to inheriting eternal life.

It urges us to this duty, first, by showing that benevolence is not to be circumscribed by national boundaries. Because the ancient Jews were prohibited from being familiar with idolatrous nations, and were enjoined to maintain a perpetual enmity with Amalek and the seven nations of Canaan, whom God had cast out before them and devoted to ruin, they came to regard themselves as warranted to hate all of mankind but their own nation, and did, in a great degree, confine their love and regard to their own kindred and people. As the Jews were, in an especial manner, the chosen people of the one living and true God, so were they particularly required to hate the ways and uproot the idolatries of the

Canaanitish nations, who were ever striving to seduce them from the worship of Jehovah.

On this point, the Divine injunctions were rigorous and inflexible; and properly so, because, as familiarity with sin lessens the hatred of it, and intercourse with transgressors insensibly begets a following in their steps; hence, God would break off all intercourse with such wicked nations, that He might preserve "unto himself a peculiar people, zealous of good works." Yet at the same time, the laws which God enjoined upon the Jews, in respect to strangers who happened in their land as travellers, or who came to sojourn there, were of the most lenient and tenderly protective kind. "Thou shalt not oppress the stranger; for ye know the heart of a stranger, seeing ye were strangers in the land of Egypt."

The time, however, had now arrived for breaking down this national seclusion. The purpose of God, in fencing off the Jews from other nations, and constituting them emphatically a theocracy, had been accomplished. The Messiah had come. The Christian dispensation was opening up to view, and that dispensation was not designed for one nation or people only, but for the whole world. Christianity knows no geographical boundaries, no treaty limits, no barriers of language, customs, climes, pursuits; it recognises no distinctions of sex, of colour, of estate, of education; it represents us all as of one blood, the offspring of a common Father, for whom is provided a common Redeemer, and before whom lies a common death, a common judgment, a common eternity. To meet this wonderful enlargement of God's scheme of grace, which lay folded up in the Jewish theocracy, as the germ in the seed corn, there was required a new promulging and a more vigorous enforcement of the duties of the second table of the Divine law. That promulgation of the law our Saviour made when He summed up the decalogue in two commands, on which He told us hung " all the law and the prophets;" and that vigorous enforcement of this second great command, our Saviour made in the touching parable now before us. And what our Lord thus taught He practised. National boundaries did not circumscribe his compassion. The Roman centurion, the Syro-Phœnician mother, the woman of Samaria, partook of His benevolence; and herein He has left us an example not to permit our charities to be pent up within the narrow bounds of our own state or nation, but, overleaping these, to find in every child of Adam, no matter what his birth, his education, his position, his abode, a " neighbour," an object of regard, and, if need be, of compassion. The acknowledgment of the lawyer, that he who had "showed mercy" to the wounded man, had most proved himself a neighbour, even though he was a Samaritan; and the solemn injunction, " Go and do thou likewise;" make it imperative on us to practise similar compassion to all our race, and like liberality of mind and heart and purse.

The parable teaches us, secondly, not to circumscribe our benevolence by our religious sympathies.

Those of the same " household of faith" may have more claims upon our kindness, but not to the exclusion of others. The Apostle's injunction is, "Do good unto all men;" and he adds, because of the nearer affinity into which religion draws us, "especially unto them that are of the household of faith."

Nothing could exceed the bitterness of the religious enmity between the Jew and the Samaritan. With rival temples, rival priests, rival altars, rival sacrifices, rival kingdoms, each stigmatized the other as idolaters, and waged mutual persecutions with a deadliness of hatred peculiar to religious animosities. Yet in this parable, the wounded Jew, whom the Priest and Levite of his own nation heeded not in the hour of his extremity, was succoured and relieved by the hated Samaritan. He did not stop to calculate the force of his religious differences; he did not pause on his journey to taunt and revile this helpless Jew; but, as soon as he saw his necessitous condition, "he had compassion on him." Religious differences, then, should have nothing to do with enlarged Christian benevolence. Sectarian charity is selfish charity, because based on motives of personal or denominational aggrandizement. Had the Samaritan thus reasoned, he never would have relieved the plundered Jew. Had Jesus thus thought, he never would have spoken this parable; for this rebukes that narrow spirit, and inculcates a broad philanthropy that disregards the fences and boundaries of sects and denominations, and that is willing to expend itself on every one that needs attention, because each sufferer whom our charities can reach is the "neighbour" whom we are bound to relieve. He who confines his benevolence within the limits of his religious creed, casts dishonour upon the God whom he pretends to worship, disregards the plain commands of the Bible, and manifests a narrowness of mind and illiberality of spirit, degrading to the Christian name.

This parable teaches us, thirdly, not to limit our sympathy and benevolence by personal friendships. Between the Jew and the Samaritan there was no social intercourse. The Jew cursed the Samaritan publicly in the synagogue; declared that he who received one into his house was laying up curses for his children; would no more eat of their food than they would taste swine's meat; and this enmity, manifesting itself through all the minute intercourse of adjoining nations, was fully reciprocated by the Samaritan, who sought in every way to annoy and vex the Jew. But all this weighed not in the case before us. Nor should such personal considerations weigh with us.

In his sermon on the mount, our Lord remarked, "Ye have heard that it hath been said, Thou shalt love thy neighbour and hate thine enemy;" this was the moral code of the Pharisees and Scribes, in which God's law had been mutilated by human traditions; but Christ recovers His law from these Talmudical perversions, by the authoritative command, "But I say unto you, love your enemies; bless them that curse you; do good to them that hate you, and pray for them which despitefully use you and persecute you." This is the sublime morality of the Gospel, so contrary to the spirit of the Jews; and the reason which Christ gives for its exercise is as sublime as the precept.

"That ye may be the children of your Father which is in Heaven: for He maketh His sun to rise on the evil and on the good, and sendeth rain on the just and on the unjust." Let your kindness be as limitless and as unconstrained by personal feelings as God's, for it is a necessary qualification to our being the children of God, that we should love our enemies. The hate of men we must meet with love, their cursing with blessing, their despite with goodness, their persecution with prayer. The kindness and sympathy of Jesus were not restricted within the circle of his immediate friends: "He went about doing good" to all classes, in all places, at all times, under all circumstances; yet often "had not where to lay his head;" often "was an hungered;" often "wearied," and always "a man of sorrows and acquainted with grief." He went even to Samaria, and there opened living fountains in the hearts of those who heard and believed on Him, even though at first rebuffed and almost insulted. In the very hour of his betrayal and arrest in Gethsemane, He imparted healing mercy to one of that midnight band who had gone out to bind Him; and on the cross He gave pardon and life eternal to the thief who, but a short time before, was reviling His holy name.

The broad command, then, enforced by this parable, and corroborated by the other teaching of Jesus Christ, is, that we are to show kindness, mercy, charity, irrespective of nation, kindred, friendship, or creed. That each man has a claim upon his fellow man, both by the common law of humanity and the superadded law of God.

In what an elevated position does this parable place the Christian dispensation! How nobly it contrasts, on the one hand, with the spirit of the Jews, whose hatred of other nations called out the reproaches of Tacitus and Juvenal and Diodorus Siculus; and, on the other, with the tenets of the best and wisest of the heathen philosophers, with whom revenge was a virtue, forgiveness of injuries a weakness, and love of enemies unknown.

The sentiment of the heathen poet—" Homo sum, nihil humanum a me alienum puto"—has been justly applauded as one of the finest of human apothegms; but it falls short, far short, of the Divine teaching of Jesus—" Love your enemies, bless them that curse you, do good to them that hate you, and pray for them that despitefully use you and persecute you;" for while the former maxim is founded on curiosity and selfishness, the latter is based on the manifestations of a Divine love, and its required imitation by those who would be called " the children of God." But this true spirit of love can be found only in hearts renewed by the Holy Ghost. It is not the product of natural amiability; it does not result from the gushings of human sympathy; it is not evoked by tender education. It is only as we love Christ, that we can love all men in Christ, and for Christ. If we indeed love Him with all our heart we love everything which He loves; and everything which engages His affection becomes magnified in importance and invested with new interest to us. When, therefore, we mark how deeply and self-sacrificingly He loves our race, how much affection and labour and care and blood He has expended on it; surely we find the highest possible motives for loving our fellow men. Love for them filled the Divine heart of Jesus; love for them evoked the mightiest operations of the Holy Ghost; love for them called forth the highest reach of the love of God the Father; and then are we most God-like when we imitate Him in manifesting a holy and sanctified affection towards our fellow men. Hence that strong assertion of St. John—"If a man say, I love God, and hateth his brother, he is a liar; for he that loveth not his brother whom he hath seen, how can he love God whom he hath not seen?"

This parable also furnishes a great missionary argument; not by way of direct precept, but by induction. If the law of Christ's Gospel requires us to love our neighbour, to the extending to him of all needed succour for the supply of his physical necessities, surely it requires, with all the added force of the supereminent value of the soul over the body, that we should love the souls of our neighbours, and give them the spiritual succours which they need for salvation. And as the word "neighbour" has been so broadened as to comprehend all mankind, irrespective of creed, colour, country; so must our love, if we would have it co-extensive with Gospel requirements, go out world-wide; so must it busy itself about the millions of our race who are now lying "half dead" in trespasses and sins; so must we, like the Samaritan, give to them those means of grace, and those aids in securing eternal life, which God has put in our power; so should we seek to bring them to the "Inn," the Church, and thus show forth our love to Christ, by evincing tenderest love for those for whom Christ died, but who are yet unblessed with Gospel light, and uninvited by the offers of salvation. He is not a true lover of his race who draws back or refuses to come up to the missionary work; for, as mankind can only be made holy, and consequently happy, through the applied blood of the cross, as this blood of cleansing can only be applied through faith in the Lord Jesus, and as he can be believed on only as he is preached to the nations, so a true philanthropy, that which strikes down to the root of things, is that which would exert itself to send out living preachers or spirit-speaking Bibles into all the corners of the earth, until all should know the Lord, from the rising to the setting sun. Christ's heart was a missionary heart, and every one who has Christ formed within him the hope of glory, has a missionary heart also.

In conclusion, though we do not believe in the fanciful interpretation of this parable, to which we have alluded, we may at least use it as illustrative of the exceeding love of our Lord Jesus for us miserable sinners. If we admire the conduct of the Samaritan, infinitely more must we admire the love of Christ. He beheld us robbed of the image of God, wounded by sin, lying helpless in our fallen humanity, and when we were so dead in iniquity that we could not help ourselves; when the Patriarchal dispensation stalked by on the other side, and deigned no help, when the Levitical dispensation came and looked on us through its shadowy ceremonies, and then, leaving us in our blood, passed by also on the other side; then Christ came, and though we were His enemies, He pitied us, bound up, by the oil and wine of Divine grace, our ghastly wounds; Himself bare our infirmities, took the whole charge of our cure, and healed us, not like the Samaritan, by giving money from His scrip, but blood from His heart, riven by the soldier's spear; blood from His head, drawn out by His acanthine crown; blood from His hands and feet, started by the spikes of the accursed tree; and by this precious bloodshedding He obtained for us relief from our enemies, spiritual health here, and life eternal beyond the grave.

The Pharisee and the Publican.

THE PHARISEE AND THE PUBLICAN.

"Two men went up into the temple to pray; the one a Pharisee, and the other a publican. The Pharisee stood and prayed thus with himself, God, I thank thee that I am not as other men are, extortioners, unjust, adulterers, or even as this publican. I fast twice in the week, I give tithes of all that I possess. And the publican, standing afar off, would not lift up so much as his eyes unto heaven, but smote upon his breast, saying, God be merciful to me a sinner. I tell you, this man went down to his house justified rather than the other: for every one that exalteth himself shall be abased; and he that humbleth himself shall be exalted." LUKE XVIII. 10–14.

THE two characters introduced into this parable were well known as types of the two extremes of Jewish society; and the contrast is the more striking, because of the preference given to the humble Publican over the haughty Pharisee.

A brief examination of the characteristics of the two classes will enable us to obtain clearer ideas of the persons brought to our notice, and of the truth which this parable was intended to convey. The Pharisee, as he thrusts himself more prominently forward, will first claim our attention.

The great body of the Jewish people were divided into three sects: the Pharisees, the Sadducees, and the Essenes; corresponding somewhat to the three schools of Grecian philosophy: the Pythagoreans, the Epicureans, and the Stoics. "Unlike the philosophy of the Greeks, however, which had scarcely anything but a human ground on which to stand and labour, the Jewish sects made a Divine revelation the object of their philosophical research, and so were saved from the grosser errors and absurd wanderings into which the Greek schools were led, while in pursuit of the airy visions of their own heated brain."

Until the Babylonish captivity, the Jews, as a body, were united in opinion; but after their dispersion, they imbibed many erroneous dogmas, and, grafting the fragments of a Greco-Oriental philosophy upon the long-accumulating traditions of the elders, they sought by these to interpret the Holy Scripture; and thus, for more than a century before Christ, the people became divided in doctrines and split up into factions, both political and religious. The three prominent parties were named severally, the Pharisees, the Sadducees, and the Essenes. Of these, the Pharisees were the wealthiest, the most learned, and the most influential, and were so called from a Hebrew word which signifies to separate, because they separated and distinguished themselves from others, by affecting uncommon sanctity, and by wearing a peculiar garment. Thus St. Paul calls the Pharisees "the straitest sect of our religion," and Josephus says that "they were the most religious of any of the Jews, and the most exact and skilful in explaining the laws."

The two sources whence we obtain our knowledge of Phariseeism are the writings of Josephus and the books of the New Testament. Josephus was himself a Pharisee, and he has presented the views and characteristics of that sect with force and minuteness in his several writings. His opinion was that of one interested in the case, and his representations are the most favourable that could possibly be made; yet, when closely examined, we cannot fail to discover how fully the leading features of this sect as portrayed by their apologist and expounder, and as drawn in Holy Writ, agree. The colouring is different, but when denuded of all masks and sophistry, the lineaments are the same. We will take the Bible view of their case, because it is Divinely true, and because it is important to a right understanding of this parable, that we should look at them through the delineations of the Holy Ghost.

From the New Testament, then, we learn that this sect was held in high repute as expositors of the law; that they were very casuistical in unfolding the Scriptures; full of proselyting zeal; rigorous in ritual observances; oppressive in their exactions; ostentatious in their charity and religion; pompous and self-inflated in their affected holiness; covering up an intense love of sensual pleasures by a pretended stoicism; diligent in the performance of every outward rite, that they "might be seen of men," while "inwardly they were ravening wolves;" haughty and imperious to inferiors, yet cringing parasites of royalty and power; neglecting the weightier matters of the law, and minutely critical in tithing and doing what the law did not require; "serpents" in wisdom, but leaving the trail of their slimy deeds behind them; "vipers" in the sudden and unexpected stings which they fastened wherever they thought they could strike their fangs with impunity; "graves," over which the people walked and knew not the hollowness beneath until they fell into the pit; "whited sepulchres," which indeed "appear beautiful outward, but within were full of dead men's bones and all uncleanness." They substituted human traditions for God's Word; made their boast of the law by wearing broad phylacteries, and yet dishonoured the law; turned their prayers into instruments of covetousness and extortion; "compassed sea and land to make one proselyte," and then made him "twofold more a child of hell than themselves;" united in the one aim of destroying Jesus, and effected their purpose through bribery, blasphemy, perjury, and a bitter vindictiveness, that could slake its thirst for blood only in the opened veins and riven heart of the Messiah. So that it is unquestionably true, as has been well remarked by Mosheim, "that the religion of the Pharisees was for the most part founded in consummate hypocrisy; and that in general they were the slaves of every vicious appetite; proud, arrogant, and avaricious; consulting only the gratification of their lusts, even at the very moment when they professed to be engaged in the service of their Maker." Yet their pretended claims to the guardianship of the law; their rabbinical learning; their great outward sanctity, gave them such influence with the people, that if they gave out any report against a high priest or king, they were believed; while their political influence was so vast, that at times they virtually ruled the people through the almost automaton hands that held the sceptre. No wonder, then, that John the Baptist, and our blessed Lord, whose omniscient eye took in at a glance their whole character, denounced them in the strongest terms as "serpents," as "generations of vipers," as unable to escape the damnation of hell?

We turn now to contemplate another class. As the Pharisee was in the highest repute among the Jews, for sanctity, the Publican was regarded as the lowest of the race, in vice. At the time of our Saviour, Judea was a province of the Roman Empire,—subject, therefore, to Roman taxation; and the Publicans were the officers employed to collect the taxes. There were at this time two sorts of people called Publicans; the Mancipes, and the Socii. The "Mancipes" were those who farmed the taxes of the several provinces; had the oversight of the inferior Publicans; received their accounts and collections, and transmitted them to the Quæstores Ærarii, who presided over the finances at Rome. These Mancipes were sometimes Roman knights; and Cicero makes honourable mention of them in his orations, Pro Lege Manilla and Pro Plancio.

The "Socii" were a lower class of Publicans, to whom the Mancipes let out their several districts in smaller sections, and whose duty it was to collect from the people the sums levied by the senate. Both of these are properly styled "Telonai;" though the former are those whom the Greeks call "Architelonai;" which term St. Luke applies to Zaccheus.

While, then, the Mancipes or Architelonai were gene-

11

rally men of probity and morality, and mostly of the Equestrian order, the Socii or lower class of Telonai, were frequently freedmen or slaves, and are spoken of with great contempt by heathen, as well as Jewish writers. Theocritus says of them—" Among the beasts of the wilderness, bears and lions are the most cruel; among the beasts of the city, the publican and the parasite." The reason of this general hatred was their rapacity and extortion; for they oppressed the people with unlawful exactions in order to enrich themselves.

Besides, Publicans were peculiarly odious to the Jews, who looked upon them as the instrument of their subjection to Rome, and who consequently regarded them as out of the pale of civilized society. Accordingly (in the New Testament), we find them joined with harlots and sinners, and other profligate persons; hence the objection made to our Lord, that He was " the friend of publicans and sinners," was designed as a reproachful slur upon His character. The Publican in the parable was one of this lower or despised order, with whom the self-righteous Pharisee thought it sinful to converse, and whom he regarded as " the offscouring of all things."

In conformity with the custom of the Jews, both the Pharisee and the Publican went up into the temple to pray at the hour of prayer. In common discourse, the word " temple" comprehended all the chambers, courts, and colonades connected with the sacred edifice on Mount Moriah. When, therefore, it is said that the Pharisee and the Publican, that Peter and John, that Paul and Timothy, went up into the temple, nothing more is meant than that they went into one of the courts of the temple, and not into the sacred building itself, which contained the Holy and Most Holy Place; for into the Holy Place none but priests were admitted, and into the Holy of Holies only the High Priest could enter, and he but once a year, and then only with the blood of the atonement and the censer of burning incense. Into the temple, strictly so called, our Lord himself never entered, though He frequently visited its courts and walked and taught in its porches.

The "hour of prayer" was the "third and ninth hour" of Jewish time, corresponding to the nine o'clock in the morning and three o'clock in the afternoon of our computation; and the place where prayers were wont to be made was that part of the temple called "the court of the Israelites," which was divided into two portions by an ascent of fifteen steps—the lower being appropriated to the women, and the higher to the men.

But though the Pharisee and the Publican came with the same ostensible purpose to the temple, yet how widely diverse in their devotions! "The Pharisee stood and prayed thus with himself." There is something quite emphatic in the phrase prayed "with himself," as if his prayer was for his own satisfaction, for the gratification of his own pride, for the laudation of his own merit. He in whose heart there is no godly humility, will always pray "with himself," rather than to God. The Publican "stood," also, because it was not permitted to pray in the temple in any other posture; though elsewhere kneeling and bowing of the head were practised. "I will either," says an old divine, speaking of the posture in prayer, "I will either stand as a servant before my Master, or kneel as a suppliant to my King; but I will not dare sit as an equal."

The prayer of the Pharisee (if such it can be called) was, "God, I thank thee that I am not as other men are, unjust, extortioners; or even as this Publican. I fast twice in the week, I give tithes of all that I possess." There is in this prayer great self-complacency, ostentatious devotion, and a boastful liberality. There was no humility of soul, no confession of sin, no craving of Divine pardon. It was rather the proud heart condescending to tell God how good it was, and how much it had done for Him; while, at the very moment of prayer, disdain for a fellow worm dwelt in his heart and was uttered by his lips. He "went up" to the court of the temple, and "stood" in the attitude of prayer, to pronounce in the ear of God a eulogy upon his own virtues.

The Publican, "standing afar off," at the other side of the Men's Court, was so abased in his own estimation that he "would not so much as lift up his eyes unto Heaven, but smote upon his breast, saying, God be merciful to me a sinner." Here is manifested conscious guilt, deep penitence, profound humility, sincere confession, and earnest petition. The words which he utters are few, but he condenses in them the whole force and fervour of his soul. The prayer is brief, but effective. It comes from a heart awakened by the Holy Ghost to a sense of its guilt, and made conscious of merited wrath; the cry for mercy proves that there was a felt deserving of judgment; the appeal to God evidenced a knowledge of sin as committed against Him, and of pardon as flowing only from Him; the calling of himself "a sinner" was a confession of iniquity, which was the first step to repentance; while repentance and conversion were not far distant from him who was so overpowered by conscious vileness and needed grace, as to pray, with smiting upon his breast, "God be merciful to me a sinner." This petition therefore, in its closest analysis, develops all the elements of genuine prayer, and illustrates the fact, how the deep yearnings of the heart can be condensed into one terse and vigorous ejaculation, that shall enter into the ear of the Lord of Sabaoth.

What a contrast to the prayer of the Pharisee! There is here no boasting, no self-laudation, no ungenerous comparison of himself with others; but self-renunciation, self-abasement, and an unreserved casting of himself upon the mercy of God as his only shelter from the curse of His broken law.

The result of these two prayers our Lord gives us in the concluding words of the parable, saying, "I tell you this man (the Publican) went down to his house justified, rather than the other; for every one that exalteth himself shall be abased, and he that humbleth himself shall be exalted."

The prayer of the Publican secured for him the favour of God; and, being pardoned through the abounding mercy which he so earnestly craved, he became, in the sight of God, as one who had not sinned, as a righteous or justified person, to whom pertained the promise of eternal life, and from whom had been removed the condemning power of the law, for he was "justified freely" by the grace of God.

The Pharisee received no such answer to his prayer. He had prayed "with himself," and of course God did not hear him, to answer him; he sought no mercy, and consequently none was received. So he went down from the temple to his house as he went up, a proud, self-righteous hypocrite.

This parable has two very important designs, viz., to rebuke religious pride or Phariseeism, and to point out the true way in which sinners should sue for pardoning grace, agreeably to the moral drawn by our Saviour Himself: "Every one that exalteth himself shall be abased, and he that humbleth himself shall be exalted."

Religious pride or Phariseeism exhibits itself in a great variety of ways; and though its marks cannot always be read in the outward character, its ravages in the soul are naked and open to the eyes of Him with whom we have to do.

Following the course of thought suggested by the parable, we remark, that the first sign of religious pride or Phariseeism, is to "trust in themselves that they are righteous." The Pharisees vainly supposed that they made themselves righteous by their own works; and not only so, but, by a delusion stranger still, they supposed that God would look upon those works precisely as man looked upon them. They had so completely corrupted the Word of God by their traditions, that they had lost a true knowledge of some of His most necessary attributes. As for understanding the nature of true righteousness, either as resulting from a perfect obedience to God's law, or as a casting of the soul upon God's mercy, through faith in an anticipated Redeemer, it scarcely found lodgment in their minds. They reduced their religion to human standards; estimated their good works at a human valuation; and then measuring themselves by themselves, and comparing themselves among themselves, came to indulge much self-conceit; and because friends flattered, and parasites praised, and the ignoble crowd stood in awe of their apparent sanctity, they esteemed themselves to be the most religious men of the day, the possessors of a righteousness that would fully justify them in the sight of God. In this low standard of religion, and in this self-righteous judgment, they are followed by many professedly good people at the present day. Because such persons have been guilty of no great crime; because they are not notorious evil livers; because they are zealous for the outward services of religion, and the visible means of grace; because they are regular in the discharge of public duties, and possess great worldly integrity blended with an unimpeached morality and an attractive amiability, they readily, under the flattery of friends, think within themselves that they are righteous. The adversary of their souls lulls them into security with this deceptive thought; makes them more and more pleased with their state; keeps from them as much as possible whatever will alarm their fears, or break up their delusion; and thus causing them to tread in slippery places, "their feet shall slide in due time." The true Christian casts away all his personal righteousness in which he once trusted, as filthy rags, and trusts for his righteousness to the imputed merits of his dear Redeemer, made his by that appropriating faith which is itself the gift of God. He loathes himself; his language is, "Behold, I am vile." He is ready to put his hand upon his mouth, and his mouth in the dust, and cry "Unclean! unclean!" He sees in himself nothing but vileness—in God nothing but holiness; in the law nothing but righteousness; and in Christ alone, the Redeemer of his soul from the impending curse of God. Thus he finds no righteousness of a justifying character in himself; it is all derived from Christ, and he is accounted as righteous "only for the merit of our Lord and Saviour Jesus Christ, by faith." So long as a man "trusts in himself that he is righteous," he will never seek to be clothed upon with Christ's righteousness; but this is the only righteousness which will avail with God, or secure our salvation: hence the absence of it, like the simple lack of the wedding garment, will insure being cast into outer darkness, "where there is weeping, and wailing, and gnashing of teeth."

A second mark of religious pride or Phariseeism is, to "despise others." This is a natural and necessary result of self-righteousness, a great part of which consists in comparing one's self with those around, and drawing invidious conclusions, as the Pharisee in the temple did, in reference to the Publican.

There are, it must be confessed, proud and haughty professors of religion, who look down upon their fellow Christians, because they occupy lower stations in the Church or in social life, because they are less educated and refined, or because of their less apparent piety. They are keen-sighted in detecting the errors and failings of their friends and neighbours; and they delight to depreciate real talent and true worth, in the hope that, by so doing, they will elevate their own position and character. Hence, they are devoid of that "charity" which "suffereth long and is kind," which "vaunteth not itself, is not puffed up, doth not behave itself unseemly, seeketh not her own, is not easily provoked, thinketh no evil;" without which, says St. Paul, "the tongues of men and of angels," "the gift of prophecy," the possession of a "faith" that "could remove mountains," the bestowal of "goods to feed the poor," and the giving of one's "body to be burned," is profitless and vain; for prophecies "shall fail," tongues "shall cease," knowledge "shall vanish away," but "charity never faileth," for it is the greatest of the three abiding graces of the Christian life.

The despising of others proves us to have an unkind and censorious spirit, widely at variance with the Gospel of Christ. It proves us to be under the influence of malign and selfish passions, which are, in all instances, of Satanic origin. It proves us to be devoid of the Spirit of Christ, who was no respecter of persons; and St. Paul tells us, "If any man have not the spirit of Christ, he is none of His." It proves us to be deficient in self-knowledge, or in an understanding of our true position before God, or of our true relations to Jesus Christ. It proves that we are puffed up in our fleshly minds, thinking of ourselves above that we ought to think. It proves, in fine, that we have not the first element of the true Christian, but that all our professions, from the foundation-stone to the turret, being laid upon the shifting sand, will soon fall and bury us in its ruins.

A third trait of religious Phariseeism is, the cultivation of a mere ostensive piety.

The Pharisees practised their religion "to be seen of men." The wide phylacteries, the enlarging the borders of their garments, the long prayers, the sounding alms-trumpet, the washings and ablutions, the sanctimonious visage, the rigid fastings, the scrupulously paid tithes, were all done for show, to make an outward impression upon the popular mind; and this was carried to such an extent, that our Saviour compared them to whited sepulchres, "which indeed appear beautiful outwards, but within are full of dead men's bones, and all uncleanness."

Nor has this feature of Phariseeism been done away. It exists in full vigour at the present day. We would not be uncharitable, but are we not warranted by the Bible and daily observation in saying, that a large portion of the religion of Christendom is a surface religion; a praying of the lips, and not of the heart; a bowing of the knees, but not of the soul; a singing with the voice, but not of the spirit; and a going up to the courts of the Lord, not with singleness of purpose to worship Him who is a Spirit in the beauty of holiness, but because it is the decent custom of society, and to be gazed at by the great assembly? Religious forms are necessary to the fencing in and protection of the faith, but whoever trusts in them, rather than in the faith which they enclose, is leaning upon the hope of the hypocrite, which "will perish with the giving up of the ghost." We are made true children of God, not by becoming strict rubricians, or minute ritualists; tithing, as it were, the anise, mint, and cumin, to the exclusion of the weightier matters of the law; but by being born again of water and the Holy Ghost. We must observe rubrics, and conform to rites, and obey canons, as *means* whereby we gain important religious benefits; but not as an *end*, to rest in them alone. Whoever trusts to the forms of religion alone for salvation, trusts to the mere scaffolding of the Church, which shall be taken down when the whole building, "fitly framed together, groweth unto an holy temple in the Lord." God recognises no religion that dwells not in the soul, that springs not from His Holy Spirit, and that does not work by faith and purify the heart.

A fourth trait of Phariseeism is, to boast of one's goodness.

We have been struck, on reading some of the ancient Rabbins, with the unblushing egotism of the Pharisees. Humility was unknown, self-praise was a virtue, and their perpetual ambition was to seek out the chief seats and high places of earth.

The sound common sense of modern society puts a strong restraint upon this egotistical spirit, so that it does not betray itself as much now as then; still there is much of it abroad, masked under affected humility, seeking to win praise by a false meekness, that only half conceals the pride of heart that lurks beneath. But no true Christian is a boasting Christian. One of the first works of the Spirit of God upon the heart is to take down the idol self, and erect Christ on its vacant pedestal; and when Christ takes possession of our heart, we feel so vile and sunken in His presence, so worthless and unprofitable, so leprous with sin, and hell-deserving with an ever accumulating guilt, that we, like the Publican, scarcely dare lift up our eyes to Heaven, much less to boast of our goodness or make a parade of our virtues. A boasting Christian is a living libel on the cross of Christ. Instead of talking of our goodness, or praising our piety, let us look at our sins in the light of God's countenance, and bewail our shortcoming beneath the outstretched arms of the Crucified.

When we can work out our salvation, we shall be privileged to boast; but so long as salvation is "not of works, but of grace," being in very truth "the gift of God," "boasting is excluded." For the poor, humble, Christ-dependent penitent is justified by God, before the praying, fasting, tithing, alms-giving, yet boasting Pharisee.

The other lesson which this parable teaches, is the spirit in which sinners should approach God, as indicated by the prayer of the Publican, and the words of our Saviour, "He that humbleth himself shall be exalted." By reason of original sin, which "is the fault and corruption of every man that naturally is engendered of the offspring of Adam," we have alienated ourselves, and that radically, from the love and favour of God. Return to Him we must before our sins can be pardoned, and our souls be saved. But how shall we return? We cannot come to Him as claimants of His favour, for we have no claims where we have forfeited every right and title to regard. We cannot come as purchasers, bartering our own goodness for God's mercy, for our boasted righteousness is as filthy rags, vile and worthless; nor can we throw ourselves just as we are upon God's clemency, and run the risk of acceptance and consequent salvation, for God out of Christ "is a consuming fire;" and such presumptuous conduct would be only rushing "upon the thick bosses of Jehovah's buckler." The only way of access to the mercy of God is through the blood of Jesus Christ. This is the way of His own appointment, to which He has annexed all His promises and blessings, and out of which, seek it as much as men may, they will find no salvation. We can be saved only in God's way; and every attempt to scale the gate of heaven by schemes of man's devising, is insulting to God, as it virtually discredits His wisdom, mercy, goodness, and truth; and is ruinous to man, for the Bible distinctly declares that there is "none other name under heaven given among men whereby they can be saved."

We must come to God, then, conscious of our condition as sinners, confessing our iniquities, forsaking and truly repenting of our sins past, pleading for mercy for Jesus Christ's sake, and resting the strength of our plea on the infinite merits and perfect sacrifice of the Lamb of God, "who taketh away the sins of the world." This is taking God at His word, and believing on the Lord Jesus Christ as our only hope and salvation; and when, through the operation of the Holy Ghost, we are enabled to lay hold on this "hope set before us" in the Gospel, then do we find a peace and joy which the world can neither give nor take away. These are the authenticating seals of the Spirit, "whereby we are sealed unto the day of redemption," certifying to us, under the hand of the Third Person of the adorable Trinity, that "there is now no condemnation to them that are in Christ Jesus, who walk not after the flesh but after the Spirit." This is the only way to approach God, through repentance and faith; and these are the gift of God, to be sought for by earnest prayer and supplication; for it is only in Christ that God is found "reconciling the world unto Himself."

Great, then, is the encouragement which the truly penitent and believing have to come to Jesus. What though, like the Publican, they be regarded as the offscouring of all things? Christ came " to save sinners :" What though they feel their vileness so as to cause them to smite upon their breast in anguish, and be afraid to lift up so much as their eyes to heaven? the deeper the consciousness of guilt, the more they feel the need of a Saviour, and the more precious becomes His salvation. We cannot be too humble, for " He resisteth the proud, but giveth grace unto the humble." We cannot be too full in our confessions, for " He that confesseth and forsaketh his sins shall find mercy." We cannot be too penitential for our transgression, for it is "the broken and contrite heart with which God is well pleased." We cannot be too strong in our faith, for "without faith it is impossible to please God." We cannot be too importunate in our supplication, for "the kingdom of heaven suffereth violence, and the violent take it by force." Come, then, in humility, in godly sorrow, in true repentance, in simple faith, in earnest prayer to the Throne of Grace, and, like the Publican, we shall find acceptance with God, **and go down** to our house justified before **Him.**

The Labourers in the Vineyard.

12

THE LABOURERS IN THE VINEYARD.

"For the kingdom of heaven is like unto a man that is a householder, which went out early in the morning to hire labourers into his vineyard. And when he had agreed with the labourers for a penny a day, he sent them into his vineyard. And he went out about the third hour, and saw others standing idle in the marketplace, and said unto them, Go ye also into the vineyard; and whatsoever is right I will give you. And they went their way. Again he went out about the sixth and ninth hour, and did likewise. And about the eleventh hour he went out, and found others standing idle, and saith unto them, Why stand ye here all the day idle? They say unto him, Because no man hath hired us. He saith unto them, Go ye also into the vineyard; and whatsoever is right, that shall ye receive. So when even was come, the lord of the vineyard saith unto his steward, Call the labourers, and give them their hire, beginning from the last unto the first. And when they came that were hired about the eleventh hour, they received every man a penny. But when the first came, they supposed that they should have received more; and they likewise received every man a penny. And when they had received it, they murmured against the good man of the house, saying, These last have wrought but one hour, and thou hast made them equal unto us, which have borne the burden and heat of the day. But he answered one of them, and said, Friend, I do thee no wrong: didst not thou agree with me for a penny? Take that thine is, and go thy way; I will give unto this last, even as unto thee Is it not lawful for me to do what I will with mine own? Is thine eye evil, because I am good? So the last shall be first, and the first last; for many be called, but few chosen."

Matt. xx. 1–16.

THE materials out of which this parable is constructed require but little explanation, except what is necessary to understand the Jewish method of computing time. They reckoned the day from sunrise to sunset, dividing it into twelve portions or hours; consequently, "early in the morning," the time at which the "householder" first went out to hire labourers, answers to our six o'clock; the "third hour," to our nine in the morning; "the sixth hour," to our noon; "the ninth hour," to our three in the afternoon; and "the eleventh hour," to five o'clock, or an hour before sunset, reckoning it at equinoctial time.

At these several hours "the lord of the vineyard" went out to the market-place (or bazaar, as it is termed in the East, the ordinary resort of porters and labourers waiting for employment), to get workmen for his vineyard, and hired five different sets of labourers.

"When even was come," the steward was directed to "call the labourers and give them their hire, beginning from the last unto the first." The eleventh-hour labourers therefore advanced, and "received every man a penny"— a sum equal to about fifteen cents of our money, and which was then the usual wages of a labourer, and the pay of a soldier. Seeing this, those who had laboured all day supposed that, when their turn to be paid came, they would receive more, "and they likewise received every man a penny." They had laboured three, six, nine, and eleven hours more than the first paid labourers; had toiled, some of them, through "the burden and heat of the day," and they thought that they had a right to more wages; and though they took the stipulated penny, yet they "murmured against the good man of the house," as if he had done them great injustice. Turning, however, to one who, perhaps, was foremost in complaining, he said, "Friend, I do thee no wrong. Didst thou not agree with me for a penny?" I did not compel you to labour; I hired you at the usual wages; you agreed to my offer; you have done your part, which was, to labour until sunset, I have done mine, which was, to pay you a penny. Where is the injustice of this? Therefore, "take that thine is, and go thy way. I will give unto this last even as unto thee. Is it not lawful for me to do what I will with mine own? Is thine eye evil, because I am good?"

Many interpretations have been given to this parable. The different hours specified have by some been referred to the several ages of man; the call to labour in the Lord's vineyard being made in many cases, "early in the morning" of life, as with Samuel and Timothy; in others, at the third hour, or youth, as in the cases of Joseph and Josiah; in others at the sixth, or manhood hour, as was done to the Apostles of the Lord; in others at the ninth, or declining hour; and in some extraordinary cases, as the penitent thief at the hour before life's sunset.

Other commentators refer the periods at which the labourers were hired to the several ages of the world; as that the first call was made in the world's "early morning," in Eden; the third-hour call was in the day of Noah; the sixth-hour call, in the times of the Mosaic dispensation; the ninth-hour call was in the day of Christ's advent; and the eleventh was the mission to the Gentiles.

Various other interpretations have been made of these calls; but it will be unnecessary as well as unprofitable to consume time in running out any of these analogies, **as we** shall thereby be led away from the scope and import of the parable, as they unfold themselves in the circumstances under which it was delivered, and the moral which our Lord deduced. The points which are distinctly brought out in the parable, and which it is important for us to know, are these:

1st. That there is a vineyard in which to work. Under the similitude of a vine stock, or a vineyard, the Bible frequently represents the Jewish and the Christian Church. It seems to be a favourite idea of the olden prophets, being used by David, Solomon, Isaiah, Jeremiah, and Ezekiel; and our Lord often employs the same imagery to illustrate the relations which the Church holds to himself and to the world. The fitness of this language to express what is designed is peculiarly felicitous; for a vineyard was most prized and esteemed of all possessions; required most anxious care at all seasons of the year, and yielded to the diligent husbandman a larger return than any other culture.

The Christian Church is now what the Jewish Church was in the Levitical dispensation, "the vineyard of the Lord of Hosts." It is fenced off from the world by the forms of a public profession of faith in Christ; planted with the "choicest vine," even Christ, "the true vine," and dressed by husbandmen of God's calling and appointment, whose duty it is so to superintend the culture, as that it shall bring forth fruit to the glory of "the Lord of the vineyard."

In this vineyard, or visible Church of Christ, there is much work to be done, more than sufficient to tax all the energies of mind and body; and the call is, "Go work to-day in my vineyard." There is the work of weeding out and cultivating one's own heart until it becomes fruitful with all the graces of the Spirit. There is the work of maintaining purity of life and faith in the particular church with which we are connected. There is the work of bringing those around us under the influences of Gospel truth and Gospel institutions: the vast *home* work of the Church, embracing all agencies and instrumentalities necessary to the tillage of the domestic field. There is, lastly, the work of spreading the religion of Jesus "into the regions beyond;" the great *foreign* work of the Church, by which it is to act upon its Lord's commission, "Go ye into all the world, and preach the Gospel to every creature." "The whole world lieth in wickedness," and the earthly instrumentality whereby it is to be converted to God is in the keeping of professing Christians. They are to be "co-workers with God;" and, if they fail to labour to the extent of their ability, the responsibility of lost souls and of disobeyed commands will rest upon them for ever.

2d. All who are not labouring in Christ's vineyard are "idle." Not that they are physically idle; not that they are intellectually idle; nor yet that they are morally idle, for that is impossible, as every man in one sense is morally active. The soul is ever working; thoughts are busy there, passions wrestle there, affections move there, and never is there a moment when there is vacuity and repose. But by "idle" is meant unprofitably employed. All unprofitable employment of our time is virtual idleness, even in a worldly and business aspect; how much more so in a heavenly and spiritual one! Everything is morally unprofitable which has not a tendency to advance the glory of God and the salvation of our souls. Unconverted men, though they may be busy about their farms, their studies, their merchandise, are not doing anything for the glory of God, or for the salvation of their own souls; hence, all unconverted men are spiritually "idle."

They may be diligent in working out a worldly morality, but they are spiritually idle! They may be sedulous in building up a self-righteousness by works of charity, of ritualism, of penance, of will-worship, of Pharisaic devotion, but they are only busy idlers in the sight of God. Their works are vain—their labour shall not profit—and their toil shall only end in their deeper ruin; because they are not working in the field of the Church, and consequently are not obeying the injunction of the Divine "Householder," "Go ye also into the vineyard."

3d. It is never too late to go into the vineyard of the Church. This remark is made not to encourage presumption, but to rebuke despair. The uncertainty of life, the possibility of grieving away the Holy Spirit, the danger that our mental powers may not be preserved to us in our last sickness, or that we may be suddenly summoned to the bar of God, warn us with great force against any delay in making our peace with God. To postpone, therefore, a profession of Christ's religion because we may, perchance, enter the vineyard at the eleventh hour, is most daring rebellion and impiety towards God, and a solemn trifling with our soul, which should fill us with trembling and alarm. When we say, therefore, that it is not too late to go into the vineyard, we do not mean that it will not be too late if we put it off to a future day; for we know nothing of the future, not even "what a day may bring forth;" but we mean that if we have put it off to the present time, *it is not too late* NOW *to go to Christ."*

All the invitations of the Gospel are addressed to us in the *present* tense. The language of the Bible is, "Behold, *now* is the accepted time; behold, *now* is the day of salvation." *To-day*, if ye will hear His voice, harden not your hearts." "Exhort one another daily while it is called *to-day*." "Son, go work *to-day* in my vineyard." There is no to-morrow in all the offers of grace, or in all the overtures of the Spirit. To-morrow is a fiction of time—it never comes. It is a present work that we have to do—there is a present time allotted to us for doing it; there is a present Spirit vouchsafed to begin and carry on the work. Avail ourselves of these *present* privileges, and the future shall be bright with heavenly glory; neglect them, and the future shall be dark with eternal woe. You may have passed the "early morning" of your life, and "the third hour" may find you out of the vineyard; we call to you, then, in this third hour, this dew-time of youth, "Go ye also into the vineyard." You may have reached the meridian of life, and the "sixth hour" may find you still "idle;" and we call to you, therefore, in the noon of manhood, "Go ye also into the vineyard." You may have progressed into the afternoon of life, and "the ninth hour" may find you still unengaged in Christ's service; and we call to you, therefore, in this waning period of the day, "Go ye also into the vineyard." Or it may be that "the shadows of the evening are stretched out," and the sun of your existence, already far down in the western sky, is hastening to his setting; and at this eleventh hour you are and have been "all the day idle;" and we cry out to you, therefore, with but one hour of daylight in your possession, and the night of death fast coming on, "Go ye also into the vineyard; and whatever is right, that shall ye receive." Few, however, who pass the third and the sixth hour out of the vineyard, enter it at the ninth or the eleventh. We know of many who gave themselves to God's service in life's morning, in life's noon-tide; but the number of those who become His in the evening of their days, are very few; and the Bible records but one eleventh-hour convert, the thief on the cross: one! that none might despair; only one! that none might presume.

4th. God will reward all who labour for Him, when their work is done. It is not until even comes that the Lord of the Vineyard will "call the labourers and give them their hire." We often labour in this world without seeming to receive any reward; nor should we expect to receive it here. But, though long delayed, it will come at last, for "He is faithful that promised." It is, to a great extent, withheld from us here, because our work is not all done when we are removed from the vineyard. We live and we work in our influence and in the agencies and instrumentalities which we set in motion, long after we have passed away. Though dead, we yet speak to future generations; and, as it is a principle of the Divine economy, to hold us responsible not only for our actual words and overt deeds, but for everything that results from our example, our influence, our labours, so is it impossible to mete out the rewards which pertain to us through Divine grace, until, in the final closing up of earthly scenes and accounts, it shall be seen what we accomplished for Christ; not merely what we did for him living, but what we did for him through means and institutions and influences which emanated from us, and which were in active operation long after we had slumbered in the dust. Hence it is that the day of judgment is placed at "the end of the world:" because then only shall all the lines of influence, good and bad, be fully run out; then, only, will all the results of our lives, good and bad, be fully developed. Take, for example, the work done by Paul. Could he have been rewarded (speaking after the manner of men) during his lifetime? Is not the power of Paul still felt? Is not the influence of Paul still at work? and, though he died eighteen centuries ago, does he not speak to the dwellers in the nineteenth century, and to the inhabitants of England and America, as forcibly as he did to those who lived in the dawn of the Christian era, and who heard his oral teachings in Damascus, Corinth, and Rome? So of Augustine, Wiclif, Luther, Cranmer, Martyn, Simeon, and a whole galaxy of sainted ones, who now shine "as stars in the firmament." They have gone to their rest, and left their work, as the world would say, unfinished; but not so; their work is still going on, and will continue until time shall be no longer. It matters very little, therefore, whether we see much of the fruit of our labours while we tabernacle in the flesh, but when the even of the world comes, when the Lord of the Vineyard shall say, "Call the labourers" to the judgment-seat, and "give them their hire," then shall we receive "according to that which we have done, be it good or bad." Then can the sum total of our work be cast up; then the whole amount of labour be known; then the reward be rightly bestowed.

Lastly, the reward that we shall receive will be nothing that we can claim of right, but will be bestowed upon us by the free sovereign grace of God.

And here comes out the true intent and purpose of the parable. In the arbitrary division of the Bible into chapters, made by Cardinal Hugo in 1240, the chapter containing this parable was unfortunately cut off from the 19th chapter, whereas it is, in fact, a continuation of it. In that 19th chapter we find that a "Young Ruler," with much external reverence for Christ, had come to him with the inquiry, "Good Master, what shall I do to inherit eternal life?" Our Lord told him what to do, and put his sincerity to the test by ordering him "to sell all that he had, and give to the poor,"—a test which discovered the latent covetousness of his heart, and one which he did not attempt to carry out, for "he went away sorrowful, for he had great possessions."

This striking example of clinging to the seen and the earthly, rather than to the unseen and the heavenly, gave occasion for Christ to say, "Verily I say unto you, that a rich man shall hardly enter into the kingdom of heaven;" which so amazed the disciples that they exclaimed in wonder, "Who then can be saved?" But Peter, foremost among the disciples in speaking as in acting, said to the Saviour, "Behold, we have forsaken all, and followed thee; what shall we have therefore?" We who, unlike the rich young man, have left all and followed thee. In the spirit of a hireling who was looking to wages rather than to work, he seemed to think that something was deserved by them who had made such sacrifices, and who at the first call had gone into the vineyard; and, in the working of a self-complacent mind, he wished to know what they would receive. Our Lord replies to them and says, "Every one that hath forsaken houses, or brethren, or sisters, or fathers, or mothers, or wife, or children, or lands, for my name's sake, shall receive a hundredfold, and shall inherit everlasting life;" adding, "but many that are first shall be last, and the last shall be first;" and then follows the parable under consideration, designed to show that the rewards of grace are not for the first called alone, and do not follow the length of Christian service, but that while all shall receive the promised wages, viz., eternal life, God will do as he wills with his own infinite blessings, bestowing them when, where, and how he will, according to his own good pleasure. The value of the work stands not in the amount of labour performed, in the number of hours employed, or in bearing the burden and heat of the day, but in the *animus*, the spirit in which it is done; and that spirit should be humility, not boasting of long service, or arduous service; not grudging at others' preference or others' wages, but regarding any pay as undeserved, and all reward as out of God's infinite grace, and not for the worthiness of individual merit. And as the work stands only in humility, so the reward stands only in grace. Do what we may; heap up labour upon labour, and sacrifice upon sacrifice; yet there is so much of sin mixed with all that we do, that were we to receive according to the real merit of the works performed, they would each be cast out of God's sight as sinful, and we ourselves be driven from his presence. If the reward then is of grace, "it is no more of works, otherwise grace is no more grace; but if it be of works, then is it no more grace, otherwise work is no more work."

Would that we could feel this more! It would humble our proud hearts; it would bridle in our rampant spirits; it would abate our self-complacent minds, flattering ourselves tnat we deserve more, and grudging whatever is bestowed upon others; it would bring us more like docile, feeble, little children, to the feet of Jesus, causing us to cling to him by a simple faith, and to lean only upon the merits of "His blessed passion and precious death."

And then, too, how will it enhance the value of the reward to know that we deserved nothing! That the best, the most diligent, the most faithful, was, after all, but an unprofitable servant, and that the reward is the expression of the overflowing love and bounty of our God, given to us, not for our service or for our deservings, but on account of Christ's pleadings and in virtue of his perfect sacrifice.

The Barren Fig-Tree.

THE BARREN FIG-TREE.

"A CERTAIN man had a fig-tree planted in his vineyard; and he came and sought fruit thereon, and found none. Then said he unto the dresser of his vineyard, Behold, these three years I come seeking fruit on this fig-tree, and find none: cut it down; why cumbereth it the ground? And he answering, said unto him, Lord, let it alone this year also, till I shall dig about it, and dung it: and if it bear fruit, well; and if not, then after that thou shalt cut it down." LUKE XIII. 6–9.

THIS, like several other of our Lord's parables, has a double signification: one immediate, pertaining to the Jews; one ulterior, referring to all time.

It primarily refers to the nation of Israel as a people whom God had chosen to be "His people," whom he had assiduously cultivated by special and long-continued mercies, and from whom it was very natural that He should expect fruit in some measure answerable to the blessing and labour bestowed.

They proved, however, barren and unfruitful and when He looked that they should have borne fruit, He found nothing but the most aggravated sterility. In consequence of this, they were cut down as "a barren fig-tree;" rooted up from their ancient home, and scattered, like autumn leaves, by every wind under the expanse of heaven.

In a more enlarged sense, this parable evidently refers to the unfruitful professors of Christ's religion, or to those who are barren of all fruit of righteousness, under the influences and within the enclosure of the Gospel vineyard.

The professors of Christ's religion are emphatically "planted in the vineyard of the Lord," the Church; for under the figure of a vineyard, the Bible represents both the Old and New Testament Church. In this spiritual vineyard they have better soil, better care, better protection, than in the world without. There the Gospel is fully preached; there the sacraments are duly ministered; there the dews of the Spirit more surely descend; there the early and the later rain of reviving grace falls; there the Sun of Righteousness shines with full-orbed splendour, and the winds of the Spirit blow, and the husbandmen of God labour, to bring the trees of His planting to maturity and fruitfulness. Whatever is necessary to enrich the soil has been abundantly lavished, so that when we find any therein who are barren, we know that it is no fault of the ground, or of the sun, or of the rain, or of the husbandman, but of the tree itself; it is sapless, graceless; and a professor of religion, whose heart is devoid of spiritual vitality, and in whom there are no pulsations of a godly life, can no more bear fruit than a tree planted in the richest soil, and tended by the closest care, which yet has no sap, no vegetable blood vitalizing its trunk, and circulating through all its branches. The one case is just as impossible as the other.

What Christ seeks, and what He has a right to expect of all the trees of His vineyard, is, *fruit*, good fruit; not the leaves of profession only, which fall with the frosts of time; not the blossoms of promise merely, which drop off ere they come to maturity; but "fruit meet for repentance," "fruit unto holiness," "fruit unto eternal life."

That there are unfruitful professors, is evident to all who look into the condition of the visible Church. We see them occupying the same position year by year, yet never discover any fruits of righteousness. Their lives give no evidence of piety; they are indeed outwardly moral and religious, decent in all the externals of Christian duty, but there is an evident lack of inward grace. You discover no ardent love for Christ; no kindling up of soul under the preaching of Divine truth; no warm outsprings of heart towards fellow Christians; no generous liberality in the cause of Jesus; no delight in talking about the Saviour; no enjoyment in private prayer or meditation; no desires after greater conformity to the Divine likeness; and no strong cryings of soul after more faith, more love, more grace, more consecration of spirit. Where we mark the absence of these things, we have indubitable evidence of an unfruitful professor, a barren fig-tree.

But, giving to the parable a wider scope, still we may say that all who live in Gospel lands, and within the sound of the church-going bell, are, in one sense, planted in the vineyard of the Lord, in contrast to those who dwell in heathen lands, where the Gospel of the Son of God has not been proclaimed. All those who live in Christian countries, and within reach of the means of grace, even though they do not avail themselves of it, dwell, as it were, under "the droppings of the Sanctuary," and partake more or less of its influence.

The influence of the Bible, the influence of the Sabbath, the influence of the Church, the influence of Christian institutions, the influence of a sanctified press, the influence of the godly lives of individual Christians, have a power fully moulding effect upon society. These influences combined, shape and fashion to a great extent the views and opinions of the people, and restrain, modify, and govern even those who are ashamed to acknowledge their power; nay, even the sceptic, the licentious, the profane, the rabid infidel, deny it as they may, are under their potent sway, and are kept from committing the gross outrages which their several creeds permit, by the overawing power of Christian principle. It is a blessed thing to be connected by any links with the people of God, for the streams of mercy which flow to them, and the streams of godly influence which flow from them, make broad bands of verdure on each side of their borders.

From each one upon whom God has bestowed these numerous favours, the Master of the vineyard expects and seeks for fruit: it was to make us fruit-bearing that He surrounded us with these privileges and blessings, and we are guilty of great ingratitude if we suffer ourselves to be barren; for if we yield no fruit of righteousness after so much has been done, the fault is all our own.

Yet, in the midst of the anxiety of the Lord of the vineyard to obtain fruit, He manifests the greatest forbearance. "Lo, these three years I come seeking fruit, and finding none!" implying that He had given ample time for it to manifest its fruitfulness if it had any: days, months, years have passed, and yet no fruit appears. He does not, at the first indication of barrenness, cut us down; there is no hasty procedure with our Lord; He is long-suffering and full of forbearance, waiting to be gracious. Men act in hot haste, and repel injuries with prompt chastisement; but God arises to judgment only after long delay, and when the overtures of mercy have been signally disregarded. Beautifully has the Psalmist illustrated this, where, speaking of the perverseness of the children of Israel, and God's long-suffering towards them, he says, " But He being full of compassion, forgave their iniquity, and destroyed them not; yea, many a time turned He His anger away, and did not stir up all His wrath."

Thus is it now. You have perhaps been receiving blessings and mercies from your youth up, and many a blossom of hope has cheered the eye of watching friends. You have been watered and nursed as tender plants in the heritage of our Lord, and many a bud of promise has indicated the beginning of spiritual life; yet manhood, and mid life, and old age have been reached, while, as yet, no fruit appears. During all this while Christ has waited to be gracious. He has stood by looking at you in pity, calling to you in love, making the ground around you fertile with the rich blessings of the Gospel, but the barrenness is not removed, the fruit does not appear. When the angels sinned, there was no long-suffering and forbearance exhibited towards them; their punishment followed close upon their sin, for such high-handed rebellion required high-handed justice.

But He has not dealt so with us. His bearing has ever been that of a God waiting to be gracious. "The long-suffering of God," says St. Peter, "waited in the days of Noah while the ark was building, even one hundred and twenty years;" and the entire history of the Jews is a record of God's forbearing mercy. In the days of Moses the Lord inquired, "How long shall I bear with this evil congregation which murmur against me?" Hundreds of years afterwards Nehemiah exclaims, "Many years didst thou forbear them:" and later still, the Prophet Jeremiah adds, "The Lord could no longer bear, because of the evil of your doings." The New Testament exhibits the same feature of the Divine goodness. "God endureth," says St. Paul, "with much long-suffering the vessels of wrath fitted for destruction:" and St. Peter declares that the Lord is long-suffering to usward, not willing that any should perish, but that all should come to repentance.

Thus is it now. God patiently waits upon sinners, to be gracious; He kindly stands at the door of their hearts knocking for entrance, and there you have kept Him until He says, "My head is filled with dew, and my locks with the drops of the night." But mercies having failed, forbearance being no longer a virtue, God now comes to some determination: "Behold, these three years I come seeking fruit on this fig-tree, and find none; cut it down, why cumbereth it the ground?"

There are two reasons why God should cut down the barren fig-tree: its own uselessness, and its cumbering soil that might be better occupied. It was worthless in itself, and made the ground worthless on which it stood. The spiritually unfruitful man, be he a professor of religion or not, is useless in himself, and takes up room or cumbers the vineyard with his presence; for as there is no middle ground of action, all who are not doing moral good, are doing moral harm; according to the striking words of Christ, "He that is not with me is against me." Life is wasted to him who brings forth no fruits of righteousness. It may be crowded with what the world esteems noble and generous deeds; it may teem with the fruits of honour and fame; the life of such a man may call forth eulogies, and his death panegyrics, while his name may be given in charge to applauding history: yet, if he has been toiling for the glories of time alone; if he concentrated his energies upon the ever-changing present; if he has made no provision for his soul, and secured no peace with God through Jesus Christ, he is a barren fig-tree, a useless cumberer in God's moral vineyard.

The test of moral usefulness consists in doing works that shall survive the things of time and sense. The region of such labours is the soul, the higher and eternal interests of our being. Here, is where fruitfulness must be seen. We must do deeds that shall live after the trump of the Archangel shall sound; deeds that conscience can approve in the hour of death—that Christ can applaud in the day of judgment—that will be remembered with delight through eternity. It will not be asked in the last day, did you build a city, or erect a kingdom, or lead an army to victory; but did you bring forth fruits of rightcousness, did you cultivate the graces of the Spirit, did you do the humble works of a child of God. Have you laboured to extend the kingdom of Christ, and win souls to His sceptre; and if you have, though poor in this world's goods, and looked down upon by this world's nobles, you shall prove yourself to be a tree of God's planting, soon to be transplanted into the Paradise above.

Not only are the lives of unconverted men useless as regards their souls, they are also cumberers or wasters of the ground. Their lives and their influence prove an hindrance to the Gospel. They oppose its progress in their own hearts, and throw the whole weight of their authority and example upon the side of the world, the flesh, and the devil. Every unrenewed man virtually and publicly declares, that he is opposed to the religion of Jesus Christ; that he has no confidence in the ordinances of the Church, no belief in the revelation of God. This, we repeat, is the virtual declaration of each unrenewed man; it is the language of his daily life. This may seem harsh judgment, but it is only plain Bible truth.

Suppose an individual should present himself before you, and show you deeds properly drawn and duly authenticated, which were to place you in possession of a great yet distant estate. You listen to his story, read the deeds, examine the seals; if now you proceed no further, and take no steps to secure this property, but on the contrary turn away from the whole subject—you say as strongly as actions can say, that you do not believe the report of the messenger, and that you discredit his pretended titles; and by your neglect of him you virtually give the lie to all that he has said and shown you. This would be the judgment of every unbiassed mind. Apply this to religion. The ambassador of Christ comes to you with the Word of God. He points out in it the title-deeds to an inheritance reserved in Heaven for you; he shows you the means by which to secure it; he offers to conduct you through the processes necessary to attain it; he solemnly pledges the veracity of God to its truth; and he establishes the genuineness and authenticity of his message by evidence that cannot be overthrown. If now you turn your back upon Christ, and refuse to believe on His name, you virtually declare your disbelief in the whole thing; or if, professing to believe it with your lips, you put off the work of salvation to a future day, you in effect say, I do not believe that God will be as strict as He says He will; I will try His long-suffering a little longer; and though the Holy Ghost says, "*Now* is the accepted time, behold, *now* is the day of salvation," yet I will run the risk of postponing repentance towards God and faith in the Lord Jesus Christ, because He knows that I intend some time or other to become a Christian, and He will not therefore cut me down as a cumberer of the ground. In this delusion many sinners pass months and years, until they are "suddenly destroyed, and that without remedy." We are too apt to forget that there is a time beyond which God's Spirit will not strive, there is a boundary line over which mercy never steps.

At the very point when the forbearance of God seems

to end, an intercessor appears; Christ comes into view, and pleads for "one year" more of probation. "Let it alone this year also: and if it bear fruit, well; if not, after that thou shalt cut it down." He does not pray that it should never be cut down, but not *now*. Every sinner is at this moment under the condemnation of eternal death; and the reason why he is not executed is, that Christ pleads, "Let him alone this year also!"

This, however, is a reprieve, not a pardon; a reprieve for a short time, yet long enough to make full trial. During this reprieve God is giving him the culture and tillage necessary to fruitfulness; the means of grace, the bleeding Saviour, the striving Spirit, the ordinances of the Church. His position is one of extreme peril, and of extreme solicitude: of peril, because the time is short— the isthmus of probation between the land of hope and the world of despair is very narrow, and his feet stand on slippery places; of solicitude, because upon his resolves this year may hinge the destiny of his soul for ever.

If, through the renewing influences of the Holy Ghost, sought for and received as the free gift of God, he becomes a "tree of righteousness," and "brings forth fruit," it is well: "well" in life, "well" in the hour of death; "well" at the day of judgment, "well" throughout eternity. If not, then, after that probation ended, he shall be "cut down" as a "cumberer of the ground." And a fearful thing it will be to be "cut down," after having been by baptism planted in the vineyard, after having had years of spiritual culture under Gospel vine-dressers, and especially after having been spared yet longer on probationary ground, through the intercession of Christ Himself as the Master of the vineyard; for to the guilt of disobeying the commands of God, and of slighting the ordinances of the Church, there is superadded the setting at nought of the Lord Jesus, under circumstances of the most deliberate contempt, which cannot fail to call down the wrath of the Almighty. To all such we commend the declaration of St. Paul to the Hebrews—" He that despised Moses' law died without mercy under two or three witnesses; of how much sorer punishment suppose ye shall he be thought worthy, who hath trodden under foot the Son of God, and hath counted the blood of the covenant wherewith He was sanctified an unholy thing, and hath done despite unto the Spirit of Grace? It is a fearful thing to fall into the hands of the living God."

The Unjust Judge:
The Importunate Friend.

THE UNJUST JUDGE: THE IMPORTUNATE FRIEND.

"THERE was in a city a judge, which feared not God, neither regarded man: and there was a widow in that city; and she came unto him, saying, Avenge me of mine adversary. And he would not for a while: but afterward he said within himself, Though I fear not God, nor regard man; yet because this widow troubleth me, I will avenge her, lest by her continual coming she weary me. And the Lord said, Hear what the unjust judge saith. And shall not God avenge his own elect, which cry day and night unto him, though he bear long with them? I tell you that he will avenge them speedily. Nevertheless, when the Son of man cometh, shall he find faith on the earth?" LUKE XVIII. 1–8.

"Which of you shall have a friend, and shall go unto him at midnight, and say unto him, Friend, lend me three loaves; for a friend of mine in his journey is come to me, and I have nothing to set before him? And he from within shall answer and say, Trouble me not: the door is now shut, and my children are with me in bed; I cannot rise and give thee. I say unto you, Though he will not rise and give him, because he is his friend, yet because of his importunity he will rise and give him as many as he needeth." LUKE XI. 5–8.

THE parable of the Unjust Judge grew out of the circumstances related by St. Luke in the seventeenth chapter. The Pharisees had demanded of Christ, "when the kingdom of God should come?" This impertinent curiosity he justly rebukes; but, at the same time, takes occasion, from their question, to foretell his disciples the dire effect that would attend the destruction of Jerusalem, rivalling the horrors of a deluged world, or the ravages of Sodom's conflagration.

This announcement was calculated to depress their spirits and shake their faith: for, be it remembered, Christ offered no outward inducement to men to become His followers; He gave no flattering encomiums; He held out no rich patronage; He presented no anticipations of earthly pleasure, wealth, ease, or honours;—but, on the contrary, told them that shame and reproach awaited them; that they "would be hated of all men for His name's sake;" and that "whosoever killed them would think that he did God service."

In order, therefore, to teach them that they should not faint in the day of adversity, that there should be a deliverer and a deliverance, and that the way and means of securing much of their needed help was in their own reach, he relates to them the parable of the Unjust Judge. The elements of the parable are quite simple, and need but little elucidation. Of the judge, two things are said—that "he feared not God, neither regarded man."

This was a proverbial expression, used even by such classical writers as Homer and Euripides, denoting consummate and unblushing wickedness; indeed, most of the heathen writers employ the term to signify one totally abandoned to all evil.

Take away from man "the fear of God," and you fill the soul with every inward sin, and make it "a cage of unclean birds." Take away from man "a regard for man," a proper respect for human opinion, when sound and wholesome, and you surround him with every outward sin, and make him a selfish despot, grinding out from his fellow men whatever may contribute to his own lusts or aggrandizement, reckless of their happiness, solicitous only for his own. Strike out from the heart both these elements—the fear of God and a regard for man—and you make him a monster with a human shape, but a devil's heart. When such sit upon the bench of law, or in the seat of equity, we may take up the lamentation of Isaiah, and say, "Judgment is turned away backward, and Justice standeth afar off, for truth is fallen in the streets, and equity cannot enter!"

The other character introduced to us in this parable is a widow—a name which stirs the fountain of sympathy by telling us of sorrow, loneliness, and bereavement. Like a vine torn by the scathing lightning from the tree around which it clung, and left to trail in the dust, yet leaving still some tendrils clasping the rifted trunk, so is woman when Death writes "widow" on her broken heart.

The introduction of this widow here gives increased interest and pathos to the parable. Left to struggle alone with the world, her natural protector gone, she has evidently been overreached or defrauded by one of those craven-hearted men, who, while they dare not oppress their own sex, yet cowardly triumph over unprotected womanhood. The cases of such were specially provided for by God, and judges were bound by the Divine law to see that justice was meted out to the widow. "Ye shall not afflict any widow or fatherless," was the command of Jehovah; and among the curses pronounced upon Mount Ebal, was that uttered by the Levites, "Cursed be he that perverteth the judgment of the stranger, fatherless, and widow; and all the people shall say, Amen!"

The widow came to this judge to be avenged of her adversary. The word which our English translators have rendered "avenge," is from a Greek verb, which signifies to execute right or justice, to maintain one's right, or to defend one's cause. The Geneva Bible of 1557 translates it, "do me justice of mine adversary."

The old English writers use the words *avenge* and *revenge* to signify, not evil intent and malice, as the terms now import, but simply the assigning to a plaintiff what is just, and thereby delivering him from the evil acts or purposes of his adversary. This poor widow then came to the unjust judge for simple justice, and he, by the law of God and man, was bound to give it to her; but either through indifference or indolence, for a long time he refused to give her audience. But put off once, she came again; rebuffed to-day, she returned to-morrow; and with an energy born amidst sorrow and nursed by oppression, she persisted in her appeal until the judge listened to her cry. To this he was moved, not by duty or compassion, but by her importunity acting upon his selfishness; for he gives the reason of this conduct when he says, "Though I fear not God, neither regard man, yet because this widow troubleth me I will avenge her, lest by her continual coming she weary me." There is a great deal more of meaning in the word "weary," as used here, than appears upon its face to an English reader: hence, to understand its full force as an operating motive upon the mind of the judge, we must resort to its primitive signification. The original word literally means, to strike one under the eye, and was a term used by the boxers of the Grecian games to designate a stunning blow in that part of the face, which, more than any other, was galling to a pugilist; it came at length to express by metaphor whatever is irksome, wearisome, or galling. The same word is used by St. Paul in the Corinthians, where speaking of his self-discipline he says, "I *keep under* my body," as if he had said I so ill treat or beat down my natural appetites and evil lusts that I keep the sinful desires of the flesh in subjection to the rule of my spiritual life, and thus my body is "kept under," or mortified in all its corrupt manifestations.

It is a very homely but expressive rendering which good old Tyndale gives in his version three hundred years ago. "Yet because this widow troubleth me, I will avenge her, lest at the last she come and *hagge on me*." *Hagge* is an Anglo-Saxon name for fury or goblin, answering somewhat to the Hecate of mythology, and is used by Shakspeare to signify a witch or enchantress. To hag any one, then, is to harass or torment them with real or fancied terrors; and this is what the martyr Tyndale meant, when he put the expression, "lest she come and hagge on me," into the mouth of the unjust judge.

Let us turn now to the parable of the Importunate Friend at Midnight.

The subject of our Saviour's discourse at the time this was uttered was prayer. He had Himself been "praying in a certain place;" and His disciples, standing probably at a respectful distance, yet observing His words and actions, felt a desire to know something of prayer themselves; reasoning, with much truth, that if He, their Lord and Master, needed to pray, much more was such devotion necessary for them. In addition to this incentive, they were stimulated still further to prefer the request, from the fact that John had taught his disciples to pray—had given them probably a form of prayer as the guide to their devotion; and, therefore, not to be behind John's disciples in the privileges of grace, they approach Jesus with the request, "Lord, teach us to pray, as John also taught his disciples."

Jesus immediately complies, by giving to them as a formulary what is commonly denominated the Lord's Prayer; that remarkable collection of petitions and ascriptions, which contain within themselves the elements of every prayer that can ever be offered by the faithful heart to our Father in Heaven. Each want of the renewed soul, each object of its most anxious desire, everything for which it can pray aright, lie enfolded in some one or other of the petitions of this prayer, as the majestic oak lies wrapt up in the acorn. The more we meditate upon the paragraphs of this prayer, the more profound and comprehensive do they appear; no human mind can grasp the full meaning of any one of the sentences of this prayer, or sound the depths of its spiritual mysteries. It carries in itself the proof that Christ is Divine, for only a mind possessing Divinity could frame a prayer that should concentrate every possible aspiration of the soul and every known attribute of the Godhead; giving to a few rude disciples a set of words which they readily comprehended and used, which yet, at the same time, is a form of prayer suited to every age of life, every period of time, every class of persons, every nation of earth, and to every condition of the soul, from the time that it draws the first breath of spiritual life, until at the hour of death it exchanges the prayers of earth for the praises of heaven.

Having given His disciples this model prayer, and thus taught them for *what* they should pray, the necessary element of acceptable petition, He proceeds to show them *how* they should pray, and this He does in two ways: first by parable, then by precept; the parable giving more emphasis to the precept, and the precept more point to the parable.

It is not unusual in those hot countries to journey in the night, thus avoiding the burning rays of the sun, and enjoying the refreshing coolness which then prevails. The coming in, therefore, of a friend at midnight is quite in keeping with oriental usages, and supplies an important element of the parable. Had the friend thus surprised by an unexpected visit gone to his neighbour in the day time, to ask for "three loaves," he would easily have obtained them; but going at midnight, when his house was closed, its doors barred, his family at rest, and rousing him from the first sweet sleep of the night, was a test of friendship and liberality of no ordinary kind.

To the request, then, for "three loaves," to supply the necessities of this traveller, the man "from within" answers,

"Trouble me not; the door is now shut, and my children are with me in bed; I cannot rise and give thee." These reasons for declining do not weigh against the necessities of his hungering, fainting friend, therefore he goes not away at this rebuff, but presses his request more and more with shameless earnestness, until the householder, wearied with his importunity, rises, and "gives him as many as he needeth."

The key-word of this parable, then is, IMPORTUNITY—an earnest persevering effort to obtain his request. This was the point to which the Saviour wished to direct the attention of his disciples, and by the means of this parable He designed to enforce the duty of earnest, persevering prayer, and in this respect the parable is not unlike that of the Unjust Judge, and though there are points of difference, yet so far as it regards the setting forth of importunate prayer, they may be regarded and treated as one.

That spirit which these parables enjoin is still further enforced by the precept with which our Lord follows up the similitude of the Midnight Friend: "And I say unto you, ask, and it shall be given unto you; seek, and ye shall find; knock, and it shall be opened unto you. For every one that asketh, receiveth; and he that seeketh, findeth; and to him that knocketh it shall be opened."

The end which our Lord had in view in uttering the parable of the Unjust Judge was, as He declares, "that men ought always to pray, and not to faint;" and from the two parables, combined, we learn these truths: First, That men "ought always to pray;" Secondly, That we must "not faint" at the apparent delay of God, and the pressure of our adversary; Thirdly, That this prayer must be importunate; and lastly, that instant and earnest prayer will always prevail, and that they who ask shall receive, they who seek shall find, and to those who knock the door of grace shall be opened.

First. "Men ought always to pray." We usually give form to our petitions by praying on our knees, with closed eyes and solemnly uttered words; but to pray always in this manner is impossible, physically and mentally; hence our Lord must mean something else than the formal and distinctive act of prayer when he said, "Men ought always to pray;" and St. Paul also must have had in his mind something else than set, closet petitions, when he exhorted the Thessalonians, "Pray without ceasing," and the Romans to be "instant in prayer."

Prayer is the expression of the soul's desires; but "God is a Spirit" and the soul is immaterial, and there is needed, therefore, no intervention of words or posture, no utterances of the tongue, no attitudes of the body, in order to have intercourse with Him. There may be prayer without words, without a closet, without the bended knee, without the shut eye. There may be prayer in the thronged street, in the busy market, in the din of the workshop, in the bustle of the store, amidst the books of the office, and the activities of professional life. When the soul is so attuned to God's will that there is an ever-growing harmony between it and God, and an ever-increasing conformity of mind and heart to Jesus Christ, then is that soul in a praying frame, ready at any moment to commune with its Heavenly Father; now darting out a desire, now ejaculating a petition, now breathing out a holy wish, and now silently reflecting back the manifestations of Divine love, with a glow of emotion and tenderness of sensibility peculiarly affecting. He who cultivates this spirituality of mind lives in an atmosphere of prayer, and breathes the spirit of supplication. He is always in a praying condition. It requires no violent wrenching off of his mind from things seen and earthly, before it can be fastened on things unseen and eternal; but it passes from his avocations to the Throne of Grace with an easiness of transition evincive of the little hold things on earth have upon his heart, and of the powerful attraction of the Mercy-Seat.

It is the privilege of the Christian to have this perpetual intercourse with God, to have his soul thus brought into fellowship and communion with the adorable Saviour; and where we fail to enjoy it the cause is in ourselves, and not in God,—for His ear is ever open to our requests, being "more ready to hear than we to pray, and more willing to give than either we desire or deserve."

In this praying state men "ought always" to keep their souls, because it is the only truly healthful state of the soul, its only truly happy state, its only true preparative to the unveiled enjoyment of God in heaven.

Secondly. We must "not faint" at the apparent **delay of** God, and pressure of our adversaries. In ourselves, indeed, we should often faint, for our strength is weakness, and our strongest resolutions are but as the thread of the gossa mer around the sinewy arms of some giant passion. But we should "faint not," because we pray to an almighty God; we go to a throne of grace from which we are never excluded; we offer our prayer through the Saviour, who is always a prevailing intercessor; and we are aided by the Spirit of grace and supplication, who "helpeth our infirmities."

The widow fainted not, even though she had an unjust judge to appeal to; and because she fainted not she gained her petition. And if this weak, unprotected woman, by the mere force of importunity, wrung from the hands of a judge "who feared not God, neither regarded man," redress of her grievance, shall not God's own children, if they faint not, in due time reap, from their heavenly Father, full and satisfactory answers to their requests? Can He, who is all justice and all love, do less for His importuning children than this "doomsman of wickedness" did for the afflicted widow? Indeed, Christ Himself puts the question, "Shall not God avenge His own elect, which cry night and day unto Him, though He bear long with them?" and He answers His own question by declaring, with marked emphasis, "I tell you that He will avenge them speedily."

The "elect" of God have, as we learn both from the Bible and experience, "an adversary," that great adversary "the Devil, who goeth about like a roaring lion, seeking whom he may devour." This "adversary" of God and man is none other than that "archangel ruined," who at the head of legions of other fallen angels is plotting, though impotently, the overthrow of the moral government of God on earth. To this end they assault the Church of God and "His own elect" with peculiar virulence and power, level against them every fiendish weapon, spread out every deceiving lure, and seek to entrap their souls into eternal ruin. They torment the children of God with fears, and doubt, and spiritual darkness; they harass them with innumerable temptations, and leave no point unassailed, from the infusing of secret unbelief to the open and iron-hearted persecution of the saints by fire and fagot, by sword and scaffold, by dungeon and death. Every child of God feels the enmity of this adversary, and groans to be delivered from his power; some he vexes more than others, but all are made to bear the marks of his violence, and to endure his hatred and reproach. But think you that God will suffer this to go on unavenged? Can he, as a Father, see His children prostrated by this prince of darkness, and not hasten to their rescue? Can He, as a covenant God, behold those who have laid hold upon His covenant assaulted and persecuted by this great adversary, and not avenge them? "I tell you," says Christ, "He will avenge them speedily!" and though, from God's "bearing long" with the machinations of this adversary, it may seem as if He did not regard His suffering people, yet there is only a seeming hiding of His power, for He has declared, "Vengeance is mine, I will repay;" for when His people are almost faint and despairing, then shall He arise to judgment, and making bare His arm, shall put His hand on the throat of His enemies. This was proved in the destruction of Jerusalem, when those who had cried out concerning Jesus, "Crucify Him! Crucify Him!" coupled with the horrid imprecation, "His blood be upon us and on our children," and who had visited their wrath upon the first Christians, were suddenly shut up within the walls of the city, and subjected to a series of trials, and sufferings, and deaths till then unheard of in the annals of retributive vengeance.

In every age since, not a persecution of the Church has existed which has not been followed by the avenging curse of God. Nay, further, not a leader or originator of any of the great persecutions which have been directed against Christianity in its first planting among the nations, or in its subsequent revivals, who has not been made "to drink of the wine-cup of the wrath of God." Collect the biographies of all the sword-armed or torch-bearing antagonists of the Church, whether you find them among Roman emperors or Roman pontiffs; whether among Gallic princes or Gallic cardinals; whether among Spanish kings or Spanish inquisitors; whether among English sovereigns or English prelates, and you shall find that all have experienced the vengeance of Almighty God.

There is scarce an exception to this remark, from the time of Pontius Pilate, who, like Judas, "went out and hanged himself," and Herod Agrippa, who was eaten up of worms and died; down to the imbecile Charles IX., before whose crazed vision the bloody scenes of St. Bartholemew's day ever glared its spectral horrors, and, like the ghost of Banquo before Macbeth, would not "down at his bidding;" or Mary of England, the "bloody Mary," who reigned amidst rebellions, and died amidst the taunts and triumphs of her hating subjects. It is a truth written in God's Word, " He will avenge his elect!" it is a truth written on the breastplate of God's justice, " He will avenge them speedily;" it is a truth that all history reiterates and confirms, " Jehovah shall tread down His enemies;" and so will it ever be unto the end of the world. God often " bears long" with sinners in order to test the faith of His people, and to show to the world how grievously men will sin if left for a season to themselves, but when his disciplinary course is over, his punitive begins, and there is no escaping out of His hands.

Thirdly. We learn from these parables that Christ requires earnest and importunate prayer. A few formal phrases, a few languid petitions, a few ascriptions of praise, and a few acknowledgments of mercies, are not the kind of prayers which are pleasing to God. He requires deep-felt, heart prayers, the wellings up of desires from souls that feel their sin and their need of a Saviour, and that burn with love and zeal.

It is not "eloquent prayers," elaborately carved and polished by the tools of rhetoric, for ears refined, that are pleasing to God. It is not an harangue addressed to men under the form of prayer to God, that He approves; neither is it " much speaking," or " vain repetitions," that engage His attention. Do you wish to pray aright? go to God as a sinful child, go to Him as your Father, reconciled by the death of His Son, go in faith and hope, in love and adoration; tell Him your fears, your trials, your doubts, your sins; unburden your soul at the gate of his ear; go with a broken and a contrite heart, looking only for acceptance in and through the merits and sacrifice of Jesus Christ, and you shall assuredly be heard, for the word of His promise is, " Whatsoever ye shall ask in my name, believing, ye shall receive," and " Him that cometh unto me I will in no wise cast out."

Fourthly. Instant and earnest prayer will always prevail.

To use in part the words of another, the widow was a stranger, not at all related to the judge; but Christians are " God's elect," His favoured, His " peculiar people." The unjust judge was not interested in granting her petition; but God's honour and truth is concerned in relieving the wants of His people. There was little hope of prevailing with such a merciless and unjust judge; but we address a loving and compassionate Father. The widow, moreover, had none to intercede for her; but " we have an advocate with the Father, Jesus Christ the righteous." She was in danger of irritating the judge by her entreaties; but the more importunate we are the more is God pleased, for "the prayer of the upright," says Solomon, "is His delight." She, notwithstanding all her difficulties, obtained her request; how much more shall we, who, in lieu of difficulties, have such abundant encouragements!

The same line of argument and the same inferences can be drawn from the parable of the Friend at Midnight, though we need not stop to recapitulate them here.

To unfold fully the encouragements which we have to importunate prayer, would require a volume rather than a page. We find them in the attributes of God; in the covenant made with Christ; in the manifold promises of His holy Word; in the recorded instances of its success, as in the cases of Jacob, and Moses, and David, and Daniel, and Paul; and in our own experience of God's faithfulness and truth, in reference to every earnest cry which we have uttered in His ear.

In order to the putting forth of this earnest importuning prayer there is needed more "faith on the earth." Faith is the essential basis of all prevailing prayer. There is no acceptable prayer without it. Our prayers will be fervent and effectual, just in proportion to the strength and vitality of our faith. If we have but a faint belief in God's government and care; if we have but little trust in Jesus Christ, as our only Saviour; if we believe but in part the full and free promises of grace; and if, instead of the manly, vigorous walk of faith, we take the tottering steps of an infantile belief, then will our prayers be weak, ineffectual, unedifying. But if we cling to God's Word with unrelaxing tenacity; if we yield ourselves up to Christ in undoubting confidence; if we hold fast the precious promises, and, steadying ourselves by the staff of hope, walk with firm step in the pathway of the just, then shall we reap the rich results of our devotions. Our prayers will be heard, will be answered; and blessings uncounted, unmerited, and unspeakable in richness and in glory, will descend upon our souls.

Nor should our prayers be confined to our own needs alone, for we find in the parable of the Importunate Friend a great incentive to intercessory prayer for others. The poor widow pleaded for herself; her own wrongs, her own necessities urged her to continually press her suit: but in the other parable, the one who came to borrow bread of his friend did not ask it for himself, but for a traveller who had unexpectedly presented himself at his door. His whole importunity was in behalf of another's necessities, not his own; and he continued pleading at that midnight hour, and before that bolted door, until he gained his request.

While, therefore, we should, like the widow, plead with unrelaxing earnestness for our own spiritual needs, we should likewise present importunate supplications to Almighty God in behalf of those whom His providence has placed under our care, those near and dear to us by the ties of consanguinity or affection. The promise is not, Ask for yourselves only, and ye shall receive; seek for yourselves alone, and ye shall find; knock only for personal admittance at the door of heaven, and it shall be opened; but it runs in this broad language: "Whatsoever ye shall ask in my name, believing, ye shall receive." "Verily I say unto you, that if two of you shall agree on earth as touching any thing, it shall be done for them of my Father which is in Heaven." How often do we find in the narrative of our Saviour's miracles, that He wrought special deeds of mercy upon persons brought to Him by others, and because of the faith of those who brought them!

The man who was let down on a bed before Him

through the broken-up roof of the house, was healed because of the faith of those who had borne him to Jesus. The servant of the Capernaum centurion, the daughter of the Syrophœnician woman, and many other cases, were each healed by Jesus because of the faith of those who applied to Him for aid and favour.

The preceptive part of Scripture sustains the truth thus taught by the parables and the miracles of Jesus. St. Paul begs an interest in the prayers of his fellow Christians. He told the Corinthians that they had helped to deliver him from dangers through their prayers; he assured the Philippians that he knew that his afflictions would "turn to his salvation through their prayers." He often speaks of remembering others in his prayers, and St. James distinctly urges, "Pray one for another." Intercessory prayer for each other is then the plain and bounden duty of the children of God; they should come with boldness to the Throne of Grace; they should plead the necessities of their friends with the importunity of that midnight householder; they should faint not in their application, even though at first God seems to say, "I cannot rise and give thee." Pray on; God will hear, will arise, will open to you the windows of heaven, and give you, not "three loaves" merely, but will rain down upon your soul and the souls of those for whom you intercede, "heavenly manna," that "angels' bread," which shall strengthen and sustain both you and them, until you enter the promised land above.

The Wicked Husbandmen.

THE WICKED HUSBANDMEN.

'THERE was a certain householder, which planted a vineyard, and hedged it round about, and digged a wine-press in it, and built a tower, and let it out to husbandmen, and went into a far country. And when the time of the fruit drew near, he sent his servants to the husbandmen, that they might receive the fruits of it. And the husbandmen took his servants, and beat one, and killed another, and stoned another. Again, he sent other servants more than the first: and they did unto them likewise. But last of all he sent unto them his son, saying, They will reverence my son. But when the husbandmen saw the son, they said among themselves, This is the heir; come, let us kill him, and let us seize on his inheritance. And they caught him, and cast him out of the vineyard, and slew him. When the lord therefore of the vineyard cometh, what will he do unto those husbandmen? They say unto him, He will miserably destroy those wicked men, and will let out his vineyard unto other husbandmen, which shall render him the fruits in their seasons. Jesus saith unto them, Did ye never read in the Scriptures, The stone which the builders rejected, the same is become the head of the corner: this is the Lord's doing, and it is marvellous in our eyes? Therefore say I unto you, The kingdom of God shall be taken from you, and given to a nation bringing forth the fruits thereof. And whosoever shall fall on this stone shall be broken: but on whomsoever it shall fall, it will grind him to powder." MATT. XXI. 33–44.

"A certain man planted a vineyard, and set a hedge about it, and digged a place for the wine-fat, and built a tower, and let it out to husbandmen, and went into a far country. And at the season he sent to the husbandmen a servant, that he might receive from the husbandmen of the fruit of the vineyard. And they caught him, and beat him, and sent him away empty. And again he sent unto them another servant; and at him they cast stones, and wounded him in the head, and sent him away shamefully handled. And again he sent another; and him they killed, and many others; beating some, and killing some. Having yet therefore one son, his well-beloved, he sent him also last unto them, saying, They will reverence my son. But those husbandmen said among themselves, This is the heir: come, let us kill him, and the inheritance shall be ours. And they took him, and killed him, and cast him out of the vineyard. What shall therefore the lord of the vineyard do? He will come and destroy the husbandmen, and will give the vineyard unto others. And have ye not read this Scripture, The stone which the builders rejected is become the head of the corner: this was the Lord's doing, and it is marvellous in our eyes? And they sought to lay hold on him, but feared the people; for they knew that he had spoken the parable against them: and they left him, and went their way."   MARK XII. 1-12.

"A certain man planted a vineyard, and let it forth to husbandmen, and went into a far country for a long time. And at the season he sent a servant to the husbandmen, that they should give him of the fruit of the vineyard: but the husbandmen beat him, and sent him away empty. And again he sent another servant: and they beat him also, and entreated him shamefully, and sent him away empty. And again he sent a third: and they wounded him also, and cast him out. Then said the lord of the vineyard, What shall I do? I will send my beloved son: it may be they will reverence him when they see him. But when the husbandmen saw him, they reasoned among themselves, saying, This is the heir: come, let us kill him, that the inheritance may be ours. So they cast him out of the vineyard, and killed him. What therefore shall the lord of the vineyard do unto them? He shall come and destroy these husbandmen, and shall give the vineyard to others. And when they heard it, they said, God forbid."   LUKE XX. 9-16.

THERE are two aspects under which this parable may be viewed: one as it respects the Jews; the other as it regards the world at large. It was delivered in the court of the temple, to the chief priests and scribes who had gathered around Jesus to cavil at His words; and just after His triumphant entry into Jerusalem.

The Jewish application of this parable is evident from collateral Scripture and historical facts, as will appear from a very brief analysis. The "certain man," or "householder," as Matthew expresses it, is God; and the "vineyard" is the Jewish Church. Under the appellation of a vineyard, David, Jeremiah, and Isaiah speak of their nation; and there is much show of truth in the supposition that our Lord, when he framed this parable, alluded to the words of Isaiah, "For the vineyard of the Lord of Hosts is the house of Israel, and the men of Judah His pleasant plant; and He looked for judgment, but behold oppression; for righteousness, but behold a cry."

The "husbandmen" to whom he let it out were the priests and Levites and scribes, to whom were committed the moral and religious culture of the nation. The going "into a far country," means in the original that He left them for a time, which indeed was done, when the Shekineh, the emblem of His glory, was removed from them. The sending of servants, "when the time of the fruit drew near," "to the husbandmen, that they should give him of the fruit of the vineyard," for the rent of the same, as was and is customary in Eastern countries, refers to the Prophets whom God sent to His people through the whole period of the Levitical dispensation, beginning with Moses, and ending, eleven hundred years after, with Malachi.

The treatment which these ancient ministers received is well described by the conduct of the husbandmen towards the servants sent to receive the fruits of the vineyard; they "beat one," "stoned another," "killed another," treated one "shamefully," "wounded" another, and "cast him out of the vineyard." Both the Prophets Elijah and Daniel complain that the Jews have slain the prophets with the sword. Jerusalem especially had this reputation, as our Lord's apostrophe testifies: "O, Jerusalem, Jerusalem, that killest the prophets, and stonest them that are sent unto thee;" and St. Paul, when he enumerates the long list of worthies in his catalogue of the faithful, in the eleventh chapter of Hebrews, says that they "had trial of cruel mockings and scourgings, yea, moreover, of bonds and imprisonment: they were stoned, they were sawn asunder, were tempted, were slain with the sword; they wandered about in sheepskins and goatskins; being destitute, afflicted, tormented, they wandered in deserts, and in mountains, and in dens, and in caves of the earth;" and though the Apostle in this passage does not design to refer so much to individual cases as to the great varieties of sufferings experienced in the persecution under Antiochus Epiphanes, yet we know of instances of each of these kinds of torture in the history of God's ancient servants: for Elijah, Elisha, Ezra, Nehemiah, Jeremiah, Micaiah, and Eleazar "had trials of cruel mockings and scourgings," Sampson and Daniel were in "bonds and imprisonment," Zechariah was "stoned" in the court of the Lord's house; Isaiah, according to ancient tradition, was "sawn asunder" with a wooden saw, by order of king Manasseh; the "Lord's priests" at Nob were hewn in pieces with the sword of Saul, and "the prophets of the Lord" were cut off by Jezebel, the wife of Ahab; Elijah, and Elisha, and John the Baptist, "wandered about in sheepskins and goatskins;" and all of them were more or less "destitute, afflicted, tormented;" for this was the way in which these wicked husbandmen, the Kings and Priests and Levites, treated the servants sent by God "to receive the fruit of the vineyard."

After repeated messages and great forbearance, the lord

of the vineyard asks, "What shall I do?" and he resolves, "last of all I will send my beloved son; it may be they will reverence him when they see him." And so in the last days of the Jewish economy, when temple, and altar, and synagogue, and priest, and Levite, and ritual were to be done away, and to give place to the higher, holier ministry, temple, and service of the Christian Church, God, who loved His vineyard notwithstanding the treatment which His servants had received, determined to give the Son of His bosom, "His only begotten" and "well beloved Son," to die for His rebellious children. "It may be," He says, "they will reverence my Son;" the dignity of the person sent and of the person sending, ought to inspire a reverential regard, and reason might have well argued, "they will reverence my Son." This Son came; He left "the glory which He had with the Father before the world was," the courts of heaven, the worship of angels, and came to the husbandmen of earth to receive the fruit of His vineyard. "But when the husbandmen saw Him they reasoned among themselves, saying, This is the heir; come, let us kill Him, that the inheritance may be ours."

Yes, Christ was "the heir;" "heir of all things," as St. Paul says; heir in His mediatorial character, and by Divine appointment; but in order to kill this heir the chief priests and scribes and Pharisees "counselled together." It was the one vengeful purpose of their lives, the one great aim of their efforts, begun by Herod at the birth of this heir, and consummated by Pilate and Caiaphas when they hung Him on the accursed tree.

In pursuance of this foul design "they cast Him out of the vineyard," saying, "Away with Him," delivering Him into the Roman power, and with the cry, "Crucify Him! crucify Him!" they "killed Him" on Calvary.

"What, therefore," asks our Saviour, "shall the Lord of the vineyard do unto them?" His audience, not as yet perceiving the force of the parable, replied, "He will miserably destroy those wicked men, and will let out His vineyard unto other husbandmen, who shall render Him the fruits in their season:" thus unwittingly condemning themselves, and pronouncing their own well-deserved doom. Nor was it long before their own sentence was carried into execution; for by the irruption of the Roman army into Judea, the vineyard of God's planting—the Holy City—was destroyed; its temple, the glory of the whole earth, was burnt with fire; its palaces were razed to the ground; its streets were filled with ruins; its walls were broken down, and with a havoc unparalleled in the history of the world, those husbandmen were destroyed by fire, by pestilence, by famine, and by the sword. The siege of Jerusalem began about the feast of the Passover, one of the three festivals when all the males of the nation were required "to present themselves before the Lord:" and when, therefore, more than three millions of people were pent up within its walls. Of these, over eleven hundred thousand were killed, and nearly a hundred thousand others were carried captive into Egypt, Rome, and the colonies of

Augustus. Not only was their land, the beautiful and almost consecrated hills of Judea, given to others, to the Roman, the Syrian, and the Egyptian, but their Church was broken up, the veil of its temple was rent in twain, its oblation ceased, its priesthood was abolished, its splendid ritual was done away, and those who were once restricted to the outer courts of the Jewish sanctuary, are now made to draw nigh unto God, even into the inner courts of a more glorious temple, built up by Christ of "lively stones," on Himself, "the chief corner stone," a temple whose only High Priest is the Lord of Glory, whose only sacrifice is "the Lamb slain from the foundation of the world," whose incense is "the prayers of saints," whose choral service are the hymnings of the redeemed, whose "walls are salvation, and whose gates praise."

This parable must have tingled upon the ears of the priests and Pharisees, and when they came to understand its import, they immediately, "the same hour, sought to lay hands on Him, for they perceived that He had spoken this parable against them;" and had they not "feared the people," they would immediately have caught Him, and cast Him out of the vineyard, and killed Him.

But this parable has a Christian, as well as a Jewish aspect. It is true that we have not killed the Prophets; we have not cast the Heir of the Lord of the vineyard out of the vineyard; we have not imbrued our hands in His blood; but if sin is the same in all ages, as we know that it is; if man's nature is the same through all generations, as experience proves; then need not the sinner congratulate himself that he is guiltless of the blood of Jesus, for there lies in his heart a principle which, if fully developed, would lead him to do precisely what the Jews did, slay the prophets, and cast the Heir, even Christ, out of His vineyard. Both hate God, both disobey His laws, both set aside His Gospel, and both say in their acts, if not in words, "we will not have this man to reign over us."

Each human heart is a vineyard of God's planting, and through His Holy Word He has sent to you Prophets and Apostles to receive the fruit of your tillage; have you listened to the words of His servants, and returned to Him the hire of your vineyard? Nay, has not Christ himself stood at the door of your heart knocking, and saying, "Rise and let me in;" and have you not suppressed as much as possible all thoughts of Him, and refused Him entrance? And where, in the sight of God, is the difference between the Jews and yourself? but that, in the former, the overt act of insult and murder was superadded to the inward feeling of enmity and rebellion?

Every one who does not receive Christ into his heart, does virtually "cast Him out of His vineyard." Every one who refuses to listen to the call of God's ministers, does in fact evil entreat the servants of the Lord. Every one who withholds from the "Householder" the wages of righteousness, does, to that extent, strive to take from Him the inheritance. Each one of these assertions, strong as they may seem, is borne out and sustained by the Word of God. "He that is not with me," says Christ, "is against me." "He that heareth you," says the same blessed Saviour to

His disciples, "heareth me; and he that despiseth you, despiseth me; and he that despiseth me, despiseth Him that sent me." "Will a man rob God?" asks the Prophet Malachi; "yet ye have robbed me; but ye say, wherein have we robbed thee? in tithes and offerings;" *i. e.* in not rendering to God that which He requires; and His requirement of each human being is, "Thou shalt love the Lord thy God with all thy heart, and mind, and strength, and thy neighbour as thyself." There is no evading this responsibility on the one hand, and this accountability on the other—the one you must bear through life, and the other will meet you at the bar of God; and there you will be judged, not so much for what you did as for what you did not do; not so much for overt acts as for the inward feelings of your soul towards your adorable Redeemer.

We have seen, though briefly, what the Lord did to the wicked husbandmen; and what shall he do to the impenitent now? They give no heed to the messages He sends, yield to Him no revenue of praise, and in their hearts crucify His Son afresh, and "put Him to an open shame." They break His laws, reject His love, refuse His salvation, choose to "walk in the light of their own eyes, and after the counsels of their own hearts," and what shall He do to them? The Apostle answers for us: "He that despised Moses' law died without mercy under two or three witnesses; of how much sorer punishment suppose ye shall he be thought worthy who hath trodden under foot the Son of God, and hath counted the blood of the covenant wherewith he was sanctified an unholy thing, and hath done despite unto the Spirit of Grace: for we know Him that hath said, Vengeance belongeth unto me; I will recompense, saith the Lord."

We are emphatically taught by this parable that God will hold us responsible for our treatment of Jesus Christ. He held the Jews, the husbandmen of his ancient vineyard, responsible for their conduct towards his servants and his Son; and fearfully have they been made to endure, even to this day, the severity of that self-assumed curse, "His blood be on us and on our children;" and they will continue to endure it "until the fulness of the Gentiles be brought in." But as the sin of unbelievers now is more aggravated, in many of its aspects, than that of the Jews in the time of Christ's earthly ministry, so will God, in accordance with the principles of eternal justice, hold every living soul, who has heard of Christ, responsible for his conduct towards that blessed Jesus.

Even those who take a comparatively low view of our moral relations to God, acknowledge that we are responsible for the right use of our time, our money, our talents, our influence; and shall God hold us strictly accountable for these, in one sense, minor and inconsiderable things, and not make inquisition of us for our treatment of that "unspeakable gift," "his well-beloved Son?" The supposition is impossible! God must cease to love "His only-begotten Son," must ignore His law, must annul His covenant, must vacate His attributes, must revoke His word, must change the very elements of His being, before He can suffer the rejectors of Christ and His Gospel to go unpunished; and hence the force of that declaration of Christ, after His resurrection and just prior to His ascension, "He that believeth and is baptized shall be saved, but he that believeth not shall be damned."

The simple keeping of Christ out of our heart is, small as it may appear to worldly men, the crowning sin of the ungodly; and until He is admitted there, and believed on by a faith that "worketh by love and purifies the soul," all other changes will be of no avail. We may correct this evil habit, and prune away that sin; we may turn from debauchery to purity, from profanity to reverence, from covetousness to charity; we may polish our characters till we shall appear beautiful to ourselves and others; we may even have a sentimental regard for Christ, and experience a sort of respect for His ordinances, and join with outward devotion in the praises of the sanctuary; yet, build up these characters as high as we may, adorn them with every worldly grace, set them off with every earthly virtue, unless Christ is formed in our hearts the hope of glory, they are nothing "but whited sepulchres, which, indeed, appear beautiful outward, but within are full of dead bones and all uncleanness."

On the other hand, no matter what may have been our former course, no matter what the turpitude of our character, though our sins be black as midnight, and numberless as the stars, and gross as lust itself; yet, if we now repent and open the door to Christ, and receive Him into our hearts in the fulness of a faith that trusts in Him alone, and will "make mention of His righteousness only," all will be well: "though your sins be as scarlet, they shall become as snow; and though they be red like crimson, they shall be as wool;" for this blessed Jesus had declared, "Him that cometh unto me I will in no wise cast out."

Keep, then, this "beloved Son" no longer out of the vineyard of your heart, but, as He stands at the door and knocks, let your language be, in the words of an older poet—

> " No longer, Master, shalt thou knock to me;
> Once more *I feel thy need.* Oh, enter in,
> As my proud heart forsakes its idol sin,
> And contrite grown, now listening waits for Thee.
> I know that I have turned a heavy ear
> Unto thy gentle knocking; sometimes cried
> With a rough voice, Why this persisting here?
> Go Thou thy way, and keep the outer side.
> This have I said to Thee, who for me died!
> But, *Master! I repent;* come Thou anear,
> And by the love Thou hast borne me alway,
> Let me *forgiven be*, and *sanctified;*
> And henceforth humbly serve Thee and obey:
> Oh! Master, *enter; even while I pray.*"

The Sower.

16

THE SOWER.

"BEHOLD, a sower went forth to sow; and when he sowed, some seeds fell by the way side, and the fowls came and devoured them up: some fell upon stony places, where they had not much earth: and forthwith they sprung up, because they had no deepness of earth: and when the sun was up, they were scorched; and because they had no root, they withered away. And some fell among thorns; and the thorns sprung up and choked them: but others fell into good ground, and brought forth fruit, some a hundredfold. some sixtyfold. some thirtyfold."

MATT. XIII. 3–8.

"Hearken; Behold, there went out a sower to sow. And it came to pass, as he sowed, some fell by the way side, and the fowls of the air came and devoured it up. And some fell on stony ground, where it had not much earth; and immediately it sprang up, because it had no depth of earth: but when the sun was up, it was scorched; and because it had no root, it withered away. And some fell among thorns, and the thorns grew up, and choked it, and it yielded no fruit. And other fell on good ground, and did yield fruit that sprang up and increased; and brought forth, some thirty, and some sixty, and some a hundred." MARK IV. 3–8.

"A sower went out to sow his seed: and as he sowed, some fell by the way side; and it was trodden down, and the fowls of the air devoured it. And some fell upon a rock; and as soon as it was sprung up, it withered away, because it lacked moisture. And some fell among thorns; and the thorns sprang up with it, and choked it. And other fell on good ground, and sprang up, and bare fruit a hundred fold. And when he had said these things, he cried, He that hath ears to hear, let him hear." LUKE VIII. 6–8.

"Hear ye therefore the parable of the sower. When any one heareth the word of the kingdom, and understandeth it not, then cometh the wicked one, and catcheth away that which was sown in his heart. This is he which received seed by the way side. But he that received the seed into stony places, the same is he that heareth the word, and anon with joy receiveth it; yet hath he not root in himself, but dureth for a while: for when tribulation or persecution ariseth because of the word, by and by he is offended. He also that received seed among the thorns is he that heareth the word; and the care of this world, and the deceitfulness of riches, choke the word, and he becometh unfruitful. But he that received seed into the good ground is he that heareth the word, and understandeth it; which also beareth fruit, and bringeth forth, some a hundredfold, some sixty, some thirty."

MATT. XIII. 18–23.

"The sower soweth the word. And these are they by the way side, where the word is sown; but when they have heard, Satan cometh immediately, and taketh away the word that was sown in their hearts. And these are they likewise which are sown on stony ground; who, when they have heard the word, immediately receive it with gladness; and have no root in themselves, and so endure but for a time: afterward, when affliction or persecution ariseth for the word's sake, immediately they are offended. And these are they which are sown among thorns; such as hear the word, and the cares of this world, and the deceitfulness of riches, and the lusts of other things entering in, choke the word, and it becometh unfruitful. And these are they which are sown on good ground; such as hear the word, and receive it, and bring forth fruit, some thirtyfold, some sixty, and some a hundred."

MARK IV. 14–20.

"Now the parable is this: The seed is the word of God. Those by the way side are they that hear; then cometh the devil, and taketh away the word out of their hearts, lest they should believe and be saved. They on the rock are they, which, when they hear, receive the word with joy; and these have no root, which for a while believe, and in time of temptation fall away. And that which fell among thorns are they, which when they have heard, go forth, and are choked with cares and riches and pleasures of this life, and bring no fruit to perfection. But that on the good ground are they, which in an honest and good heart, having heard the word, keep it, and bring forth fruit with patience." LUKE VIII. 11–15.

THE many mighty works which our Saviour did in and around Capernaum, drew together large multitudes to see and hear Him. Some, like the Scribes, and Pharisees, and Herodians, mingled with His audience "to entangle Him in His talk;" others came to bring their maimed or diseased friends to be healed; others, impelled by curiosity, grouped around Him to see the wondrous miracles which He performed: while few assembled to listen to His words of heavenly wisdom, or to be instructed in the things concerning the Kingdom of God.

Knowing the hearts of all men, He was aware of these varying dispositions in His hearers, and distinguished in each the motive which led them to His teaching. Accordingly, He addressed to them a parable which met their several cases, and illustrated their different receptions of His truth.

So great, however, was the crowd, that, in order to avoid the press, Jesus was compelled to get into a ship, and push out a little from the land, while His audience sat down upon the sea-shore; which, gently rising from the beach, made a fine natural amphitheatre, where each could see and hear.

How picturesque the scene which meets the eye of the mind! The dense crowds of the people, mingling all ranks and classes; the turbulent Galilean; the restless Gadarene; the sanctimonious Pharisee, the brisk Scribe, the dark-browed Herodian, all clustered in waiting silence on the borders of the lake. To the right was the town of Capernaum, with its busy market and toll-booths, where the clay cottage of the fisherman leaned against the stone walls of the palace. Behind Him lay the Sea of Galilee, dotted with boats passing to and fro between Tiberias, Genesereth, Dalmanutha, and Capernaum. Around Him were the bronzed-faced sailors, leaning upon the tackling of their ship, with their nets dragging at its side; and there He stood, a fishing-boat His pulpit; the sloping banks of Tiberias His temple; the rippling waves and rustling winds His choir; preaching the doctrines He had brought from Heaven, and speaking, "as man never spake," of the things which make for our eternal peace.

But hark! He waves His hand to command silence; the shifting multitude stand still; the hum of voices is hushed, for Jesus opens His lips, and truths such as earth never heard before, leap from his tongue with an eloquence as simple and majestic as His own character.

The truths were divine—the illustrations earthly; perhaps his eye at that very moment caught the form of some Galilean farmer, traversing his newly ploughed field, and casting his seed about him on the right hand and on the left; some falling upon the still standing thorns; some upon the rocky ledge; some on the beaten footpath; and some into the upturned furrows; while birds hovered behind him to pick up the uncovered seed which lay scattered upon the rock or the wayside. Taking this scene as His text, He uttered the simple yet exquisite parable of the Sower wherein He designed to represent the different soils of the human heart, and the different receptions and results which the seed of the Gospel meets with as it is sown broadcast over the world.

Our Saviour here distinguishes several kinds of hearers who attend upon the Gospel ministry; and in some one or other of these four classes may every man in Christendom find his true position. The causes of this diversity are skilfully analyzed, and the results of such kinds of hearing are distinctly classified in his exposition of the parable, which, in answer to their request, He subsequently made to His disciples.

Let us, then, as little children, sit at the feet of Jesus, while he unfolds to us this beautiful parable. His mild eye invites inquiry, and we look up and ask, "Lord, who are meant by the wayside hearers?" He replies, "When any one heareth the word of the kingdom, and understandeth it not, then cometh the wicked one, and catcheth away that which was sown in his heart. This is he which received seed by the wayside."

The peculiar wording of the parable, as recorded by St. Luke, intimates a subdivision of this class of wayside hearers into the indifferent, who allow the fowls of the air to pick up and devour the seed; and the infidels, who treat it with contempt and tread it under foot. Of this latter class we shall not speak, as none will probably read these pages; of the former, "the indifferent," we desire to give a few marks and warnings.

The wayside is a public thoroughfare, beaten smooth and hardened by the feet of travellers, so that seed dropped there cannot sink in, but is speedily picked up by the birds, or trodden down by men.

Of many a human heart may it be said, it is a wayside, where all thoughts travel; where evil imaginations, and sinful feelings, and corrupt desires meet and exchange salutations; where the "lusts of the eye" stand peering at the corners of the street; where the "lusts of the flesh" look in at the windows of her house, "which is the way to hell, going down to the chambers of death;" where the "pride of life" flaunts its train and trappings, that it may excite the buzz of admiration, or the homage of the vulgar. The heart of such a man is trodden down and made hard like a wayside, by overrunning thoughts and sins. When he enters the house of God, his heart is thronged with evil imaginations; when he bows in prayer, his spirit prays not; when he stands up to sing God's praise, his soul only sends back echoes of earthly ditties; and when the minister sows broadcast "the seed of the word," it falls upon his affections as upon a wayside, to be either trodden under foot by negligence, or else picked up by the evil one, who cometh like the fowls of the air to snatch away the newly dropped grain of gospel grace. How many ostensible worshippers of God there are who, Sabbath after Sabbath, sit under the droppings of the Sanctuary, and yet heed them not, because of the pre-occupancy of their thoughts and affections by the great adversary of souls! The word reaches only the outward ear, it never vibrates on the tympanum of the soul. On these wayside hearers, the word of God has no effect at all, and herein they differ from the three remaining classes, in one of which it has at least a momentary effect; in another it has an imperfect effect; and in the last a good and productive result. But on this class it is entirely devoid of benefit. Once their hearts were susceptible and tender; once they were stirred with the story of a Saviour's love and death; or trembled at the threatenings of a sin-hating God. Whence then this change? Whence this stony-heartedness, this indurated wayside soul? They have resisted again and again the strivings of the Spirit; they have stifled the oft-recurring convictions of sin; they have not sought to understand the truth—they have even affected to disbelieve it; they have allowed other and worldly impressions to overpower their minds, and have yielded to the hostile influences of sin, which, like hovering birds, have waited to catch up and bear away the seed as fast as it fell upon their hearts. This course, persisted in for a series of years, while, at the same time, all the outward duties of life, and all the external requirements of religion, have been perhaps attended to, has conspired to make them gospel-hardened, and no pleadings of Divine love can rouse them, no thunders of Sinai break up their indifference.

The one prominent characteristic here is *heedlessness*—a perfect inattention to truth, a complete negligence of the means of grace, a continued carelessness concerning their souls, and a total thoughtlessness about God, and Christ, and the Holy Ghost. Such a process inevitably lays waste the soil of the heart, beats it down, hardens it, and makes it barren of all spiritual life.

Of all mournful spectacles, this is among the most mournful; for, combined with a seeming respect for the Gospel, and a high-toned morality, and an honourable discharge of life's duties, there is a wilful resistance to the Holy Ghost; a deliberate rejection of the blessed Saviour; a hardened impenitence towards Almighty God; and for such men, though they may flourish on earth "like a green bay tree," there is reserved the fearful and eternal punishment of an insulted God.

But our inquiring glance is again directed to the Saviour, and we ask, "Lord, who are designated by the stony-ground hearers?" "They are those," he replies, "who, when they have heard the word, immediately receive it with gladness, and have no root in themselves, and so endure but for a time; afterward when affliction or persecution ariseth because of the word, immediately they are offended, and so fall away." The several Evangelists, in recording this parable, have a slight variation here: St. Matthew says, "stony places," St. Mark, "stony ground," St. Luke, "rock." The idea designed to be conveyed by each is, however, one and the same, viz., a rock with a superficial covering of earth, just enough to fructify the seed, and give it a temporary germination, not enough to allow it deepness of root, and consequent permanence and fruit. So there are many hearts which are, indeed, stony, but which are yet coated over with a thin layer of sensibilities and emotions, just enough of the soil of goodness to start into vegetation the seed of the word, but not enough to give it depth of root or perfectness of growth.

A great multitude of those who attend the ordinances of grace have delicate and excitable natures: their minds are, to a certain extent, interested, their imaginations are pleased, their sensibilities are touched, and, at times, they seem powerfully affected by the truth; their feelings are all quickened into excitement, they listen with intense interest, tears start to their eyes at the story of the Saviour's love and death; they resolve to break off from their sins, and turn to God, to abandon their evil companions, and to unite themselves with the Church of Christ; the seed has fallen upon the thin soil, it has taken root, but ere long some gay associate, some irreligious jester, some scheme of pleasure, or some plan of business, calls off their minds, and the seed which began to germinate so rapidly for good, perishes as soon as the hot sun of persecution is up, because "it has no deepness of earth."

Much of the religion of the world is the product of mere sensibility, acted upon by an excited imagination; it is a piety springing up from the thin soil of morality, that lies upon the top of man's rock-like heart.

Such "stony-ground hearers" may, for some time, appear well, especially if the seed has fallen into some cleft of amiability; but let persecutions arise, let tribulations sweep over the Church, and their slender stalks of grace are uprooted, and lie withered and destroyed. Or let such be exposed only to the minor persecutions of ungodly friends and relatives, let them be ridiculed and contemned, let them be avoided and neglected, let the tribulations through which every child of God must pass as he travels heavenward, come upon them, and "they endure but for a time," being soon "offended" at a religion which exposes them to such trials; and, rather than bear the taunts of men, they dare the frowns of God, and so return to the world which they once promised to renounce.

In the wayside hearers the seed is caught up by the wicked one; in the stony-ground hearers the seed takes root, springs up, and is then wilted by the scorching sun. In the one case Satan "catcheth away that which was sown, lest they should believe and be saved;" in the other case he brings to bear outward and inward trials consequent on a reception of the truth, compared here to the scorching rays of the sun, or to the burning desert wind, which began to blow when the sun was up. "As that heat, had the plant been rooted deeply enough, would have furthered its growth and hastened its ripening; so these tribulations would have furthered the growth in grace of the true Christian, and ripened him for heaven. But, as the heat scorches the blade which has 'no deepness of earth' and has sprung up on shallow ground, so the troubles and afflictions which would have strengthened a true faith, cause a faith which was merely temporary to fail." So, having no "root in himself," or inward root, he "but dureth for a while," "and in time of temptation falls away."

There is great emphasis in the words, "having no root in himself." Such persons have no deeply rooted convictions of sin, no deeply rooted sense of the need of a Saviour, no deeply rooted resolves of abandonment of their iniquities, no deeply rooted faith in the Lord Jesus, no deeply rooted principles of a Christian life. And where these radical elements are wanting, there all will be loose, shifting, and superficial. Only those who are rooted and grounded in Christ, whose hope, whose faith, whose love, whose joy, like so many roots, strike down deep into the gospel soil, and twine around the very heart of Jesus, drawing thence their life-sap, and circulating it through all the arteries of the soul, can bear the storms of adversity, the sun of persecution, and so endure unto the end.

Beware against trusting to these shallow impressions; beware of this mere surface religion; beware of these slight and transient resolves of reform, which, like "the morning cloud" and "the early dew," soon vanish away.

But listen! Christ is describing the thorny-ground hearers, and says they are such "as hear the word, and the cares of this world, and the deceitfulness of riches, and the lust of other things entering in, choke the word, and it becometh unfruitful."

Here we have a good soil, and depth of soil, but a soil in which are already planted the germs or roots of evil. Consequently, when the seed of the word is sown in it, it springs up indeed, but the thorns spring up with it and choke it, so that it "becometh unfruitful."

This applies to the nominal members of the church of Christ: "Those who do not quite cast off their profession, and yet come short of any saving benefit by it; the good they gain by the word being insensibly overcome and overborne by the things of this world."

This, then, is the picture of one in whose heart grace is struggling for existence against the cares of this world, the deceitfulness of riches, and the lusts of other things. The originals of this portrait are to be found in every Sabbath congregation. They are punctual in their accustomed place in the house of prayer; they maintain a devout appearance; the seed is received into their hearts, it takes root, it springs up, but alas! side by side with the upshooting blade of grace is the choking thorn-stalk, drawing its life-sap from the same soil, and by its speedier, ranker growth impoverishing that soil to the damage and sterility of the tender sproutings of the good seed.

Instead of pausing at the first appearance of these thorns, and plucking them up by the roots; instead of bestowing a careful husbandry upon the soil, watching the incast seed, and rooting up everything that would choke its growth; they suffered the operations of business, the plans of wealth, the schemes of ambition, the love of feastings, parties, amusements, and the cares and anxieties of life, to grow up unchecked, until they overtopped the plants of grace, sucked out the strength of the affections, impoverished the soul, and left the good seed to become choked, and "bring no fruit to perfection."

Several things are mentioned here as choking the work of grace in the heart,—1. The cares of this world, viz., those feverish anxieties, active energies, fruitful plans, fretting worriments, perplexing aims, connected with providing for the wants of our worldly existence, everything in fine that hinges upon the question, "What shall we eat, and what shall we drink, and wherewithal shall we be clothed?" These cares must necessarily take up a large portion of our time. Our physical necessities, our social relations, our public responsibilities demand much and earnest attention; and inattention to them is sinful, and directly violates the precepts of the Bible.

The curse is upon the earth, and the brow of man must sweat with labour to force from it a precarious subsistence.

All this is granted; but because these duties of self-support and family support are so important, shall we make them paramount? Because we must live on this earth a little while, shall we adopt the epicurean maxim, "let us eat and drink, for to-morrow we die," and centre all the interests of life in a mere animal existence? Is the body alone to engage attention? Have we no higher aims than what centre in flesh and blood? Here then lies the defect in this class of thorny-ground hearers—they do not keep the things of time and sense in subordination to things spiritual and eternal. They do not regard the wants of the soul and its care as the first object to be attended to; watching against whatever encroaches on it, or is detrimental to its interests: but, on the contrary, are so careful of the interests of business and daily life, that they check even the sproutings of grace itself, lest it should interfere with success in worldly schemes. Religion will never prevent a due attention to legitimate business and necessary cares of this life; and these, on the other hand, will never interfere, when duly regulated with the strict performance of our religious duties. The moment that the cares of this life, be they what they may, crowd out humble, frequent, heartfelt prayer, or make distasteful the reading of God's Word, or irksome the duties and services of the Christian's daily life, or unprofitable the hours and employments of the holy Sabbath, that moment must the man take his stand, and either root out the thorns, or suffer the thorns to choke the soul.

2. Another enemy of the Christian life is found in " the

deceitfulness of riches, and the lusts of other things entering in." The deceitfulness of riches prepares the way for a whole retinue of soul-strangling lusts. Observe, here, it is not riches, but the deceitfulness of riches. Riches themselves are God's gift—are valuable in their legitimate use; but they become deceitful when we put our confidence in them, rest our happiness in them, trust our hopes to them, and regard them as the chief good of our existence.

"They that will be rich," says St. Paul, "fall into temptation and a snare, and into many foolish and hurtful lusts, which drown men in destruction and perdition." How earnestly should we take heed to a warning so solemn and so awful as this! That riches are deceitful we all know; they promise much comfort, but he who has the most money has the least enjoyment of it. They cannot heal disease; they cannot ward off evils; they cannot restore the unbalanced mind; they cannot heal family feuds; they cannot give peace to the burdened conscience; they cannot purchase an entrance into Heaven. They take to themselves wings and fly away; the tempest wastes them, the fire burns them, the ocean wrecks them; they are yours to-day, to-morrow you may but clutch at their shadow. Yet, though we assent to these truths, the great aim of the majority is to get rich; and when that desire seizes upon the soul, like Aaron's rod, it swallows up all other aims, and becomes the ruling passion. Then the labour is to get money; then is heard the horse-leech cry of avarice, "give! give!" Then are the sympathies for the poor, and the sensibilities to sorrow, seared, lest gold should ooze out through those tender channels. Then is mammon erected into an idol, and worshipped with more than Eastern devotion. Then is the man consecrated to lucre, "filthy lucre;" and he takes more delight in the company of Bunyan's Mr. Muck-rake, talking of gains and bargains, than in associating with angels, communing about God and Heaven. "How hardly," says Christ, "shall they that have riches enter into the kingdom of Heaven!" It is a fearful thing when the lust of wealth gets headway in the soul. It must be narrowly watched, immediately checked: for if we do not guide our wealth into channels of benevolence, and baptize it for Christ and His Church, it will drive us into spiritual unfruitfulness, and ruin our immortal souls.

Especially in these days is this warning needed. The vast increase of the precious metals by the discoveries in Australia and California; the remarkable unfoldings of mercantile and commercial wealth through the many new avenues of trade and the use of a steam marine; the rapid development of the agricultural and industrial resources of our country by the building of railroads, canals, telegraphs; the wonderful stimulus imparted to all branches of trade and all the pursuits of men, by the inventions and science and energy of the present century, have had, in some respects, a very sad moral influence, and have done much to keep the Church in a comparatively lethargic state. Everything, now, is excitement, hurry; the long-established methods of trade are found too slow and quiet; dashing operations, bold schemes, hazardous adventures are rife on every side. The game of business is deeply, and very seldom fairly, played. Young men are inveigled into courses that, a few years ago, would have been denounced with horror. Clerks are taught the tricks of trade and the artifices of decoying, to the utter destruction of their moral sensibilities; and consequent upon this, are habits of wasteful expenditure, of dissipation, of dishonesty, of rash speculation, of ruin.

In social life, this deceitfulness of riches manifests itself in personal and household display: in building sumptuous dwellings, furnishing them with gorgeous furniture, giving luxurious balls and parties, keeping up a liveried equipage, dressing in costly garments, aiming to dazzle and outshine at the fashionable watering-places, an affectation of foreign manners, bolstered up by a smattering of foreign travel, picked up from Murray's Guide Books, during a three-months' tour in Europe.

These things are grievous thorns, growing up in the heart, choking the plants of Divine grace. The man who yields to their influence at all soon becomes entirely absorbed. There is so much of rivalry, of jostling, so much to excite and spur on effort, that a course of social extravagance, once entered upon, progresses with an ever accelerating speed, until the majority are landed in bankruptcy and disgrace. Nor is this great evil confined to what are termed the upper classes. The grades of society beneath are ever striving to climb upwards; and they toil up the rounds of the social ladder, deeming no position on it beyond their reach, and ready to make any sacrifice to attain their desire. Hence they ape the manners and habits of the wealthy, seek to pursue a course which will recommend them to their notice, and the whole burden of their daily toil is to secure a standing in fashionable circles. Is it possible, with such processes as these going on in the soul, for the seed to bring forth fruit? What has the religion of Christ to do with such scenes of luxury, prodigality, and heartless sociality? What has the Spirit of God to do with the struggling after rank and name and wealth that so occupy the heart?

There is as much incompatibility between worldliness and spirituality as between fire and water. One must, of necessity, destroy the other. This is no new truth, though the present times enforce it with new emphasis. Long ago the Searcher of Hearts declared, "Ye cannot serve God and Mammon;" "whosoever will be the friend of the world is the enemy of God;" "he that is not with me is against me;" "he that taketh not up his cross and cometh after me, cannot be my disciple;" "seek first the kingdom of God and his righteousness, and all these things shall be added unto you."

You must, therefore, take your stand in this matter. If you prefer that your heart should bring forth thorns—fit only for the burning of hell—yield to the influences of the world, and they will spring up with rank luxuriance, and cover your moral nature with the brambles of iniquity. Go on and enjoy the pleasures of sin; say to your soul, "take thine ease, eat, drink, and be merry." Shut down the window of your heart that looks out upon the future, and curtain it around with the painted tapestry of present delights; and then, throttling conscience and hoodwinking reason, cajole yourselves that all is well for time and for eternity. Lull yourself with these opiates of the deceiver, until death shall break the spell, and you wake up, a lost spirit amidst eternal burnings.

If these inevitable issues to such a course are too fearful for you to risk, then, in the name of Christ, and in the power of the Holy Ghost, and through the vouchsafed grace of Almighty God, set about the work of plucking up these thorns, and of cultivating these sproutings of the true seed. Address yourselves to watchfulness, and prayer, and self-examination, and careful culture of your souls, and, distrusting your own strength, rely only on the Divine aid, to enable you to labour with unrelaxing diligence and unsleeping vigilance in the effort to "work out your salvation with fear and trembling, for it is God that worketh in you, both to will and to do of his good pleasure."

Under these three classes, viz., the wayside hearers, the stony-ground hearers, the thorny-ground hearers, may be ranked all who sit under the ministry of the gospel, who are yet out of Christ.

And here observe that the failure in each of these cases to bring forth fruit was not any defect in the seed sown, nor in the sower who scattered it, nor in the sun and rain and dew which visited all alike; the difficulty was not so much without the man as within him. In one case there was no receptive power, in another there was no deepness of soil, and in the third there was pre-occupancy of the ground by the rank and choking thorns. Man's ruin is in every instance self-produced, and the consciousness of this will be one of the most fearful elements of his everlasting woe.

But we once more look up to our Divine teacher, and say, "Tell us, Lord, we beseech thee, who are the good-ground hearers?" and He responds in those cheering words, they are those who, "in an honest and good heart, having heard the word, understand and keep it, and bring forth fruit with patience," "some an hundredfold, some sixty, some thirty."

Though the Scriptures positively declare that "there is none that doeth good, no, not one," yet there are those, speaking after the manner of men, who may be said to have "an honest and good heart;" *i. e.*, they receive the truth without questionings and disputings; they do not twist and cavil at the word; they treat it honestly, and act upon it with simple-minded sincerity, and a desire to profit. Such persons, when they hear the word, give it their attention, and hence, applying their hearts to wisdom, "understand it," recognise it as God's word, and embrace it as suited to their wants; thus forming a contrast to the way-side hearers, who understood not the word of the Kingdom, and consequently did not believe it. But this under-standing of the truth can only result from the teaching of the Spirit; because "the natural man," says St. Paul, "receiveth not the things of the Spirit of God; for they are foolishness unto him; neither can he know them, because they are spiritually discerned." The fact, therefore, of their understanding the word, proves that the Holy Ghost has been at work in their hearts, making them receptive of truth, and enlightening their minds, making them to comprehend the truth.

The spirituality of this work is still further evinced by the additional mark mentioned by our Lord, that such "having heard the word, *keep it;*" do not allow Satan to "catch it away," as the birds picked up the seed dropped upon the wayside, but "keep it" in their memories, pondering it over in careful, prayerful meditation; "keep it" in their hearts, as the man of their council and the guide of their lives; hiding it there, that they may not sin against God.

There is much force in the word here translated "keep it." It means, to occupy, to dwell in, and in classical usage is applied to the "tutelary gods," who had an abiding place in every household; and as, among the heathen, no family or individual was considered safe without the guardianship of one or more of these tutelary gods dwelling in their halls or rooms, so should no Christian feel himself safe from the evil influences of his great adversary, without having the seed of the word occupy and dwell in his soul; not to be an occasional visiter, not a temporary tenant, but permanently abiding there in full, undisturbed possession.

Our Christian character does not depend so much on our hearing as on our keeping the word. It will not benefit us to have it pass *through* the mind: it must *dwell* there; be kept there with a jealous guarding and a scrupulous care, as the greatest treasure confided to our hands.

The necessary result of this indwelling of the "good seed" in the "good ground" is, that it will be productive; but the seed will not fructify equally in all, nor will the soils produce a like amount of harvest. There are circumstances of early education, natural disposition, social position, mental temperament, business relations, idiosyncrasies of character, intellectual advantages, which are ever operating upon the soil of the heart, increasing or lessening its fertility; consequently some bring forth thirtyfold, some sixty, some a hundred. Our own experience testifies to the truth of this. We see one Christian fertile in the graces of the Spirit, abundant in fruit, rejoicing in hope; and another, who manifests but little increase, producing but small results; but in all cases there is some increase. Increase is the absolute condition and requirement of the Christian life. This alone evidences that we have received the seed, that we have kept the seed, and that the soil is good; and while the ratio of increase is variable, the increase itself is the necessary exponent of Christian vitality.

This fruit manifests itself in two ways: first, in a growth in grace, whereby our hearts become more and more conformed to the image of God's dear Son, through the indwelling of the Holy Ghost; and secondly, by increasing efforts for the extension of the Redeemer's kingdom. But this inner and outer work of the soul are so interlaced that they cannot be separated. Where there is a growth of holiness in the heart, there is always found deeper love for Christ, and where that exists, there of necessity springs up a love for the souls for whom Christ died, and a desire to labour for and with Christ in so bringing men to the truth, as that our blessed Saviour "shall see of the travail of his soul, and be satisfied."

But this fruit, says our Lord, is brought forth "with patience." Patience is that grace which enables one to bear afflictions, calamities, and oppositions with constancy and calmness of mind, and with humble submission to Almighty God. It is an essential element of Christian character, and as such is much insisted on by the Apostles John, and James, and Peter, and Paul, as well as by Christ himself. Impatience is the mark of an unpoised mind and uncurbed will. It is a dangerous trait even in a worldly character, because it leads to rash and hasty measures, and produces a chafed and irritated spirit. Much more then must it be adverse to godliness of heart, and to all productive efforts in the cause of Christ. With what truth might the Apostle say to us as to the Hebrews, "Ye have need of patience!" and with what earnestness would he repeat to us, what he urged upon them, "run with patience the race set before you!" for, unless we persevere with unshaken steadfastness, enduring patiently the reproach and opposition of the world, stemming with even mind and submissive will the difficulties that lie before us, we cannot bring forth fruit, we cannot glorify God, we cannot secure "the prize of our high calling in Christ Jesus."

In gathering up into a few closing reflections the

teachings of this parable, we remark, first, that we are personally responsible for every particle of the seed of the word sown in our hearts; secondly, that no "wayside" hearer can be saved; thirdly, that no "stony-ground" hearer can be saved; fourthly, that no "thorny-ground" hearer can be saved; and lastly, that only the fruit-producing hearer can enter into the kingdom of heaven.

In which class are **you**?

The Tares.

THE TARES.

'THE kingdom of heaven is likened unto a man which sowed good seed in his field; but while men slept, his enemy came and sowed tares among the wheat, and went his way. But when the blade was sprung up, and brought forth fruit, then appeared the tares also. So the servants of the householder came and said unto him, Sir, didst not thou sow good seed in thy field? from whence then hath it tares? He said unto them, An enemy hath done this. The servants said unto him, Wilt thou then that we go and gather them up? But he said, Nay; lest while ye gather up the tares, ye root up also the wheat with them. Let both grow together until the harvest: and in the time of harvest I will say to the reapers, Gather ye together first the tares, and bind them in bundles to burn them: but gather the wheat into my barn." MATT. XIII. 24–30.

"Jesus sent the multitude away, and went into the house; and his disciples came unto him, saying, Declare unto us the parable of the tares of the field. He answered and said unto them, He that soweth the good seed is the Son of man; the field is the world; the good seed are the children of the kingdom; but the tares are the children of the wicked one; the enemy that sowed them is the devil; the harvest is the end of the world; and the reapers are the angels. As therefore the tares are gathered and burned in the fire: so shall it be in the end of this world. The Son of man shall send forth his angels, and they shall gather out of his kingdom all things that offend, and them which do iniquity; and shall cast them into a furnace of fire: there shall be wailing and gnashing of teeth. Then shall the righteous shine forth as the sun in the kingdom of their Father. Who hath ears to hear, let him hear." MATT. XIII. 36–43.

THIS parable, like that of the Sower, is drawn from the walks of agriculture, and needs no explanations to unfold the terms used or the personages introduced. The field, the wheat, the tares, the servants, the householder, the enemy sowing tares at midnight, are each intelligible to the common mind, involving no points of thought, or usages of life, diverse from those with which we are daily conversant.

There is one peculiarity about this parable, however, which it has in common with that of "The Sower," viz., its subsequent interpretation by our Lord himself, in answer to the special request of His disciples. Since He, therefore, who uttered it, has condescended to unfold it, it is more glorious to follow His footsteps than to mark out any new path of our own. When He instructs, we have nothing to do but listen, practise, and obey.

"The field," says our Saviour, "is the world;" a thought so great that we are really startled at its magnitude; and looking at it in its merely human aspect, as the utterance of a Jew, whose nation was separated from all other nations by theocratic institutions, which constituted them "a peculiar people," and who, from this national standpoint, regarded the Gentiles as "aliens from the commonwealth of Israel, and strangers to the covenant of promise," there is something in it morally sublime; indicating a mind of vast breadth, a soul devoid of prejudice, a heart that expanded its affections to the circumference of earth, and a faith that looked upon the far off, yet certain result, with the calmness of anticipated triumph.

But Christ was not a narrow-minded Jew, bound down by national prejudices. He was God as well as man; and His utterance here was the Divine annunciation of a truth brought from heaven, and by Him revealed to man. So that it is a prophecy as well as an assertion; it is the glorious prediction of His own assured success, as well as the statement of an ultimate fact; and uttered as it was in the day of His humiliation, with but a handful of followers, amidst the scorn and neglect of His own countrymen, it showed the God bringing the future before the eye of the present, with a clearness of vision and distinctness of statement which could only result from an omniscience that saw "the end from the beginning."

The narrow province of Judea sufficed for the Jewish Church, which was only designed to be the temporary depository of God's law and promise, the forerunner of that dispensation which the Messiah, "the hope of Israel," should, "in the fulness of time," establish "for all nations." The laws and ritual of the Jewish Church absolutely precluded it from ever becoming universal; it was a church which, as a church, could only flourish in certain latitudes and longitudes, and contained within itself the elements of its own dissolution. Its great office was, to be the depository and keeper of revealed truth; to prefigure Christ by type and ritual; to announce His advent by an ever augmenting voice of prophecy; to receive Him into its bosom when He appeared; and then to give place to a dispensation, which, rejecting the Jewish ritual and the Jewish boundaries, should be equally adapted to every land and clime, and become the sole religion of the world. In this world-wide field was to be sown "good seed" by "the Son of man." This "Son of man" is none other than

Jesus Christ; that being one of His peculiar titles, and by which He most frequently designated himself; thus rightly appropriating the title under which Daniel prophesied of the Messiah's kingdom and glory.

"The good seed are the children of the kingdom:" *i. e.* those individuals in whom the good seed of God's word had so taken root and fructified as to identify themselves with it, in such manner that they might well be called "the good seed;" not indeed in the abstract, as that which was sown, for as children of the kingdom they were not sown, but as being the fruit of that which had been sown by the Son of man, and which, in the parable of the Sower, is called "the word of God;" this, falling into "good ground," takes root and springs up, and develops itself into "children of the kingdom," who are thus, by a figure of speech, called the "good seed." Wherever "the word of God" finds lodgment in the heart and receives, through the agency of the Holy Ghost, fructifying power, there will it ever bring forth a child of the kingdom. This is its only and its legitimate fruit; hence, St. Peter speaks of Christians as "being born again, not of corruptible seed, but of incorruptible, by the word of God, which liveth and abideth for ever;" "and this," he adds, "is the word which by the Gospel is preached unto you." Thus the preached Gospel is that good seed, which, in the field of the world, will ever produce the children of the kingdom. It is said to be sown by the Son of man, because the word, which is the seed, "proceedeth out of His mouth," and because it is by His authority and commission that the blessed Gospel is preached, or scattered broadcast, throughout the world; for His irrevocable promise to His ministering servants, the seed-sowing husbandmen of His Church, is, "Lo, I am with you always, even to the end of the world;" so that, through all time, to all classes of people, throughout all the habitations of men, the ministers of the Gospel have the promised presence of "the Son of Man," giving efficiency to their sowing, fructification to the seed, and causing it in every part of this world-field to bring forth "the children of the kingdom."

This is one, and the bright side of this parabolic picture. We turn with reluctance to the other, wherein we behold another kind of seed, another sower, and widely different results.

"The Son of man," who sowed the good seed, had "an Enemy," here called "the Devil," who, after the wheat had been cast into the ground, and while the sowers slept, came stealthily into the field, and "sowed tares among the wheat, and went his way." From the Bible we learn that the devil is a person, not an idea. That he was once an angel of light—now a fallen spirit; that he is the deceiver of the world, the enemy of God, the earthly antagonist of Jesus Christ; that he is "the spirit that ruleth in the hearts of the children of disobedience;" that he is full of guile, subtlety, and falsehood; that he is "a murderer from the beginning," and "the father of lies;" "the accuser of the brethren," and "as a roaring lion walketh about seeking whom he may devour." His great aim is to thwart the moral purposes of God in man's creation; which he first attempted, and with apparent success, in the garden of Eden, in that fearful assault upon the faith and obedience of Adam and Eve. But when, at the very moment of his seeming triumph, there was uttered the hope-inspiring promise, that "the seed of the woman should bruise the serpent's head," then were all his mighty energies gathered into one effort to oppose that "seed of the woman," even Jesus Christ, and overthrow Him and the kingdom which He came from heaven to establish. This was the one aim of all his multifarious movements before and at the coming of Christ; this caused him to make that daring assault on Jesus himself, when the blessed Saviour was weak through protracted fasting, and unsustained by human aid, in the wilderness. This led him to enter into Judas to betray his master, into the high priests and scribes to condemn Him, into the people to cry out "crucify him," into Pilate to deliver Him to his soldiers to be hung upon the accursed tree. And ever since has he waged a relentless conflict with the Great Head of the Church and His ministers, and the children of the kingdom—being unremitting in toil, unrelaxing in vigilance, unsparing in deception, unblushing in effrontery, unscrupulous in his wiles to entrap the souls of men, and lead them as captives to his own abodes of eternal sorrow. This is that arch-enemy of God and man who sowed "tares" in the field of the world; and it marks the great wiliness of this enemy, that he sowed that kind of seed which, in its upspringing, would require some time to develop its true characters, its first appearings being so like the good grain, that only when it had taken too deep root to be plucked up without injuring the wheat also, could its real character be detected. The "tares" spoken of were not another kind of seed from the wheat, but of the same kind, only a bastard or degenerate wheat. Thus we find that all the grievous heresies and defections that have been produced in the Church are not the results of bald and undiluted falsehoods, but of degenerate or bastard truths, retaining enough of the truth to catch the conscience, yet using the little truth only as a means of making more deadly the error which it was designed to advance.

The danger of any soul-destroying error is in proportion to the amount of truth which it enfolds; the nearer the truth, while it yet avoids it, the more deceptive does it become. It is when Satan "transforms himself into an angel of light" that he most effectually seduces the children of the kingdom; and never did he come so near uttering the truth in its letter, and yet fail to speak it in its spirit, as when he thrice tempted the blessed Saviour, backing one of his assaults with a quotation from the Word of God.

The ingenuity of the deceptions, and the protean shapes of evil which the devil assumes, are such as no unaided mind can either comprehend or unravel. It requires the aid of God's Holy Spirit to enable us, like Milton's Ithuriel, so to touch him with the spear of truth, under whatever form he may be disguised, as to cause him " to return of force to his own likeness, discovered and surprised.'

As in the case of the Son of man, the seed which was sown was not "the children of the kingdom," but that which produced them; so here, the tares scattered by the devil were not "the children of the wicked one," but that which brought them forth; those evil principles and thoughts, which in their germination result in men of such sinfulness and guilt, as well to deserve the denunciation, "Children of the wicked one." In this class are included all who are not the "children of the kingdom;" for there are but these two moral families in God's household,—termed sometimes, "children of light," and "children of darkness;" those who "walk by faith," and those who "walk by sight;" "men of the world, who have their portion in this life," and men who "confess themselves to be strangers and pilgrims upon earth, seeking a better country, that is, a heavenly;" men "alive unto God," and men "dead in trespasses and sins;" the "friends," and the "enemies" of Christ. We may thus search through the Word of God, and though we find these two classes described under diverse names, yet we never discover any third or middle family; a matter which our blessed Lord has set at rest in the most positive terms by saying, "He that is not with me, is against me, and he that gathereth not with me, scattereth abroad." It is indeed a fearful thing to be one of the children of the wicked one; to have such a moral paternity as only the devil can furnish; to be one of his fiendish household, copying his example, animated by his precepts, following his rules, and day by day preparing for the weeping, and the wailing, and the gnashing of teeth, which shall be the portion of the children of the wicked, for ever and ever.

In consequence of this double sowing, we find springing

up in this world-field, wheat and tares; and to the question of the servants of the householder, "Wilt thou then that we go and gather them up?" the reply is, "Nay, lest while ye gather up the tares, ye root up also the wheat with them. Let both grow together until the harvest." In this answer, as we understand it, lies the real force and import of the parable; which seems to have been uttered to show that in the visible Church of Christ on earth, there will ever be the bad mingled with the good, and that those who look for an unalloyed communion here will not find it until after the harvesting, "at the end of the world."

We draw then, from this statement, these four propositions:—1st. That in the visible Church there is a present intermixture of the children of the kingdom, and the children of the wicked one. We use the the word Church here precisely as it is used in the XIXth of our Articles of Religion, where it says, "The visible Church of Christ is a congregation of faithful men, in the which the pure word of God is preached, and the sacraments be duly ministered," &c. Here, the term *visible* distinguishes it from the invisible Church, composed of those who "are very members incorporate in the mystical body of Christ, which is the blessed company of all faithful people," and who are known only to God himself. The word *men* confines it to this earth, in contradistinction to that community of which "the whole family in heaven and earth is named," embracing angels and the spirits of the just made perfect, as well as beings still on earth. The word *faithful* restricts the term Church to those who believe in the Lord Jesus, and consequently excludes all associations of imposture—infidelity or heathenism; and the expression "in which the pure word of God is preached, and the sacraments be duly ministered," &c., mark it as the Church militant, not the Church triumphant; the Church warring in the wilderness this side Jordan, not the Church at rest beyond its swellings in the Canaan above. But though the visible, militant Church, be in general terms "a congregation of faithful men," yet it manifestly embraces many who have no real faith towards God, and no true love to Jesus Christ, and no new birth of the Holy Ghost. And such has been the fact through the entire period of the Church's history. We need but casually read the records of the Old and New Testaments to see how many there were who by hereditary descent, or outward profession, became members of the visible Church, under the Patriarchal, the Levitical, and the Christian dispensations, who yet had neither part nor lot in the blessings of the covenant of grace, because their heart was not right in the sight of God.

In the band of our Lord's Apostles was a Judas; in the little Church of Samaria, a Simon Magus; in the Church of Pergamos, those "who held the doctrines of Balaam;" in the Church of Thyatira, a Jezebel-like woman; in the Church of Sardis, those whose works "had not been found perfect before God;" and in the Churches of Rome, Corinth, Colosse, Ephesus, Philippi, Thessalonica, were those "who had a name indeed to live, but who yet were dead in trespasses and sins." And what was true then is true now. In every Gospel field we find tares growing up with the wheat; in every ecclesiastical net are enclosed fishes good and bad; in every fold of Christ are there sheep sound and tainted; and into every ark of the Church, as into the ark of Noah, do there enter beasts clean and unclean. This is indeed a lamentable fact, and one that should make us walk humbly in the presence not only of God, but of a carping, sneering world; and yet it is a fact which, in the end, both illustrates and promotes the glory of the grace of God: for by this state of things, not only are the goodness, mercy, long-suffering, forbearance, and other attributes of God more gloriously displayed, than if he immediately visited sin with prompt punishment; but the character of His children, and their meetness for heaven, are greatly benefited by the very processes of trial and temptation through which, in consequence of this intermixture of good and evil, they are called to pass. Thomas Fuller, in the fifth book of his "Holy State," gives these six reasons why God permits the wheat and the tares to grow up together in the field of the Church until the harvest:—"1st. Hypocrites can nevei be severed but by Him that can search the heart. 2dly. If men should make the separation, weak Christians would be counted no Christians, and those who have a grain of grace, under a load of imperfection, would be counted reprobates. 3dly. God's vessels of honour for all eternity not as yet appearing, but wallowing in sin, would be made castaways. 4th. God, by the mixture of the wicked with the godly, will try the patience and watchfulness of his servants. 5thly. Because thereby He will bestow many favours on the wicked to clear His justice, and render them the more inexcusable. Lastly: Because the mixture of the wicked grieving the godly, will make them the more heartily pray for the day of judgment."

The second proposition is, that the bad members of the Church in many respects resemble the good, but have a different origin and a different termination.

The tares mentioned in the parable are probably the darnell or degenerate kind of wheat which, in its early blade, closely resembles true wheat; and the Rabbins say, that the tares of Palestine are like the wheat, except that the ears are not so large, nor the grains so many, nor the quality so good. So, in the Church of God, the bad or unsound members simulate the good in very many particulars. Their outward profession, appearance, and participation of ordinances are the same. They are perhaps liberal in the support of church institutions, show great regard to the sanctuary and sacraments, go through the same outward round of religious duties, and thus grow up together until the harvest. But they differ from the children of the kingdom in their origin; they have not been born again by that spiritual regeneration which is effected by the Holy Ghost. The seeds which have sprung up with such semblance of goodness are tares sown by the wicked one, producing counterfeit graces and spurious doctrines, with which multitudes rest satisfied, because at least it gives them an outward position in the Church of God. Sometimes these seeds are received unwarily at first, and when they spring up, they look so much like the true wheat, that the recipients never trouble themselves to examine whether the resemblance continue, or whether, after all, it is not darnell that they are cultivating, instead of wheat. Many there are, who rest their salvation on the fact, that once they had convictions, and, as they supposed, conversion; and, wresting to their own destruction the doctrine that man cannot fall from grace, they settle down their hopes upon a past experience, and say, once in grace always in grace, and thus grow up as rank and noxious tares, fit only for the burning.

But God has not left us to uncertainty in this matter. Though we may be deceived about others, we have at least the means of detecting the falsity within ourselves. He has given us the proper tests and criteria by which we may discriminate between the good and the bad seed, so as to know whether or not we are the children of the kingdom, or the children of the wicked one.

If we are really anxious to know the truth and the whole truth, as to our souls' sanctification and justification, we can know it by marks and evidences of that personal spiritual kind, beyond the art of the devil to counterfeit or invalidate; for the Bible distinctly declares, "Whosoever doeth the will of God, shall know of the doctrine whether it be of God."

The third proposition is, that no thorough separation can take place in this life. The command is, "Let both grow together until the harvest," and the reason assigned is, "lest while ye gather up the tares, ye root up also **the** wheat with them." While the eye of God beholds with unerring certainty who are the tares and who are the wheat, man does not; and were it left to him to root up the tares, he might leave many stalks of tares, supposing them to be genuine wheat, and pluck up many stalks of wheat, under the mistaken notion that they were tares. The terrible persecutions which have taken place between different sections of the Church, for the so-called purgation of the body ecclesiastic, afford sad examples of the way in which human servants, had they the power, would root up what they would call the "tares" in the field of the Church. We have great reason to bless God that He has removed this power from the hands of short-sighted and narrow-minded men. The Church has never used the extirpating sword but to the disgrace of its name, and to the dishonour of its Divine head. What Christ has commissioned the Church to do is, to plant and sow and cultivate with nicest skill the incast seed of the Word, but not to root up tares. This He has reserved for His commissioned angels, who, when sent forth, "shall gather out of His kingdom all things that offend, and them which do iniquity, and shall cast them into a furnace of fire; there shall be wailing and gnashing of teeth."

So far is this passage, therefore, from sanctioning persecution, it strongly, though inferentially, condemns it; it reserves the final decision to omniscient power, the final gathering to angelic reapers, ministering spirits, swayed by no human passions, and acting under the eye and finger of their Eternal King.

The fourth and last proposition is, that both the parable

and the interpretation given by our Lord, emphatically show, that a separation shall take place at some future day Whatever, then, may be the condition of the Church of God now, there is a day coming, when "judgment shall begin at the house of God." Then shall this permixtion of good and evil end; then shall the tares be gathered for the burning and the wheat for the garner; then shall there be a separation, total, complete, and for ever, of the true and false professors, who now grow up together in the field of the Church. As it is the design of another parable, viz., "The Draw-Net," to represent this special truth, we shall not dwell upon it here; but, simply announcing the fact that such a separation will take place by Divine command, under Divine direction, and for purposes of Divine judgment, we pass to the final result of such a severing of the good from the bad—first, as to the tares; and then, secondly, as to the wheat.

The "tares" are first reaped, then bound "in bundles to burn," then cast "into a furnace of fire," producing "wailing and gnashing of teeth"—figurative words, designed to show the intensity of the suffering of the wicked in the world to come; for it is only by terms borrowed from physical pain, or from implements and instruments of bodily torture, that we can set forth the unspeakable anguish of soul which they shall experience who "lie down in everlasting sorrow," "where their worm dieth not, and their fire is not quenched." The fierce struggle of contending passions; the unchecked power of evil, rising and swelling with tumultuous rage; the writhings of a spirit bereft of every hope, and haunted by despair; the goadings of a conscience quickened into intense activity by the memory of the past; the forebodings of an ever-increasing torment, waxing keener throughout eternity; the remembrance of what is lost—heaven, the soul, God's pardon, Christ's favour, everlasting bliss; and the consciousness of what has been self-induced—weeping and wailing and gnashing of teeth for ever. Oh! this, this is the fire that ever burns with gnawing, but never-consuming flame. This is the furnace, "seven times heated" by the fuel of an ungodly life, in which retributive justice shall cast the unrepenting soul, and leave it there, to memory, to conscience, to Satan, to despair. Well may the prophet say, "Woe unto the wicked, it shall be ill with him, for the reward of his hands shall be given him." With equal truth does God declare, "Say unto the righteous, it shall be well with him, for they shall eat the fruit of their doings." Their condition, after the day of judgment, shall be one of splendour and rejoicing. Freed from the body of this death, removed from a world of sin, exempt from the temptations of the adversary, full of love and peace and joy, they shine forth in their true characters, as "children of light and of the day." While on earth they were "lights in the world," but the light was obscured by their imperfections and sins, it was more frequently hidden under a bushel than set on a candlestick; but now, the clouds of error, of unbelief, of sin, have been rolled away, and, in the clear sky of heaven, they manifest their true character, and shine forth "as the sun" in the kingdom of God; and there they shall shine, says the prophet Daniel, "for ever and ever."

The Mustard Seed.

THE MUSTARD SEED.

"THE kingdom of heaven is like to a grain of mustard seed, which a man took and sowed in his field: Which indeed is the least of all seeds; but when it is grown, it is the greatest among herbs, and becometh a tree, so that the birds of the air come and lodge in the branches thereof." MATT. XIII. 31, 32.

"Whereunto shall we liken the kingdom of God? or with what comparison shall we compare it? It is like a grain of mustard seed, which, when it is sown in the earth, is less than all the seeds that be in the earth; but when it is sown, it groweth up, and becometh greater than all herbs, and shooteth out great branches; so that the fowls of the air may lodge under the shadow of it."

MARK IV. 30–32.

"Unto what is the kingdom of God like? And whereunto shall I resemble it? It is like a grain of mustard seed, which a man took, and cast into his garden; and it grew, and waxed a great tree; and the fowls of the air lodged in the branches of it." LUKE XIII. 18, 19.

FEW words, but pregnant truths! The aim of our Saviour was to find some comparison or similitude that would best illustrate the outward growth and development of the Kingdom of God. In asking the question of those around him, "Unto what is the Kingdom of God like? and whereunto shall I resemble it?" He did not design that they should answer it, for they could not, being ignorant of the nature of the Kingdom of Heaven; but by starting the question he excited their minds to action, caused them to feel more forcibly their inability to reply, and, by stimulating their curiosity, produced a deeper desire to understand the nature of that kingdom of which Jesus spoke. When, therefore, after bending to Him their attentive ears, they heard Him compare it to a grain of mustard seed, they must for the moment have been shocked at the insignificance of the resembling object, so different from their preconceived ideas of the glory and magnificence which they supposed would usher in the Messiah's reign.

Unbiassed as we are by those temporal and national views of the person and reign of Christ, which blinded the minds of the Jews; and looking at this Kingdom of God, not from a prophetic stand-point, as something yet to take its rise, but from an historic one, wherein we see it already begun, and in process; we can see the felicity of the comparison, and mark its close resemblance.

The grain of mustard seed is indeed "the least of all the seeds that are sown in the earth," which produce ligneous stems and branches; and it was in this sense, doubtless, that our Lord spoke of it,—alluding rather to the relative size of the seed, and the developed plant, than to the seed in the abstract, because the seeds of poppy and rue are smaller than those of mustard, though the plants themselves never rise beyond the character of humble herbs, whereas the mustard seed "becometh a great tree," and "shooteth out great branches."

Thus small and insignificant was the first germ of the Kingdom of God in its earthly manifestations. We say earthly manifestations, because, as it existed in the mind of the Triune God, it was a Divine idea, compassing at once all its results, and could not, therefore, be either small or insignificant. But on earth, how did Christ, who is Himself the grain of mustard seed, out of which grew the great tree of Christianity, first appear? As an infant! wrapped in swaddling-bands and lying in a manger! Could reason see anything in Mary's child, born in a stable, to foreshadow such august results? Certainly not. And when, after thirty years of obscurity, working, doubtless, the mean while, at the carpenter's bench with his reputed father, "Jesus began to teach and to preach," who saw in the plain Nazarene anything to indicate a greatness that should fill the earth with its glory? Who would recognise in Him the revolutionizer of the world? Or, beholding Him at the beginning of His ministry, selecting as His disciples,—not the titled, the wealthy, the influential —but fishermen and tax-gatherers, ignorant and rude Galileans, who would not have said, looking at the subject on mere worldly grounds, that here, surely was a great mistake, to intrust to such uncouth and uneducated men so great a treasure as the Gospel professed to be; that, if Jesus' design was to make converts and popularize His doctrines, He should have selected well-skilled Scribes, or learned Pharisees, or influential Sadducees, men who, from their social or intellectual position, would have been treated with respect, and listened to with reverence; but to call a man from his nets and fishing tackle, and tell him to go preach the Gospel; to call another from his publican's seat and tax-table, and commission him to declare the whole counsel of God concerning man's highest and eternal interests, seemed to finite minds like "casting pearls before swine," or attempting to achieve great ends by totally inadequate means. And when at last, after three years, going up and down throughout the cities of Palestine, the founder of this new religion was arrested, condemned, and crucified like a slave, who would have supposed that his tenets could survive the dispersion of His disciples, and His own ignominious death? Thus the life and death of Christ, in its human aspects, was emphatically, as to its apparent insignificance, a grain of mustard seed.

Nor does the case appear to be much better after Jesus had ascended on high. The disciples whom He left behind Him had all at one time deserted Him, and were now so timid and so few that they all assembled in an upper room for fear of the Jews. The idea, humanly speaking, was absurd, that less than a dozen illiterate Galileans could overthrow the old religions of the world, and set up a new one, which should extend from the rising to the setting sun. The mind could see in it no relation between the insignificant cause and the desired effect. They were to preach the Gospel to every creature—yet could speak no language but their provincial tongue; they were to disciple all nations to Christ—yet every one of them had lately forsaken Him and fled; they were to uproot the idolatries of earth—yet were themselves feeble and superstitious; they were to overturn the skilfully wrought schemes of human philosophy—yet were themselves untaught in the schools; they were to conquer the world to the sceptre of Jesus—yet now shut themselves up in an upper room "for fear of the Jews." Great names, literary honours, the patronage of kings, the favour of the people, they did not possess. To mortal view it was the veriest absurdity; to commission poor, illiterate, unpolished men to convert the world, then just passing from the Augustan age of its glory, to the faith of the son of a carpenter in Nazareth, whom the Jews had cast out of their synagogues, and the Romans crucified as a malefactor!

The Stoics, with Zeno at their head, had tried to reform the world, and failed; Socrates, and Plato, and the Academicians had attempted it, with no better success; Aristotle and the Peripatetic school had aimed at it, and met the same signal defeat: how preposterous, then, to send out eleven fishermen, artisans, and publicans, without books, without money, without arms, without popular favour, and expect them to succeed where the proudest wisdom and the loftiest philosophy had signally failed!

Such was the small, and, in its earthly appearings, insignificant aspect of the beginnings of the Christian religion. How like a grain of mustard seed in its littleness and apparent worthlessness! But from this "least of all seeds," we turn to behold its results in the great tree, shooting out great branches, gathering the fowls of the air under its shadow. In warm climates the mustard seed grows to an almost incredible size. The Jerusalem Talmud says, at Shichin there was a mustard stalk which had three branches, and one of them was cut down, and they covered a potter's booth with it. One of the Rabbins says:

"I have one stalk of mustard seed in my field, and I go up to it as one goes up to the top of a fig-tree." Ovalle, in his travels in Chili, thus confirms the Scripture account: "The mustard plant," he says, "thrives so mightily in Chili, that it is as big as a man's arm, and so high and thick that it looks like a tree. I have travelled many leagues through groves which were taller than man and horse, and the birds build their nests in them, as the Gospel mentions." This happily illustrates the wondrous greatness into which the religion of Christ grew from its small and obscure beginnings.

The Apostles, in obedience to the Divine command, tarried at Jerusalem until they were endued with power from on high. That power came in the descent of the Holy Ghost on the day of Pentecost. Then was it that they began to preach "Jesus Christ and Him crucified, unto the Jews a stumbling-block, and unto the Greeks foolishness." And what was the result? Fifty days from the ascension of Jesus, three thousand were converted under the preaching of Peter. In less than three years, churches were gathered "throughout all Judea, Galilee, and Samaria." In seven years the Gospel was first published to the Gentiles; and in thirty years Christianity had spread through the numerous districts of Asia Minor, Greece, southward to Egypt, and westward to Rome.

In a hundred years from the time of Christ, Justin Martyr, writing to the Emperor Adrian, declares: "There is not a nation, either Greek or Barbarian, or of any other name, even of those who wander in tribes and live in tents, among whom prayers are not offered to God the Father, in the name of the crucified Jesus." "We are but of yesterday," says Tertullian, writing a little later, "and have filled all places belonging to you. Your cities, islands, castles, towns, councils; your very camps, wards, companies; the palace, senate, forum; we have left you only your temples. Should the numerous hosts of Christians retire from the empire, the loss of so many men, of all ranks and degrees, would make you stand aghast at your desolation." In the fourth century, Chrysostom declares, "The Apostles of Christ were twelve, and they gained the whole earth. If you go to India, to Scythia, to the uttermost parts of the world, you will everywhere find the doctrine of Christ enlightening the souls of men." Such was the "great tree," "shooting out great branches," which sprung from the "grain of mustard seed!" History has nothing that can compare with it; it stands an everlasting miracle of the Most High God. Eighteen hundred years have passed since the Apostles went forth from their upper room; and how stands the religion of Jesus now? Survey a map of the world, and mark on it the countries most celebrated for law, order, civil and political rights, and there you will find the religion of Jesus. Point out on it the lands most noted for virtue and morality, for social blessings and individual happiness, and there you will find the religion of Jesus. Designate the places where learning is most encouraged, where the mind has wrought out its proudest triumphs, where intellect has scattered its richest treasures, and there you will find the religion of Jesus.

And why is this? Why is civil and religious liberty found only where the Bible is free? Why does learning flourish most under Gospel rule? Why is society the most elevated and refined where the tenets of God's word prevail? Why is all that is great, and good, and lofty, and inspiring in law, government, literature, science, art, and morality, only found among the nations of Christendom, while all that is debasing in intellect, tyrannical in power, degraded in morals; whatever strips man of his glory, society of its safeguards, government of its virtue, is found where the religion of Jesus does not prevail? Can we solve the problem on the principles of human philosophy? Gibbon tried it in his five celebrated reasons, but most signally failed. Can we explain it by the maxims of political science? Machiavel and Montesquieu, and Guizot and Bacon, each assert that its wondrous development is an anomaly in the government of the world. Can we match it by any parallel, in any country, of any religion, by any impostor? The voice of universal history answers, No! It stands alone, the wonder of the universe; the triumphal monument of Jesus, on the plains of a fallen humanity.

But its present triumphs are only a moiety of its final conquests. Prophecy, reaching far into the future, has declared that "the isles shall wait for His law;" that "the abundance of the sea shall be converted unto Him;" that "the Gentiles shall come to His light, and kings to the brightness of His rising;" that "all nations shall be blessed in Him;" and that "the whole earth shall be filled with His glory."

Thus that grain of truth, small as a mustard seed, sown at Jerusalem by the Son of man, has grown up into a tree of life, "sending out its boughs unto the sea, and its branches unto the river."

Thus has it already gathered flocking nations under its shadow; and it shall yet increase, until "the kingdoms of this world shall become the kingdoms of our Lord and of His Christ," and the Herod-hunted child of Bethlehem, the despised carpenter's son of Nazareth, the hated teacher of Galilee, the crucified malefactor of Pilate, shall reign "King of nations, as He now does King of Saints."

The Leaven.

THE LEAVEN.

"The kingdom of heaven is like unto leaven, which a woman took and hid in three measures of meal, till the whole was leavened." MATT. XIII. 33.

"Whereunto shall I liken the kingdom of God? It is like leaven, which a woman took and hid in three measures of meal, till the whole was leavened."
LUKE XIII. 20-21.

UNDER this figure, borrowed from household economy, our Lord represents the assimilating power of His truth when brought in contact with the human heart. In the parable of the Mustard Seed, He illustrated the outward, visible growth of Christianity in the sight of the world; here, however, He brings out its increase and power in a new aspect—its assimilative rather than its accretive property; its internal, penetrative, and diffusive energy, rather than its external outspreading and magnitude.

Leaven is a small piece of acid dough, which, placed in a larger mass of meal or paste, produces fermentation, and thus, by the escape of the generated gas, diffuses a lightness, or, in technical phrase, raises the dough with which it was intermixed. The word is generally used in the Bible in a bad sense; and, accordingly, there have not lacked interpreters, who, saying with Cyril, that "leaven, in the inspired writings, is always taken as the type of naughtiness and sin," have contended that the design of its use here was to indicate the damnable heresies and corruptions which should ferment in and adulterate the Church, puffing it up with vain delusions, and eventually making it a mass of apostacy and crime. This, however, is a forcing of language beyond its legitimate construction. The character of the parable, viewed in its contexts, is against such interpretation; and we hence regard the word leaven as used here in an exceptional sense to its ordinary employment—our attention being directed, not to its fermenting and puffing up properties, but to its penetrative and diffusive powers, by which the whole mass in which it is hidden soon partakes of its own nature. Using the figure, therefore, in a good sense, it illustrates, in a forcible manner, the work of grace—first in the individual heart, then in the great mass of humanity.

It is the property of grace to change the whole soul into its own likeness. The incipient operation of the Holy Ghost may be as small and apparently as insignificant as a little piece of leaven; but once hidden in the heart it will work little by little, until the man becomes a new creature in Christ Jesus. The principle of holiness, of love, of faith, of godly sorrow, or any other which is wrought by the Holy Ghost, cannot remain inactive in the heart; and the moment that any of them are introduced there, there begins a commotion, an inward struggle for ascendancy between the new principle of grace and the old principles of sin, which is continued even until death. As sin and holiness cannot commingle, they necessarily antagonize one must displace the other — they cannot co-exist in the same heart with the same power. The heart, however, is by nature depraved; it is preoccupied with evil; it is, in the words of Scripture, "full of iniquity," and sin has so blinded its perceptive powers, and hardened its sensibilities, and perverted its judgment, that it now "calls evil good and good evil," loves its present condition, "and rejoiceth in iniquity." The character of God is not loved, the Son of God is not loved, the law of God is not loved, the word of God is not loved; nothing pertaining to God is an object of regard; He is not in their thoughts; they "desire not a knowledge of His ways." But as soon as the Holy Ghost infuses into that heart, vile as it is, and dead as it is in trespasses and sin, the first element of holy love, there begins a change there, which, working silently, gradually, yet effectively, will soon leaven the soul with the power of Divine grace. One by one the old affections and passions of the soul become eradicated or changed; the things in which the man once took supreme delight, now afford no joy; the emotions which he once cherished are now uncultivated; the plans which once absorbed his energies are now neglected; the passions which once were rampant in his breast are now tamed; the desires which once engrossed his thoughts are now viewed with disgust; while the things which he formerly hated and shunned—communion with God, love to Christ, joy in the Holy Ghost, delight in the Sacred Scriptures, the cultivation of holiness of life, the walking by faith and growing in grace, are now sought for and cultivated with assiduity and delight. Grace is completely transforming in its nature and power. It causes every one whom it visits to wear its own likeness, and grow up into its own image; and when it once begins its work, though its progress may be slow, it will nevertheless go on unto perfection, resting not until Christ is formed in the soul the hope of glory.

It is perhaps important to a right understanding of this truth, that we should distinguish here between regeneration and sanctification — both, indeed, the work of the same Holy Ghost, and therefore too often confounded, though in reality quite distinct. Spiritual regeneration, or that new birth of the soul, so emphatically taught by our Lord in His discourse with Nicodemus, is the work of the Spirit of God, by which He causes the rebellion of the heart to cease, and the sinner to yield himself an humble servant of Jesus Christ. This act of faith, whereby the penitent lays hold on the Saviour as "the hope set before him in the Gospel," is the work of a moment. Up to a certain time He was a transgressor and an unbeliever; the Holy Ghost visits his soul, opens to him a view of his sins; points him to the Lamb of God, makes him hear the thunders of Sinai; holds up before him the sacrifice of Calvary; melts him with the displays of love, wooes him with the invitings of grace, warns him with the threatenings of the law; and, under the influence of one or more of these, he is led to break off from his sins, to repent, and to believe on the Lord Jesus; and the turning point is on the hinge of a single moment. There may be long and tedious processes of thought gone through before reaching that point; but when reached, the act of submission, of belief, of embracing Christ, is the act of a moment, and not a lengthened, tedious operation. Nor does it follow from this that all are able to date the hour when they were born again; for they may have been so carefully trained in infancy, and so gradually led to Jesus, that it would be impossible for them to discriminate the time when He first became precious to their souls. But, as they were born in nature, and now are born in the Spirit; as they were once enemies, and are now friends, of Christ; as they were once exposed to Divine wrath, and are now freed from condemnation; and as, when they were not in one of these states, they must have been in the other, because there is no middle path: it follows, even in the case of those who are unable to mark the period of their conversion, that their change, or regeneration, was effected by the Holy Ghost in an instant of time. All the examples of conversion in the Bible, all the terms and phrases which designate this change, and the experience of each believer, confirm this statement. Regeneration, then, is that work of the Holy Ghost, whereby there is begotten in the soul an entirely new principle of spiritual life, so that henceforth the man lives, "not unto himself, but unto Him that loved him and gave himself for him;" and so radical and thorough is this change, that the recipient of it is with truth said to be "a new creature in Christ Jesus," in whom "old things have passed away," and with whom "all things have become new."

Regeneration having been thus effected by the distinct act of the Holy Ghost, sanctification immediately begins; which, taking this newly planted principle, cherishes and develops it in its various ramifications and to various degrees of strength. This, also, is the work of the Holy Ghost, and is gradual and progressive.

In religion, as in nature, the new-born soul is a babe—a babe in Christ; it has at first to be fed with "the sincere milk of the Word," that it may grow thereby. Hence, all the directions of the Bible, in reference to the Christian's life, look to growth, progress, increase; and it is only by daily accretions of holiness that they are enabled to grow up into the stature of perfect men in Christ Jesus. Like the action of leaven upon the three measures of meal, not changing its character at once by a sudden operation, but gradually and almost imperceptibly; so the doctrines of grace are not absorbed by the heart all at once, but are gradually received, as the spiritual power is able to receive them. Each day extends the power of Divine grace; each day produces more development of Christian character; and as the assimilating process continues, there is seen one feature after another of Christ's likeness, shining out in our lives, proving that we are being renewed "after the image of Him that created us;" and this leavening process works unseen to mortal eye and unheard by mortal ear, until the whole heart is leavened, and Christ is formed in it the hope of glory.

As the operation of the Holy Ghost is thus leaven-like in its workings in the individual heart, so is it also in its effects upon the great mass of mankind. The outward growth of the Church in the gathering in of new members, in the "lengthening of its cords" and the "strengthening of its stakes," and "breaking forth on the right hand and on the left," we can see and understand; but there is a secret and hidden process prior to this open effect. There is the working of grace in the heart before the confession of faith with the lips; there is an assimilating of the soul to Jesus before there is a public putting on of Christ; and this process is ever at work in Christian communities. The minister of Christ preaches the Gospel, and it falls like seed upon the heart; but he cannot follow it into the recesses of the soul; and yet, there, hidden away, it begins its regenerating work, and, ere long, develops its full effect. The Bible is read and its truths take hold of the conscience, and in secret places the leaven of heavenly doctrine begins its assimilating power, until the heart is leavened with grace divine. Wherever the Gospel is preached, there is this leavening process going on. The world busies itself about its wars, its governments, its commerce, its literature, its fashions, its farms, its merchandise, and heeds not the silent work of the Holy Spirit in the inner chambers of a thousand hearts, effecting there those changes, and bringing out those results, which, in their aggregation, are to alter the face of earth, and make it "a dwelling-place of righteousness."

For, as the woman took and *hid* this leaven in the meal, so is the grace of the Holy Spirit *hidden* from the carnal eye; for "the natural man understandeth not the things of the Spirit of God; they are foolishness unto him, neither can he know them, because they are spiritually discerned." The working of this Gospel leaven does not appear on the surface of society; it is covered up from outward observation; but beneath the surface, in the centre of the mass, at the core of humanity, it is fermenting and working, and changing that with which it is brought in contact; and this process it will infallibly continue "until the whole is leavened."

It is a glorious thought, that this whole world shall be leavened with truth; that the secret operation of this grace shall yet penetrate, purify, pervade, and assimilate to itself all nations, kindreds, tribes, and people, and shall make this, our fallen earth, so like the renewing power which converts and sanctifies it, that it shall become a "mountain of holiness," filled with the **glory of the Triune God**.

The Hid Treasure.

THE HID TREASURE.

"The kingdom of heaven is like unto treasure hid in a field; the which when a man hath found, he hideth, and for joy thereof goeth and selleth all that he hath, and buyeth that field." — MATT. XIII. 44.

THERE are no less than seven parables in this thirteenth chapter of St. Matthew. They cluster together like stars in a constellation, forming, in the firmament of truth, a parabolic Pleiades. The first four were spoken in the hearing of the multitude by the sea-shore; but after Jesus had sent the people away, and "went into the house," He first, at the request of His immediate disciples, unfolded the parable of the Tares of the Field, and then proceeded to speak three more parables, of which that under consideration was the first.

In the earlier parables, our Lord had spoken of Christianity in its general aspects and effects. He now brings it down to the personal needs of each individual, showing that it is not merely to be observed and admired at a distance; that it is not a thing about which we may or may not be interested without involving any moral consequences, but is, on the contrary, a matter of intense personal importance—that which each one must possess or lose his soul. "The kingdom of heaven," says our Lord, "is like unto treasure hid in a field." The value of the Gospel of our Lord and Saviour Jesus Christ does not lie upon the surface. It is indeed a treasure of great worth, even when regarded only in its historic or its literary aspect; as illustrating ancient manners and customs, as enforcing certain moral precepts, as exhibiting much rhetorical elegance and power. Hence, we often find the Bible prized and lauded by those who are not animated by its spirit. Poets, philosophers, statesmen, heroes, jurists of highest name, have rendered profound praise to the inspired writings, who, nevertheless, "received not the truth in the love of it," and did not become "new creatures in Christ Jesus." The reason of their commendation is obvious. There are in the Bible such pages of history, such strains of poetry, such teachings of wisdom, such maxims of state policy, such illustrious deeds of valour, such profound principles of eternal and universal law, that even the prejudiced infidel has been forced to concede their merit; so that throughout Christendom the Bible has established itself, not only as the great moral classic of the world, but Art finds in its scenes its sublimest subjects, and Science acknowledges it as her loftiest standard.

All this, however, is not the particular value here alluded to. The Gospel has a deeper worth than what is thus patent and generally acknowledged; its real preciousness lies in its spiritual blessings, by which it imparts to the soul "durable riches and honour." The blessedness of its faith, by which the soul is united to Jesus Christ; the peace, "passing all understanding," which it imparts to the heart; the "joy unspeakable" with which it ravishes the inner man; the "hope that maketh not ashamed," pointing the drooping spirit to its bright inheritance in heaven; the abundant supplies of grace through the manifold gifts of the Holy Ghost, which are bestowed upon the prayerful seekers for the Divine favour; these are some of the inestimable blessings which constitute the riches of this "treasure hid in a field." He who admires the Bible because of its outside excellencies, admires, indeed, a most rare and costly casket, but he knows nothing of what the casket contains. It is only the man of faith, who, with the key of prayer, unlocks this casket; that truly beholds the treasure, and understands its value.

There was, therefore, great propriety in Christ making this treasure to lie hidden in a field; and this he could the more naturally do, because in Eastern countries, where there are no banks, or safe places of public deposit, and where, owing to the despotism of the rulers, or the relaxed state of society, property is unsafe, it is not uncommon for persons to make deposits of their treasures in the ground, selecting obscure and unattractive places, and there hiding them away. And as, in the convulsions which so often shake oriental nations, the owner of such a treasure might be cut off before he could have time to designate its locality to his friends or family, so, the secret dying with him, it would perhaps a long while continue there until by accident it was discovered.

The parable brings before us just this case. A person has by chance discovered concealed treasure; he sees enough to know that it is there, and that it is very valuable; but yet, respecting the law which made all that was in the earth the property of its owner, he seeks to buy the field at its ostensible value, keeping all the while the secret to himself, as a piece of knowledge to which he had exclusive right by reason of his exclusive discovery. Paying to the owner of the field the full price that he asks, the finder "sells all that he has," and buys the field, knowing that the treasure hidden there will remunerate all his outlays, and make him rich for life.

Two points are to be noted here:—First, The discovery of this treasure. The man who found it was not expecting or seeking it. He did not know of its existence; it was by the merest accident that he stumbled upon it; he may have been examining the field for the purpose of ascertaining the quality of its soil, the nature of its situation, or its agricultural capabilities, and while thus engaged, some fortuitous event brought him to the spot of concealment, and directed him to its hidden treasure. Here, we think, lies the distinction between this parable and the succeeding one. In that, the merchant was on the search for goodly pearls; it was his set aim and business; here, however, there was no seeking for hid treasure until chance brought it to his notice. Thus is it often with men in spiritual matters. From the force of early habit, or because of the propriety of the thing, or from motives of a literary or secular character, some may be daily reading God's Word, intent on giving breadth and vigour to their minds, but neither seeking nor caring for its buried treasure. They are looking at the Bible in every light but its true one, and seeking in it every blessing but that which is spiritual. While thus engaged, the Holy Ghost opens the eyes of their understanding to perceive that, which by nature they cannot know, and lo! they behold glimpses of a hid treasure, which at once awaken joy and excite increased desires after a deeper and more experimental knowledge of God's blessed Word. When the soul is thus wrought upon by the Holy Spirit, everything is changed. The field of Scripture, in which this precious treasure has so long been hidden, now becomes, in his estimation, of infinite value. It is that which puts him in possession of salvation and eternal life, which makes him an heir of God, and which gives him the riches of Divine grace for time and for eternity.

For the discovery of this he is not indebted to the research or acumen of his own powers—for by no intellectual effort could these hid treasures be brought to light—but to the Holy Ghost, who gave him that spiritual discernment and spiritual taste, by which he was enabled to discover and appreciate the peculiar blessings of grace as they lie concealed from the natural eye and the carnal mind. Such is the cause of the man's discovering the treasure, and this brings us to the second point, viz., The value which he puts upon this treasure.

In the parable it is said, that, "for joy thereof," the man "goeth and selleth all that he hath, and buyeth that field." This is precisely the feeling of the finder of Divine grace. In the joy of his discovery, he is ready to renounce everything of an earthly nature that conflicts with his possessing it, and would willingly part with that which the world most highly esteems, that he may gain it as his own. Such was the feeling of St. Paul. As a member of the Jewish community, and observing rigidly its Levitical observances, he had, at one time, to use his own language, great "confidence in the flesh," *i. e.*, great reliance on his own self-righteousness, a trusting for salvation to his rigid Phariseeism; but, when he was arrested on his persecuting journey, and made to see the truth as it is in Jesus, when the scales had fallen from his eyes, and he beheld the long-hidden treasure before him, then he quickly abandoned all that he held most dear, saying, "What things were gain to me, those I counted loss for Christ. Yea doubtless, and I count all things but loss for the excellency of the knowledge of Christ Jesus my Lord, for whom I have suffered the loss of all things, and do count them but dung, that I may win Christ." This is the very spirit of the man finding the hid treasure. He puts upon it its true value; he estimates everything else as comparatively worthless; he feels the force of the Saviour's assertion—"He that loveth father or mother more than me is not worthy of me;" and that if we would be His disciples, we must "forsake all and follow him;" and, in the spirit of these injunctions, he is ready to give up everything that impedes his progress in the Divine life, or that conflicts with his getting possession of these hid treasures of the Gospel.

The first aim of life, now, is to be "rich towards God;" to obtain that soul-wealth which consists in faith, and love, and joy, and peace in the Lord Jesus; to receive within himself "the earnest of his inheritance." Whatever pursuit formerly engrossed his mind is now abandoned, or made subservient to his new aim; whatever passions ruled in his soul, and led him captive, are now mastered or made to do willing service to his Redeemer; he no longer "lives unto himself," but unto Him that loved him, and gave Himself for him.

It is impossible to put too high an estimate on this Gospel treasure. In whatever light we regard it, whether in itself, as an emanation from God; or in its effects, as renewing the soul, and making it meet for the inheritance of the saints in light, it is of priceless value.

In comparison with it, those things which the world most prizes, and after which men most strive, are as worthless dross; they have lost their wonted place in his imagination; he has found nobler riches; and he will part with all that earth can give him, though it could multiply its gifts a thousandfold, that he may gain this priceless treasure—the salvation of his soul.

We can never estimate spiritual blessings above their real value; in truth, we can never give them their true worth; we always underrate them, because we do not and cannot now see the full blessedness and glory which they contain. So much of the Christian's happiness lies in the other world, and so large a portion of it is revealed under figures which the mind can scarcely comprehend, that we completely fail in estimating their worth. The pleasures of the world we always set down at too high a figure; they ever appear in inflated magnitude and unreal importance; but the pleasures of religion are always set too low; and the world, the flesh, and the devil aim to depreciate their value, by distorting their character, maligning their influence, and perverting their power. But it will all be of no avail to him who has truly found Christ. To all such "Christ is precious," "the Chief among ten thousand, and the one altogether lovely." His soul finds its full joy and delight in Him. Christ is formed within him the hope of glory; his heart has become a temple of the Holy Ghost; his life is hid with Christ in God; and, walking in faith, rejoicing in hope, patient in tribulation, instant in prayer, he moves on through life without any fear of the future, knowing that, when the earthly house of his tabernacle is dissolved, "he has a building of God, a house not made with hands, eternal in the heavens."

The Pearl.

THE PEARL.

"THE kingdom of heaven is like unto a merchant-man seeking goodly pearls: who, when he had found one pearl of great price, went and sold all that he had, and bought it." MATT. XIII. 45–46.

THE difference between this parable and the one of "The Hid Treasure" seems to lie in this: that in the latter, the man came upon the treasure unexpectedly, when he was neither thinking of nor looking for such a thing; while in this, the merchant-man is *seeking* after the pearls, and has made it his business and his care to secure the very articles which he most desires.

The two parables, therefore, furnish us with types of two different characters:—The man who, Paul-like, is arrested by the Holy Ghost and made to discover the hid treasure when he was neither seeking nor expecting it; and those who, Berean-like, are "searching the Scriptures daily," that they may gather thence the pearls of grace and truth. The character of the first we have already considered, and we confine ourselves now to a brief delineation of the latter.

The "merchant-man" in the parable was "seeking goodly pearls." That was the object of his daily care and labour Ordinary pearls would not answer, they must be "goodly;" these were the object of anxious pursuit, because upon obtaining them rested his reputation as a pearl dealer, as well as his profits from their sale. In his diligent search he is rewarded by discovering one "of great price," and such was its size, and perfection, that to obtain it he sold out all the goodly ones hitherto collected, and embarked his whole fortune in this one pearl, knowing, from the estimation in which the pearl was held by oriental princes, and the enormous prices which were paid for large, round, smooth, and unclouded ones, that he would be able to command greater gains by the sale of this single pearl of great price than from all the pearls of inferior value, how "goodly" soever they might be.

We occasionally meet with persons who have, like Timothy, been carefully instructed in the Scriptures "from a child," or who, like Samuel, have early been impressed with Divine truth, and who, possessing earnest and inquiring minds, anxiously seek for that which will satisfy and comfort the soul. They deliberately set themselves to seek the truth; they are not careless and ignorant persons, but of meditative minds, of tender consciences, of craving souls, who believe that there are "goodly pearls" of grace to be found in God's Word, and who diligently seek them, while at the same time they have such defective views of the character of Christ as to make them rest short of that single-hearted faith in Him which alone secures salvation. There is a moral twilight as well as a natural one; and many there are in this crepusculous state, who, like the man when half healed by Jesus of his blindness, "see men as trees walking." They have glimmerings of the truth, but have not got clear and distinct views of it; they see it looming up amidst partial darkness, but not standing out sharp and clear in outline against a noonday sky. Such persons are apt, with a great deal that is true, to mix up deadly errors. They seek to augment their own righteousness; they bring in their own morality as a ground of salvation; they wish to do something which shall merit God's favour; they seek to blend their work with Christ's perfect and finished work, and thus make a joint stock of their redemption. They lean perhaps too heavily upon rites and ceremonies, upon sacraments and ordinances: all "goodly pearls" in themselves, but not to be trusted or counted of value in comparison to the "one pearl of great price."

No matter, however, with what defective views a person comes to the Word of God, if he approaches it with a sincere desire to know God's will and do it; if there is a moral honesty about him, that will not let him rest until he find the truth, then God will meet him in His Word, and reveal Himself to his mind, and cause him to find in Jesus Christ and the plan of salvation that rests on His precious death and sacrifice, the "pearl of great price;" for Christ declares, "He that doeth the will of God shall know of the doctrine whether it be of God;" and the promise of God is, "Ye shall find me when ye seek me with all your heart."

When such persons behold this pearl of great price, then are their eyes opened by the Holy Ghost to behold its excellency and value. They are seized with a quenchless desire to possess it; their former discoveries in truth, on theories of mind, in which, as "goodly pearls," they long traded and delighted, now appear in their real worthlessness; and, willing to sell off that which they have hitherto obtained, they venture their eternal all upon this Pearl of great price. Nothing now will satisfy the soul of the true believer but Christ; he must possess Christ; he must make Him his own by a living, personal, appropriating faith: thus is he made to "put on Christ," to be "conformed to His image," and to rejoice with a joy unspeakable and full of glory.

It matters not what goodly pearls we may possess—pearls of morality, or virtue, or education, or sensibility—if we have not Christ, they are valueless for all the purposes of salvation; while he who has found Christ has found that which swallows up all lesser pearls in its priceless excellence and perfect beauty.

We are taught by these parables that we must make every sacrifice, in order to obtain the rich blessings that are found in the Lord Jesus. To this duty we are urged by every consideration that can sway human conduct, and he is derelict to every duty to God and to his own soul who, when Christ is set before him as his Redeemer, fails to go to Him as such, and to secure from Him the pardon and the peace which He only can bestow.

It is a matter of wonder and adoring gratitude that God condescends to put within our reach so unspeakable a gift. He was under no necessity to save us. But Christ loved us even when we were sinners, and by offering Himself to satisfy the demands of justice, was enabled to effect our ransom, and yet preserve unimpaired the attributes of the Most High; for, on Calvary, "mercy and truth met together, righteousness and peace embraced each other." Since God then has given us this Pearl of Great Price, since Christ offers himself to us in all the fulness of His redeeming and mediatorial efficacy; since the Holy Ghost pleads with us to accept His overtures of grace, and "buy the truth and sell it not," buy it "without money and without price;" ought not we, for whom this rich provision is made, to renounce everything on which we lean, or in which we trust, that we may obtain this hidden treasure of the Gospel, and possess for ourselves this Pearl of Great Price?

The Draw-Net.

THE DRAW-NET.

"THE kingdom of heaven is like unto a net that was cast into the sea, and gathered of every kind: which, when it was full, they drew to shore, and sat down, and gathered the good into vessels, but cast the bad away. So shall it be at the end of the world: the angels shall come forth, and sever the wicked from among the just, and shall cast them into the furnace of fire; there shall be wailing and gnashing of teeth." MATT. XIII. 47–50.

WHILE the parable of "The Tares" illustrated the fact that there is, and will be until the end of the world, an intermixture of good and evil in the field of the Church, the parable of "The Draw-Net" is evidently designed to show the final separation that shall take place in God's appointed time.

While our Lord has so constructed some of his parables as that their unfolding should elucidate nearly all the great doctrines of religion, he has, in the prodigality of his instruction, uttered many others, designed to set forth single, elemental truths; even though several of them may seem to repeat the same ideas, or overlap each other in their covering of the same ground.

Thus, we can easily draw out from the parable of the Tares all the instruction contained in the parable of the Draw-Net; but Christ, wishing to fix its especial point upon the minds and hearts of his auditors; or because many of his hearers would better understand a figure drawn from the fisher's life than the farmer's field, and acting also upon the prophetic injunction, that "precept must be upon precept, line upon line, here a little and there a little," uttered yet another similitude, and made the draw-net of the Capernaum fisherman, as well as the field of the Galilean husbandman, illustrate the character of his Church here, and the separations that shall take place in it at the end of the world.

The figure which is at present before us is that of a draw-net or seine. This is a fisher's implement, made of heavy twine, with meshes of various size, spread over a portion of the sea and sunk to a certain extent by weights, to give it depth, yet buoyed up from complete submersion by floats; which, after being stretched to a great distance, so as to enclose a large number of fishes, is gradually drawn together by its two ends, and brought to land. This operation is familiar to all who live by the sea-side, or upon watercourses, and needs no further explanation.

When we remember that most of our Saviour's disciples, to whom this parable was more immediately addressed, were fishermen, and that He had called several of His Apostles from "casting their net into the sea," to become "fishers of men," we discern a force and directness in this similitude which they could not fail to appreciate.

The point of special interest in this parable is, the ultimate separation that shall take place between the common occupants of this net, when it is drawn to land.

By the draw-net is represented the Church; by the fishes, the members of that Church; and in this net are enclosed fishes, both "good and bad;" showing, as in the parable of the Tares, the mixture of sound and unsound professors in Christ's earthly kingdom. Concerning this fact we need neither argue nor speculate. It is a revealed and an experimental truth, notorious even to human observation, much more so to Him "who searcheth the reins and trieth the hearts of the children of men."

Into the net of the Church were "gathered of every kind," even as in the parable of the Marriage of the King's Son— the "servants went out into the highways, and gathered together all, as many as they found, both bad and good." The Gospel is preached to all classes and conditions of men; and some from each of these, professedly obey the call, and unite themselves to the visible Church. This state of things continues as long as the net is in the sea; but, when it is full, when God's purposes, in reference to his earthly Church, shall be completed, then will it be "drawn to shore"—the shore of eternity; and there, under the eye of God, shall "the good be gathered into vessels," and "the bad shall be cast away."

There is a time coming, when the moral imperfection which now pertains to the Church shall be done away; when the sound and faithful professors of Christ's religion shall be delivered from the presence of the evil disciples by whom their righteous souls have been so long vexed; when, separated from all evil in themselves and around themselves, they shall be, in their finite capacity, holy as God is holy; and when the wicked, severed from the good, shall be consigned to their merited doom. This separation will be necessary on the part of God, in order to vindicate his justice. It is said of Him, "Justice and judgment are the habitation of His throne." This justice requires that the penalties, as well as the rewards of His law, should be vigorously rendered. The penalties of the law against transgressors are very stringent and severe; and not to inflict them would be to dishonour that law, both in its enactments and sanctions, and to falsify every attribute of the Divine character. Should God fail to punish the breakers of His law, He would not be just to Himself, His statutes, His creatures. He proclaims Himself repeatedly a "God of justice:" how could He be so, unless He sustained the penalties which He has denounced against sin? He has declared again and again, that His "law is holy," and His "commandment holy, and just, and good;" and that He will uphold it in its letter and spirit, in its length and breadth: how can He do this if He relax the sanctions by which it is enacted, and the penal clauses by which it is guarded? He has declared that He "will by no means clear the guilty;" and the conscience that He has put within His creatures, tells them that they have fully incurred the displeasure of their God, and deserve His reprobation: and He must fulfil His righteous promise.

It would not be just in a human lawgiver to make a stringent code, and annex to its infraction severe penalties, and yet never design that they should be carried out: this would be a mockery of justice, and a deliberate insult to the majesty of law. Nor would it be just for human laws to take no cognisance of criminals, to permit crime to go unpunished, and, by withdrawing the penalties due to the guilty, virtually exempt guilt from punishment, and place it on the same legal level with obedience and goodness. Better have no law; better give up a community to the workings of the individual passions of its members—permitting each to "walk in the light of his own eyes, and after the counsel of his own heart;" than to suffer a law to be made null and void by stripping it of its sanctions, and taking from it its punitive and coercive power. Justice requires that human laws should be enforced; the well-being of society is indissolubly blended with their administration; and if justice speaks with an uncertain voice, or with a fickle voice, or with a partial voice, or if it is dumb, then is society torn asunder limb from limb, and the body politic lies a mangled and bleeding corpse at the feet of anarchy and crime. Much more, then, is it necessary that God's law should be sustained, and that His justice should stand out in clear and full outline in the sight of the universe.

But the truth of God, as well as His justice, requires this final separation between the good and the bad. He has said that it should take place; His veracity is at stake upon the issue. But that God should falsify His word, that He should fail to do what He has said would be done, cannot for a moment be entertained by those who believe Him to be "a God of Truth," " with whom is no variableness, neither shadow of turning."

The plain declaration of the Most High is, "The wicked

shall be turned into hell, and all the nations that forget God." "The soul that sinneth it shall die." "There is no peace, saith my God, to the wicked." These, with many others of similar import, are the positive assurances of God; and hence, as "God is not a man that he should lie, nor the son of man that He should repent," so will He do what His truth has pledged Him to do, viz., "send forth His angels, and sever the wicked from among the just."

The holiness of God also demands this eventual separation. So exalted and indescribable is this attribute of the Almighty, that we seem to sully it even by speaking of it. We can scarcely talk of it without our very breath staining its glory; for all our ideas of holiness consist in the relative freedom of a person from sin, and in proportion to the sinlessness of any one, is His holiness, a state of sin being the stand-point from which we judge, because we are only conversant with a world of sin. Abstract, essential, self-existent holiness, such as belongs to God, surpasses our comprehension. A holiness that has no relation to sin, because it existed before sin; a holiness that can be measured by no standard, because itself overtops every standard; a holiness so holy that even the heavens "are not clean in His sight," so pure that "He covereth himself with light as with a garment," so august that "He chargeth even His angels with folly," so resplendent that it fills all heaven with its effulgence, and so ravishing that the celestial harpers make it the burden of their chants as they fall down before Him, veiling their faces with their wings, as they cry, "Holy, holy, holy, Lord God Almighty:" such a holiness is as much above our conception as are the ideas of eternity or infinitude. When we can depict the sun in mid-day lustre with the chromates of the painter's pallet; when we can measure the area of space with the triangulations of the geometer; then perhaps may we be able, with the instrumentalities of earth-born words, to convey an adequate idea of the holiness of Jehovah. It is a subject which we shall ever study, and in which we shall never weary; but to know it in its fulness, to comprehend it in its infinitude, cannot be done by any created mind. This attribute, so ineffably glorious, demands the severance of the wicked from the good. The God who possesses it "cannot look upon sin but with abhorrence," and has declared that nothing unclean shall come into His holy habitation; that into it "nothing shall enter that defileth or maketh a lie;" that only "the pure in heart shall see God." Consequently there must be a dividing process when the net of the Church, now enclosing fishes good and bad, shall be drawn to shore—the shore of eternity.

In like manner we might show that each one of the attributes of God requires this separation in the visible Church. But it need not be dwelt on now, because, if even one attribute required such a severance, that would be enough; for God's character is not made up of diverse and opposing elements, but is a moral unit, and each attribute so harmonizes with the others, as that a violence done to one is done to all, and that which is requisite to the integrity or upholding of one, is equally necessary to the maintenance of every other perfection of the Divine Being.

Leaving, therefore, the point which we think has been so

clearly established, viz., that the character of God requires this final separation in the contents of the Gospel net; we further remark, that it is necessary also to the happiness and perfection of His believing people. The condition of true Christians in the visible Church is one of mingled joy and sorrow. They have indeed great cause for rejoicing; they have sources of pleasure, Divine alike in their origin and their comfort; they have a hope "that maketh not ashamed;" they have a peace "that passeth understanding;" there is for them "no condemnation," because their lives are "hid with Christ in God;" and, in view of the assaults of their last enemy, they are enabled to exclaim, "Thanks be unto God, who giveth us the victory, through Jesus Christ our Lord." Yet, at the same time, it must be confessed that what the Apostle said is strictly true—"if in this life only we have hope, we are of all men most miserable." The very fact that we have been renewed in the temper and disposition of our minds, that we have been born again of the Holy Ghost, that old things have passed away and that all things have become new, only makes us realize more vividly our sad condition, to be thus dwellers in an ungodly world, and to be thus of necessity so mixed up with sin and corruption and unbelief in the walks of daily life. The true Christian finds everything about him antagonistical to his thoughts and feelings. He loves Christ supremely; the world hates Him supremely. He delights to do God's will; the world revels in its disobedience. His heart is set on things heavenly and Divine; "the heart of the sons of men is fully set in them to do evil." He longs for a release from a place where his soul, like that of righteous Lot, "is vexed with the filthy conversation of the wicked;" he is daily pained at the manifestations of sin and unbelief; he mourns at the spiritual destitution of his fellow men, and at the rampant evils that rear themselves unbridled, and raven unchecked upon the vitals of society. Sin meets his eye wherever he turns. In the Church, he sees hypocrisy, formality, self-righteousness, censoriousness, lukewarmness, and backsliding. In the family, he finds peevishness, ill temper, discord, variance, strifes, evil surmisings, and positive hatred. In the state, he perceives crimes of every sort and hue, the decalogue broken in each one of its commandments, and iniquity restrained only by the strong right arm of law. In business, he is made to witness fraud, overreachings, deceptions, lying; so that, look where he will, he is constrained to say with the Psalmist, "Woe is me, that I sojourn in Mesech, that I dwell in the tents of Kedar!"

We are ever made to feel that we are in an enemy's country; that here, as the Patriarchs confessed, "we have no abiding city, but we seek one to come;" that "we who are in tabernacles of flesh do groan, being burdened;" burdened with the remaining corruption of our own hearts; burdened with our daily short-comings and omissions of duty; burdened with our positive transgressions; burdened with our often infirmities; and burdened with seeing and hearing the ungodliness that surrounds us, and that is ever crying to heaven for vengeance.

Such being our condition, it follows that we need deliverance from this state of trial, that we may be brought out "into the glorious liberty of the children of God." As this is a world of probation, we do not expect that this severance of good and ill will take place here, for it would cease to be probation were all sin and temptation removed from our path. But must such a commixture always exist? No. A time of deliverance is at hand; the year of release draws near; and ere long the trumpet of Jubilee, proclaiming that "the acceptable year of the Lord" has come, shall ring out its silver notes of freedom and of rest. God loves us, and will not always suffer us to be overborne by the gruff and gainsaying world; He has thoughts of mercy towards us, and hence will keep us in tribulation only for a little season; His gracious words are, "Though ye have lain among the pots, yet shall ye be as the wings of a dove covered with silver, and her feathers with yellow gold;" therefore, "look up, and lift up your heads, for your redemption draweth near." His gracious purposes in keeping us in the furnace of affliction being accomplished, we shall be removed thence, having our dross purged away, and shall come out as fine gold, meet for the master's use. Then shall His suffering people be made joyful in the Lord: separated from whatever has annoyed and troubled them here, and manifesting themselves in their true character, as "children of light and of the day," they "shall shine forth as the sun in the kingdom of their Father."

It is necessary, then, to the felicity of His saints, to the full development of Divine grace in the soul, and to the accomplishment of God's purposes in their election and regeneration, that there should be a sending forth of angels "at the end of the world," to "sever the wicked from among the just." Reason and revelation assent to and confirm this truth. It is the hope of the Christian, as he takes his weary pilgrim steps towards the Celestial City; and it is the joy of the dying believer, as he puts off this tabernacle of clay, and looks forward to the mansion of rest, "into which nothing shall enter that defileth or maketh a lie."

It is remarkable that in this parable our Lord does not say what will become of the good, after they are gathered "into vessels," though He tells us what will become of the bad; as if the parable was uttered more for warning to the evil professors than for encouragement to the faithful. In the parable of the Tares, indeed, He has told us that, after the separation there spoken of, "the righteous shall shine forth as the sun in the kingdom of their Father;" and as the righteous are one and the same class in each parable, so we infer that all those who, out of the Gospel net, are gathered "into vessels," will enjoy a felicity and glory surpassing human conception, and only to be represented to the human mind by comparing them to suns, shining in full-orbed glory in the firmament of Heaven.

Most fearful, however, are the words which indicate the course of justice upon the wicked. "The angels shall come forth and sever the wicked from among the just, and shall cast them into the furnace of fire; there shall be wailing and gnashing of teeth;" the same punishment that was to be inflicted upon the children of the wicked one in the parable of the Tares. It cannot escape the notice of the Bible reader, how frequently the element of fire is made to act a part in the punishment of the ungodly. Whether those numerous passages in which this idea is brought out are to be taken literally, so that we are to learn thereby that the wicked, after the resurrection, shall indeed dwell with everlasting burnings; that the living, quenchless flames of material fire shall ever wrap themselves about their guilty yet unconsumable bodies, causing them to gnash their teeth for pain, and wail for anguish, is not for us to assert or deny. One thing is certain, that, by the use of such language, God designs that we should gather the most painful and horrific idea of woe of which it is possible for the human mind to conceive; that we should understand by this means the intensity and unbearableness of the doom which will be visited upon the ungodly, and that this punishment shall never end; for all who love not the Lord Jesus Christ shall be cast into hell, "where their worm dieth not, and their fire is not quenched."

This is the idea that we should ever keep in mind, that there is reserved for the unbelieving an anguish of spirit, which in its inflicted sorrows shall be, like furnace fire, ever preying upon, yet never consuming, its undying victim. The warning is boldly, fully given. There is no deception about its nature or its duration. The Bible holds it up before men in full view, and writes it out in such frequently repeated and magnified letters as that "he may read that runs;" so that men are left without excuse, if, in spite of remonstrance, and invitation, and appeal, and the pleadings of mercy, and the overtures of grace, they deliberately go down, step by step, to that woe which is emphatically expressed by being "cast into the furnace of fire," where "there shall be wailing and gnashing of teeth."

Dives and Lazarus.

DIVES AND LAZARUS.

There was a certain rich man, which was clothed in purple and fine linen, and fared sumptuously every day: And there was a certain beggar named Lazarus, which was laid at his gate, full of sores: and desiring to be fed with the crumbs which fell from the rich man's table: moreover, the dogs came and licked his sores. And it came to pass, that the beggar died, and was carried by the angels into Abraham's bosom: the rich man also died, and was buried; And in hell he lifted up his eyes, being in torments, and seeth Abraham afar off, and Lazarus in his bosom. And he cried and said, Father Abraham, have mercy on me, and send Lazarus, that he may dip the tip of his finger in water, and cool my tongue: for I am tormented in this flame. But Abraham said, Son, remember that thou in thy lifetime receivedst thy good things, and likewise Lazarus evil things: but now he is comforted, and thou art tormented. And besides all this, between us and you there is a great gulf fixed: so that they which would pass from hence to you cannot; neither can they pass to us, that would come from thence. Then he said, I pray thee, therefore, father, that thou wouldest send him to my father's house: For I have five brethren; that he may testify unto them, lest they also come into this place of torment. Abraham saith unto him, They have Moses and the prophets; let them hear them. And he said, Nay, Father Abraham: but if one went unto them from the dead, they will repent. And he said unto him, If they hear not Moses and the prophets, neither will they be persuaded though one rose from the dead." LUKE XVI. 19–31.

IN some respects this is one of the most remarkable parables uttered by our Lord. It brings before us the two extremes of life, the two extremes of death, and the two extremes of existence beyond the grave. Each of these couplets may be regarded as an act in the parabolic drama;

the characters employed in their representation being a beggar, a rich man, the patriarch Abraham, and attending angels; while the scene is laid in Earth, and Heaven, and Hell. The consideration of these several acts will put us in possession of the true scope of the parable, and enable us to explain its minor features and design.

There is first exhibited before us the two extremes of life. A very rich man and a very poor man. The rich man presents himself clothed in purple and fine linen, and faring sumptuously every day. Nothing could more clearly indicate his wealth and splendour; for though, in later times, robes of purple have been appropriated to royalty alone, yet in Christ's day it was the dress of the rich, the great, and the favourites in the courts of princes, who are thence often termed by Cicero and Livy "Purpurati." Robes of purple were very costly, because of the scarcity of the shell-fish (*murex trunculus*) from which the Tyrians obtained their celebrated dye, or from the rareness of the *purpura*, from which, according to Pliny, the Phœnicians extracted their rich varieties of purple.

Of nearly equal costliness was the "fine linen," in which the rich man was clothed; consisting of an under-vest or tunic, composed chiefly of the Egyptian flax or *Bambusa*, which was of a soft texture, and so expensive, being worth its weight in gold, as to be worn only by princes, priests, or persons of great estate. In saying, then, that he was "clothed in purple and fine linen," nothing more was needed to indicate the costliness and magnificence of his attire.

But he "fared sumptuously," as well as dressed royally; and that not occasionally, but "every day." His life was a daily feast, full of everything that could gratify the palate of an epicurean lord. Of course, his dwelling was in keeping with his wardrobe and his table; and when we say, therefore, that he was gorgeously arrayed, sumptuously fed, and nobly lodged, we cover the whole ground of luxurious living, and that outward splendour which is so much coveted by men.

Turn now to the Beggar. His name is Lazarus. The name of the rich man has not been mentioned (for the term *Dives*, the Latin word for rich, magnificent, is a conventional name given to him by uninspired writers), but that of the beggar has been recorded. "Seems he not to you," asks Augustine, "to have been reading from that book where he found the name of the poor man written, but found not the name of the rich, even the book of life?" The names of multitudes of the poor, whom the world knows not of, will be found recorded in "the Lamb's Book of Life," and engraven on the palms of the hands of the crucified, while the names of but few of the rich, the wise, the noble, are written there; for they are the "men of the world who have their portion in this life."

Of this Lazarus (a name derived, as some think, from a Hebrew word, signifying *a helpless person;* or according to others, from a word which is interpreted *God is my helper*), it is said, that "he was laid at the gate of this rich man, full of sores, desiring to be fed with the crumbs," or broken meat, "which fell from his table: moreover the dogs came and licked his sores."

The portal of a great mansion was often a place of resort for beggars, that the passers in and out might give them alms; a custom mentioned as far back as Homer, in the Iliad and the Odyssey, and still kept up in many parts of the Eastern world. This description of Lazarus, like that of the rich man, is brief, but emphatic, the strokes which pencil his condition are few, but masterly, and give us a full insight into his wretchedness and want. He was helpless, for the verb, *was laid*, being in the passive voice, implies that he was borne and placed there by the aid of others, consequently was himself helpless. "Was laid *at his gate,*" like a common beggar, a miserable dependent mendicant; "*full of sores,*" diseased all over his body with grievous ulcers, which must have been intensely painful by their number and malignity, increased by his daily exposure and by the want of proper sanatives and emollients; "*desiring to be fed with the crumbs,*" not asking to sit at the rich man's table, nor yet to eat with his servants, but only for the broken refuse meat which fell from the platters and was swept into the streets; "*the dogs came and licked his sores,*"— so miserable that he was unable to fray away the dogs, which, attracted by the blood and sanies of his diseased limbs, came and licked them, thus reducing him almost to the level of the brute creation. These are the outlines of a misery rarely met with, and present to our imaginations a loathsome and repulsive object.

Such was the relative condition of the two in this life. The one, with a stately mansion, princely clothing, sumptuous fare, numerous servants, courtly friends; having all that heart could wish or money buy; filling himself day by day with these objects of sensuality and pride, and neither thinking nor caring for the poor, the sick, the houseless, the hungry; absorbed in self, living for the present, reckless of the future. The other, without a home, a bed, a table, with no companions but dogs, no resting-place but the gateway, no clothing but rags; hungry, diseased, helpless; a burden to himself, an offence to the rich; gathering a scanty pittance from the alms of travellers, and satisfying a craving hunger with the crumbs which he shared with dogs and menials. Who would not envy the rich man? Who would not deprecate the condition of Lazarus?

But the scene changes, and brings us to the close of their respective lives. "And it came to pass that the beggar died; the rich man also died and was buried." Death is the common lot of all. He blends the sceptre and the spade, and in the language of Horace, knocks with equal pace at the gates of the palace, and the hovels of the poor. The beggar died first. There is, however, no record of his funeral. He was hurried into the ground, perhaps unhonoured, unwept, uncared for, "buried with the burial of an ass, drawn and cast forth beyond the gates of Jerusalem."

Not so with the rich man: "He died and was buried;" interred, doubtless, with pomp and ceremony; for the wealth which commanded friends when living, could command mourners when dead. Here, again, who would not prefer the condition of the rich man to that of Lazarus?

The one dies surrounded by skilful physicians, faithful nurses, officious attendants, and is borne to the costly tomb with all the insignia of courtly grief; the other passes away alone, is coffined in his rags, and, without a mourner to drop a tear, is hurried out of sight. Thus closes the earthly history of Dives and Lazarus. Here the curtain of life drops, and corruption and the worm return both to their native dust.

The scene again changes, and the future, with its vast consequences, opens before us.

Dives and Lazarus again come into view, but how changed their state!

The rich man! where is he? "In hell, lifting up his eyes in torment." Where were his riches, his purple robes, his sumptuous fare, his lordly mansion? Could none of these save him? Could none of these buy him a place in heaven? No! stripped of his wealth, his robes, his feasts, his friends, he is thrust into hell, where his riches and luxuries but feed the flames which burn but never consume their victim.

The beggar! where is he? His body, perhaps, had scarce the semblance of an earthly burial, yet his soul was borne "by angels into Abraham's bosom." What though princes even carried the body of Dives to the tomb? Lazarus had the higher honour, for celestial spirits conveyed his soul to glory.

The Jews expressed the happiness of the righteous at death in three ways.—"They go to the garden of Eden;" "they go to be under the throne of glory;" "they go to the bosom of Abraham;" and it was in reference to this general idea that our Lord introduced this expression, to denote the future happiness of Lazarus. He was in the bosom of Abraham, "the Father of the faithful." He whom the rich man scorned to have at his table was received into the arms of Abraham, "the friend of God;" resting in the highest felicity which the Jewish mind could imagine.

The repose of Lazarus in the bosom of Abraham is represented in the parable as being seen by Dives, for it is stated that "in hell he lifted up his eyes, being in torment, and seeth Abraham afar off, and Lazarus in his bosom." Here again our Saviour accommodates his language to the common notions of the Jews, who were taught by the rabbinical writers to believe, that the gates of Paradise were over against the gates of Hell; separated, indeed, by an impassable gulf, yet within eye-range and ear-shot of each other. As soon as the rich man saw Lazarus he recognised him, and calls him by name, and prays to Abraham to send him "that he may dip the tip of his finger in water and cool his tongue, for he was tormented in this flame;" brief words, these, yet expressive of intense woe. The tormenting flame, the parching tongue, the quenchless thirst—a thirst so great that the only boon it asks is one drop of water from the "tip of one finger"—superadded to the humbling position of a beggar, asking like a miserable mendicant for a favour from the hands of him whom, on earth, he spurned with contempt, constitute the elements of his unearthly agony. His request, small as it is, is denied. He is bid remember, that he, "in his lifetime, received his good things;" he was one of those "men of the world" described by the Psalmist, "who have their portion in this life," who flourish here "like a green bay-tree," "whose hearts were fat as brawn," and who, in consequence, lifted up their proud spirits against God, asking, with all the insulting haughtiness of Pharaoh, " Who is the Lord that I should serve Him?" All this he is bid remember, and as his busy memory wakes into more than wonted activity, he remembers his calls of mercy rejected, his opportunities of grace slighted, his vows of obedience broken, and guilt, transgression, rebellion, gather around his mind with most harassing power. Among all the **fearful torments of the** lost, none will exceed those which memory will furnish in the perpetual review of the past.

Undaunted by the denial of this request, he prefers another: "I pray thee, therefore, Father, that thou wouldst send him to my father's house, for I have five brethren, that he may testify unto them, lest they also come into this place of torment." By the first reply of Abraham, he ascertained that there was no hope for him, and abandoning all attempt to get a personal favour, he turns his thoughts to his relatives on earth, who, pursuing, as he knew, the same course which he had followed, would, like him, take up their abode in everlasting burnings. For their sakes, therefore, he pleads that Abraham would "send Lazarus to his father's house," to warn them by his end of the dreadful fate which awaited them, if they continued in their sinful course. Abraham replies, "They have Moses and the Prophets, let them hear them." In the request of Dives there was a virtual implication that he had not been sufficiently warned, an idea which is still further sustained in his rejoinder: "Nay, Father Abraham; but if one went unto them from the dead they will repent," evidently hinting that Moses and the Prophets were not a sufficient warning, and that had a messenger from the unseen world visited him, as he wished Lazarus to do his brethren, he would have repented, and avoided that place of torment; thus aiming to charge upon God what he had brought upon himself. But Abraham closes the dialogue with the solemn yet emphatic assertion, "If they hear not Moses and the Prophets, neither will they be persuaded though one rose from the dead."

The phrase "Moses and the Prophets" is a common formula to express the writings of the Old Testament; and the assertion of Abraham proves that where the teachings of these sacred books are disregarded, no amount of personal revelation will be productive of benefit; for the same evil dispositions and perverse will which hinder men from believing the truths contained in the Scriptures, attested as they are by signs and wonders of most miraculous power, would lead them, after the first startling excitement was over, to disbelieve even though one went unto them from the dead. The point at issue between Dives and Abraham, resolves itself into this question: Is a *standing revelation* better suited to man as an accountable being, than a *special* and *individual* one? This opens too wide a subject to be fully discussed here, yet it cannot be dismissed without some statements which will go far to solve the question.

We might settle the matter in a very summary way by saying that whatever plan a God of infinite wisdom has devised, is that which is best adapted to man as a spiritual and immortal being; a standing revelation is that plan which God has devised, therefore a standing revelation is that which is best adapted to man as a spiritual and immortal being.

Those who acknowledge both the major and the minor premises, as duly assumed, will unhesitatingly adopt the conclusion—for the syllogism is a perfect one, and in the simplest form.

Waiving however this strictly logical argument, which is amply sufficient for all honest and reverent minds, we can discover many reasons why there is more weight, and should be more influence, in a standing than in a private revelation, made to particular persons, in different times, places, and conditions.

A standing revelation is not so easily counterfeited; it is supported by public and notorious evidences and monuments; it is of universal application, and thus bears equally on all; it is more easily appreciated and understood, as it concentrates upon itself the interpretation of thousands of strong, educated, and prayerful minds; it is more permanent and unchanging; it is better fitted to unfold the great lineaments of Jehovah's character; and it is more consonant to the analogy of nature, wherein God operates through general laws, those standing and irreversible statutes of His physical kingdom, which we term the laws of nature, and upon the permanence of which is based all human science.

We go further, and assert that the evidence which sustains our standing Revelation is greater than any which could be given by one coming from the Spirit world. For consider what would be the nature of the evidence which such a messenger from the dead would give! It would be that of a private individual, who could tell only his personal experience, and would possess merely the authority of a traveller to the Spirit land, narrating what he had seen and heard.

But is the evidence of such an one at all comparable to the evidence of the Bible? Is the narrative of a finite creature to be preferred to the Revelation of the infinite God? Is the story of one who tells only what his limited observation has gathered better than the words of Him who knoweth the end from the beginning? Did Lazarus who rose from the dead have a better knowledge of the unseen world than He by whom He was raised?

Let us look a moment at the respective value of the two kinds of evidence. In the case of the Bible, the grounds on which we receive and believe it, are its public, unimpeached, and wondrous miracles; its numerous, comprehensive, and far-reaching prophecies; the unparalleled preservation of its sacred books; the ever accumulating mass of historical proof; its numerous collateral and corroborative monuments; its peculiar and superhuman doctrines; its perfectly demonstrable inspiration by the Holy Ghost; its reception by the universal Church; its minute adaptation to the multifarious wants of the soul; the regenerating power which it has already exercised upon the human race. And this evidence appeals to the affections of the heart, to the faculties of the mind, to the conscience, reason, and judgment of mankind.

In the case of an apparition from the dead there would only be the personal irresponsible authority of a single individual, appealing not to your judgment and reason, for that would be lost in your fright; not to the sober faculties of your mind, for those would be paralyzed with fear; but to your excited fancies, to your stimulated imagination, startled into intense action by the standing before you of one "from the dead."

Let any candid mind say if this is any evidence at all, worthy to be compared to that which underlies the massive fabric of Revelation! We know that just in proportion as the imagination is excited beyond its healthful operations, or the passions stimulated beyond their legitimate action, the reflective and judicial faculties of the mind are depressed and weakened; the perceptions of the intellect are distorted, the decisions of the judgment are perverted, the operation of the will is irregular; the law of proportion, which, when the mind is in a normal state, keeps all its faculties in their just relation and due action, is violated, and no true judgment or decision can be had or reached by an individual whose mind is either paralyzed with fear, or bewildered by excitement.

It is perfectly absurd, therefore, to place the evidence

afforded by an apparition from the dead on a footing with that which upholds "Moses and the Prophets." But, further, the very grounds on which men object to the testimony of the Bible, apply with greater force to the evidence of "one from the dead." The objections to the Bible are mainly on two grounds, viz., as a revelation of the will of God, and as a system of moral doctrines. The objection to the Bible because it is a revelation from God, lies harder against a man from the dead, than against the Scriptures, for what would his message be but a revelation? and a revelation of things beyond the cognisance of your senses, or the testimony of your fellow men! And so, of course, on Hume's principles, it must be discarded, or else you are placed in the dilemma of accepting the evidence of a solitary and individual revelation, and rejecting the vast and ever accumulating evidence which sustains the Word of God. Which is most reasonable? Which demands the greatest credulity?

If the objection to a standing revelation be on account of its doctrines, then, if the man from the dead taught the doctrines of the Bible, you would no more believe him than you would "Moses and the Prophets;" if he taught doctrines contrary to the Gospel, then, before you can receive them, you must demand for their confirmation a proof as strong at least as that by which we prove the Scriptures to be of God, and even stronger, to counterbalance the prima facie authority of Revelation. When such evidence can be produced, then will we "read, mark, learn, and inwardly digest it;" but as no such has been given, and none possibly can be, we dismiss the objection as one originating in the pride of the sinful heart, unwilling to bow to the humbling doctrines of the Cross, rather than in the deductions of a calm reason, or an unbiassed judgment.

But the falsity of these subterfuges will still more strongly appear, if we remember the fact that the very condition of things desired by the rich man in the parable has taken place, and yet the anticipated results have not followed. One has come to us from the dead! Jesus Christ rose from the dead, and, what is of great importance to our case, rose for the very purpose of confirming the doctrines of Revelation; for St. Paul so rests the whole superstructure of the Gospel on the resurrection of Christ, that he says, with great emphasis, "If Christ be not risen, then is our preaching vain, and your faith is also vain: ye are yet in your sins." Yet how few believe the words of Jesus; how few repent at His warnings of wrath, or His invitations of grace!

The very men who most clamorously say "but if one came unto us from the dead, and told us the facts concerning the unseen world, that sin is punished with unspeakable woe, and that persistence in our present course will bring us to that place of torment, we would repent," are those who most sedulously refuse to listen to the teachings of the Saviour who did come from the dead, and who tells us in the Gospel what He sees and knows of the world to come.

To the open ear of the sincere inquirer, the Scriptures

speak out clear and full, and he who yields to their guiding voice will, at death, be "carried by angels into Abraham's bosom;" but, to the wilfully closed ear, no attestations, come they whence they may, will prove effectual, for persistent unbelief will cast them all aside, and rush with infatuated step over every barrier until death ends his earthly career, and "in hell he lifts up his eyes, being in torment."

This parable is full of instructive suggestions. It teaches that the condition of the soul, in the other world, is not at all affected by the condition of the body in this. "God is no respecter of persons." Moral qualifications alone shall decide our position in eternity.

It teaches that a man may be poor and miserable and despised on earth, and yet be dear to saints, to angels, and to God. Joseph in Pharaoh's dungeon, David hiding in caves, Elijah "hunted like a partridge upon the mountains," the Apostles regarded as "the offscouring of all things;" and above all, the personal history of our blessed Lord, who was "a man of sorrows," and "had not where to lay his head," amply sustain this precious truth.

It teaches that riches, honours, friends are no security against death and hell. "*Riches,*" says Solomon, "profit not in the day of wrath;" and Zephaniah boldly declares of the ungodly, "Neither their silver nor their gold shall be able to deliver them in the day of the Lord's wrath." *Honours* are but rainbows painted on the spray of popular applause, vanishing as soon as formed; even as the Psalmist says, "Man being in honour abideth not." *Friends* are but flesh and blood, as mortal and as impotent as ourselves; " none of them" writes David, " can, by any means, redeem his brother, nor give to God a ransom for him." He, therefore, who trusts in either of these, trusts in that which will fail him in the day of trouble.

It teaches that those who revile the godly and the poor in this life, shall respect and envy them in the life to come. The rich man took no notice of Lazarus when living, but was most anxious to secure his services when in eternity. And who are they "of whom" the Apostle says " the world was not worthy?" Its kings? its poets? its heroes? its philosophers? No! but the lowly, despised, and persecuted servants of God; those who " had trial of mockings and scourgings, yea, moreover, of bonds and imprisonments, who were stoned, were sawn asunder, were tempted, were slain with the sword, who wandered about in sheep skins and goat skins, being destitute, afflicted, tormented." The world does not write these names in its history with illuminated capitals, but they are written in the " Lamb's Book of Life." They are not decked with earthly honours, but they are dressed with kingly robes, and wear kingly crowns in Heaven.

It teaches that all those who have their "good things in this life" can expect none in the next. So much are we under the dominion of the temporal and the material, that the present too often absorbs our thoughts to the exclusion of the spiritual and the eternal; and the cry of most men, like that of the departing Prodigal, is, "Father, give me the portion of goods that falleth to me." They are under the sway of sense; they do not walk by faith; they live only for the present, and come under the class described by David, "men of the world, who have their portion in this life." They have chosen their part, but it is a worldly one, and when called hence they lose it, and have no heavenly portion in reversion.

This parable conveys a solemn warning to the rich. It is to be observed that our Lord does not charge the rich man with any positive crime or immorality. He merely states that he was rich, and lived in a style corresponding to his wealth, which may be said of many a truly good man. But he was evidently one who "trusted in his riches," of whom the Saviour declared, "it is easier for a camel to go through the eye of a needle than for a rich man to enter the kingdom of God." The snare of wealth lies in "its deceitfulness," and he who would avoid its entangling meshes, must use his riches as a steward's trust, for which he must give account at the judgment-seat of Christ.

This parable should prove a consolation to the pious poor. What though he begs his daily bread, and lies in rags at the gates of the rich? Was not Jesus born in a stable? and were not the birds and the foxes better housed than He? He may have no earthly treasure, but he has "an inheritance reserved for him in heaven." His body may be full of sores, but God says to his soul, "Thy beauty was perfect through my comeliness, which I had put upon thee." He may have but "crumbs" to eat here, but he has an invitation "to the marriage-supper of the Lamb." He may have no companions now, but angels minister to him as one of the heirs of salvation, the Holy Ghost dwells in his heart as a Comforter; Christ is to him "a friend that sticketh closer than a brother;" and, from the lowest deep of earthly abasement, he can look up to God, and say, "Abba, Father." Therefore, to all the depressed and humbled Christians, we say, in the words of the once lowly and despised, but now glorious and exalted Saviour, "look up, and lift up your heads; for your redemption draweth nigh."

And finally, this parable teaches that our eternal future corresponds to our earthly character. We enter the world of spirits with precisely the same moral feelings with which we leave this. "As the tree falls, so it lies." He that at death is sinful, will be sinful still. He that at death is holy, will be holy still. This being the case, as God's Word positively assures us, and there being guarantied to us only the present moment of time in which to prepare for this unending future, with how much emphasis should this consideration speak to us of the necessity of making immediate preparations to meet our God! Before Him we may be at any moment summoned. If called hence in an unrepenting and unbelieving state, we shall enter that unseen world only to spend an eternity amidst the torments of the lost, with an impassable gulf between us and the land of bliss. An "impassable gulf!" No passing now! no passing ten thousand ages hence! no passing for ever! Once "in hell, lifting up our eyes in torment," and we are there for ever; for though there is remorse in hell, though there is sorrow there, though there is weeping and wailing there, there is *no repentance* there, *no faith* there, *no Saviour* there!

Now, there is mercy and forgiveness; now, the blood-filled fountain is open; now, the arms of Jesus are outstretched to receive us; now, the Spirit pleads and moves upon our hearts; now, the instrumentalities of grace are freely offered. Seize them now, "for *now* is the accepted time; NOW is the day of salvation."

The Marriage of the King's Son: The Great Supper.

THE MARRIAGE OF THE KING'S SON: THE GREAT SUPPER.

"THE kingdom of heaven is like unto a certain king, which made a marriage for his son, and sent forth his servants to call them that were bidden to the wedding: and they would not come. Again, he sent forth other servants, saying, Tell them which are bidden, Behold, I have prepared my dinner; my oxen and my fatlings are killed, and all things are ready, come unto the marriage. But they made light of it, and went their ways, one to his farm, another to his merchandise: and the remnant took his servants, and entreated them spitefully, and slew them. But when the king heard thereof, he was wroth: and he sent forth his armies, and destroyed those murderers, and burned up their city. Then saith he to his servants, The wedding is ready, but they which were bidden were not worthy. Go ye therefore into the highways, and as many as ye shall find, bid to the marriage. So those servants went out into the highways and gathered together all, as many as they found, both bad and good: and the wedding was furnished with guests. And when the king came in to see the guests, he saw there a man which had not on a wedding-garment: and he saith unto him, Friend, how camest thou in hither, not having a wedding-garment? And he was speechless. Then said the king to the servants, Bind him hand and foot, and take him away, and cast him into outer darkness; there shall be weeping and gnashing of teeth. For many are called, but few are chosen." MATT. XXII. 1-14.

"A certain man made a great supper, and bade many: and sent his servant at supper-time to say to them that were bidden, Come; for all things are now ready. And they all with one consent began to make excuse. The first said unto him, I have bought a piece of ground, and I must needs go and see it: I pray thee have me excused. And another said, I have bought five yoke of oxen, and I go to prove them: I pray thee have me excused. And another said, I have married a wife; and therefore I cannot come. So that servant came, and showed his lord these things. Then the master of the house, being angry, said to his servant, Go out quickly into the streets and lanes of the city, and bring in hither the poor, and the maimed, and the halt, and the blind. And the servant said, Lord, it is done as thou hast commanded, and yet there is room. And the Lord said unto the servant, Go out into the highways and hedges, and compel them to come in, that my house may be filled. For I say unto you, that none of those men which were bidden, shall taste of my supper." LUKE XIV. 16–24.

WE have placed these two parables together, because, though uttered at different times, and designed originally for different purposes, they have such a general unity of structure, similitude, and interpretation, that for all practical purposes they may be regarded and unfolded as one.

It is peculiarly interesting to observe the rich and attractive drapery in which our Lord clothes His doctrines. He presents before the mental eye that which is usually full of joy, " a great supper ;" that which is overflowing with gladness, " a marriage feast :" and, that the attractions might be heightened by the splendour of wealth and the pomp of station, He introduces royalty itself—a King preparing a bridal entertainment " for his son,"—thus taking the highest banquet of earth, to shadow forth " the marriage supper of the Lamb" in Heaven.

No people were more accustomed to make weddings occasions of festivity, than the Orientals; for they celebrated the nuptials of sons and daughters with a display and magnificence equal to their rank or wealth, extending the festivities over several days: hence the Greek word used here by St. Matthew, and translated " marriage," is put in the plural number, because these feasts continued a succession of days: as we learn from the direction of Laban to Jacob, " Fulfil her week ;" or keep her usual marriage feast : and it is recorded of Sampson, that at his marriage he "made a feast seven days; for so used the young men to do:" and the Rabbins inform us, that this seven days of feasting was "a matter of indispensable obligation upon all married men." It was customary also to celebrate the inauguration of kings and sovereigns with feasts, similar to the wedding banquets; for on the day on which they assumed the government of the land to which they succeeded, or were appointed, the kings or rulers were considered as Sponsi et Mariti; as affianced or solemnly united to their country,— which is therefore compared to a Sponsa or bride.

When Jesus Christ, therefore, was to enter upon His mediatorial reign, God made a marriage feast at the espousals of His Son with the Church, and set out the banquet with the fat things of the Gospel of His grace. And in this comparison there is much propriety; for both the old and new covenants are several times spoken of by Prophets and Apostles, as marriage contracts between God and His people. Indeed, of all human relationship, this is the most frequently and the most elaborately used, to express the oneness, intimacy, and affection that exists between Christ and the Church. St. John introduces this figure with great effect in his description of the future glory of the Church : " And I heard," says he, " as it were the voice of a great multitude, and as the voice of many waters, and as the voice of mighty thunderings, saying, Alleluia: for the Lord God Omnipotent reigneth. Let us be glad and rejoice, and give honour to Him : for the marriage of the Lamb is come, and His wife hath made herself ready. And to her was granted that she should be arrayed in fine linen, clean and white : for the fine linen is the righteousness of saints." "Blessed are they which are called unto the marriage supper of the Lamb." Well might there be " a feast of fat things on God's holy mountain," when His only begotten Son was espoused to the Church ; when he took His earthly Zion to His bosom as His bride, and gave to her the dowry of the Holy Ghost.

When the banquet spoken of in the parables was prepared, the servants, in both cases, were sent out to those who had been previously "bidden," with the message, "Come, for all things are now ready ;" in accordance with the oriental usage, by which the guests to a feast were twice called ; first, invited some time before, that they might prepare themselves; and secondly, summoned a short time previous to the banquet, that they might be there in season.

Thus were the Jews, to whom these parables were addressed, twice bidden to the Gospel feast; first, by the prophets, long before, and again, by Christ's apostles and disciples, saying, in the name of their Lord and King, "Behold, I have prepared my dinner; my oxen and fatlings are killed, and all things are ready, come unto the marriage." The message was urgent, ample, and seasonable, and we should have supposed that it would at once have been responded to with alacrity and gladness. On the contrary, however, they to whom the message came " made light of it," and " all, with one consent, began to make excuse," pleading the most trivial affairs as a reason for slighting both the entertainer and the entertainment.

What though one had "bought a piece of ground?" the ground was not a perishable, movable thing, that "he must needs go and see it" now. It would lie in the same situation and have the same quality of soil to-morrow that it had to-day.

What though another had "bought five yoke of oxen?" he could test their strength and quality to-morrow as well as now; and it was not necessary therefore that he should neglect the banquet to "go and prove them."

What though another had "married a wife?" that could not be plead in excuse for such unjustifiable neglect; for his wife was not given to him to enjoy only to-day, to be removed to-morrow, but was his for a lifetime, and hence he could the more easily spare a portion of time now, to the calls of his lord and master.

There was neither validity nor force in any of these excuses; and to the contempt and refusal of some was added insult and murder by others; "for the remnant," says one of the parables, "took his servants, and entreated them spitefully, and slew them;" which thing was true of the Jews, who evil-entreated and slew, by cruel deaths, nearly all the Apostles of our Lord.

These insults to his servants and murders of his messengers the king hears of with anger, but he lays aside his revenge until the feast is over.

Resolved that the wedding and the supper which had been prepared should be "furnished with guests," though those who were first bidden were unworthy, servants are "sent out into the highways, the streets and lanes of the city," who "gathered together all, as many as they found," "the poor, and the maimed, and the halt, and the blind;" and thus "the wedding was furnished with guests."

This circumstance has been thought by some, unacquainted with oriental manners, unnatural and improbable; but ancient and modern writers unite to attest its truthfulness. Dr. Pococke, a distinguished Eastern traveller, says that "an Arab prince will often dine in the street, before his door, and call to all that pass, even to beggars, in the name of God, to come and sit down to his table;" and to this day, in several parts of Asia, it is as common for a rich man or prince to give a feast to the poor, the maimed, and the blind, as it is in Europe or America for gentlemen to entertain those of their own rank or order.

Thus were the Gentiles, "the maimed, the halt, the poor, and the blind," as the Jews esteemed them, called to the Gospel feast, when their despisers, the Israelites, had haughtily rejected the repeated invitations; for Christ had just before declared, "many shall come from the east and from the west, and shall sit down with Abraham, and Isaac, and Jacob, in the kingdom of God; but the children of the kingdom shall be cast out."

As there was still "room," after many had been gathered out of the streets and the lanes, the servant was commanded, "go out into the highways and hedges, and compel them to come in, that my house may be filled."

Much and injurious stress has been laid upon the word

"compel," as though it were constraint under physical fear or force. The word, it is true, may admit of that interpretation, but it cannot mean here anything more than that moral compulsion which results from the stress of argument and the force of personal appeal; because the one servant to whom was given the direction, "compel them to come in," could not by his personal power force, against their will, a sufficient number of persons to occupy the seats of so great a supper. It therefore means, an internal constraint through the pressure of powerful motives.

The invited guests having taken their places, the feast proceeds. A circumstance, however, is brought out in the parable of the Marriage Supper, which is of too much practical importance to be overlooked. It is said, "And when the king came in to see the guests, he saw there a man which had not on a wedding garment; and he said unto him, Friend" (comrade, or companion, for the original word does not imply affection and regard), "how camest thou in hither, not having a wedding garment?" In all large oriental weddings, the guests were expected to appear in particular robes, generally white, which were furnished by the master of the feast. This is an ancient custom, for we find two instances mentioned by Homer, and it is also alluded to by other classical writers.

It is well known that the wardrobes of the Eastern nobles constitute an important part of their riches. Thus Job, speaking of the wicked, says, "Though they heap up silver as the dust, and prepare raiment as the clay." Diodorus Siculus, in his 13th Book, gives an account of the hospitality of Gellius the Sicilian, who at one time, when five hundred horsemen were driven by a storm to take refuge with him, supplied them all with clothes. When Lucullus, the rich Roman general, was asked if he could furnish a hundred chlamydes (short military cloaks) for the theatre, he replied that he could send five thousand. We may, therefore, naturally enough suppose that this king, having invited guests to his feast from the highways and hedges, would order his servants to see them all properly clad out of his own wardrobe, that they might be not only cleanly in their apparel, but also, being dressed alike, might all feel themselves on one level, and thus avoid those distinctions which difference of garments so often makes.

Not to have a wedding garment was, therefore, a mark of disrespect to the host, to the feast, and to the guests. Indulging these feelings of hatred, and manifesting them by an open refusal to appear in the prescribed dress, it is not to be wondered at that, when confronted with the king and questioned by him as to his appearance, the man should be "speechless,"—that conscious guilt should muzzle his mouth with shame, for his conduct manifested a state of mind and heart worthy of condign punishment; nor was it long delayed, for the incensed king ordered his servants to "bind him hand and foot, and cast him into outer darkness," beyond the glare and lights of the halls and courts; where, instead of pleasure and delight, he should have "wailing and gnashing of teeth," the fruits of a bitter but unavailing sorrow.

This wedding garment is, by some, regarded as faith, by others, a holy life, but Calvin well says, "It is needlessly contended, whether the wedding garment be faith or a pious and holy life; because, neither can faith be separated from good works, nor are good works practicable without faith. Christ, however, only meant that we must so comply with the call of our Lord, as to be renewed in spirit, after his image, remaining constantly in union with him, that the old man, with his defilements, must be put off, and the new life diligently applied to, by which means our garment might become suitable to our honourable calling."

In his Epistle to the Romans, St. Paul urges us "put ye on the Lord Jesus Christ." This we are to do after having cast off the works of darkness"—those deeds and thoughts and feelings which belong to us in our carnal and benighted state. These are the defiled garments of our depraved nature; but when, through the grace given unto us, we cast these away and come to Christ, his language is, "Take away the filthy garment from him; behold, I have caused thine iniquity to pass from thee, and I will clothe thee with change of raiment;" and that change of raiment is the wedding garment of Christ's righteousness, seamless, spotless, which he gives to each believer, and in which alone he can appear with acceptance before the Great King. Thus arrayed, the devout soul can sing with the Prophet, "I will greatly rejoice in the Lord, my soul shall be joyful in my God: for he hath clothed me with the garments of salvation, he hath covered me with the robe of righteousness."

We have reason to fear, however, that many who sit at the earthly table of the Lord's House, are aptly represented by the man "who had not on a wedding garment." They have heard the invitation, they have gone in to the banquet, but they went in the soiled and earth-stained garments of their own morality, and never sought "to be clothed upon" with that robe of righteousness which Christ bestows upon all who come to him in true penitence and faith. The eye of man cannot tell whether we are thus arrayed or not, but when "the King comes in to see the guests," all shall be revealed; for, in the language of the Prophet Zephaniah, "The Lord hath prepared a sacrifice, he hath bid his guests; and it shall come to pass in the day of the Lord's sacrifice, that I will punish the princes and the king's children, and all such as are clothed with strange apparel." And what a startling question will that be, which the Lord shall then put—"Friend," a seeming friend, because a nominal companion, "how camest thou in" the Church and at my table, "not having on the wedding garment?" You cannot say that you did not need it, for God distinctly says, "Without holiness, no man shall see the Lord." You cannot say that it was not offered to you; for it is freely bestowed, yea, even pressed upon your acceptance by the ministers of Christ. You cannot say that it will make no difference whether I have one on or not, for it is emphatically stated, that you can only secure the favour of God by being thus robed in the garment of salvation. To the stern interrogation of our Lord you, like the man in the parable, will be "speechless." Your mouth will be muzzled with shame, and your face covered with confusion, and you shall be cast out into outer darkness, beyond the light and glory of Heaven, into the blackness of eternal sorrow; and there you will be left to spend eternal ages, writhing under the wrath of an angry God.

Have we this wedding garment? The hour is not far distant when the King will "come in to see the guests;" are we prepared to meet his searching gaze by having put on Christ, as "our wisdom, and righteousness, and sanctification, and redemption?" or have we been so careless, or hypocritical, or unbelieving, as to neglect this only garment of salvation, and thus procure for ourselves eternal banishment from the presence of God?

Ascending now from particular incidents to general inferences, we remark that these parables illustrate three important points, viz., the freeness and fulness of the Gospel feast; the perverseness of the human heart in making light of and declining its invitations; and the righteous vengeance which will overtake all impugners of God's grace and mercy.

First, the freeness and fulness of the Gospel feast. The Gospel offers everything for our spiritual wants and appetites, and leaves unsatisfied no craving of the soul. Are we weak in the faith, of feeble knees, and stammering tongues, "babes in Christ?" here is found "the sincere milk of the Word, that we may grow thereby." Are we strong and masculine in our spiritual energies and capabilities, with our "senses exercised to discern both good and evil?" here is to be had "the strong meat" of doctrines and mysteries. Are we crying out with one of old, "My leanness! my leanness!" here is that bread of life, and wine of grace, that will make us muscular and robust in spiritual health. Are we "hungering and thirsting after righteousness?" our souls "shall be satisfied as with marrow and fatness;" every holy appetite shall be appeased, for at the table of the Lord are found those memorials of dying love, of which whosoever eateth in faith, does, in the language of the martyr Latimer, "Eat with the mouth of his soul, and drink with the stomach of his soul, the body of Christ." This is bringing us to a more than angels' banquet, and feeding us on more than angels' food."

And to this "feast of fat things," which God has spread upon His holy mountain, the Church, all are invited. God has sent out His servants, His ministers, to summon all to this marriage supper of the Lamb, and the invitation runs in these words: "Ho, every one that thirsteth, come ye to the waters, and he that hath no money, come; yea, buy wine and milk, without money and without price;" "Come, for all things are ready;" "And the Spirit and the Bride say, Come, and whosoever will, let him come, and take of the water of life freely," for the assurance of the Bridegroom is, "Him that cometh unto me I will in no wise cast out." Nothing can be more full and free than the invitations of grace: God's ministers are commissioned to go into all the world, to call men everywhere to repentance, to offer pardon to the guiltiest, peace to the most rebellious, mercy to the scarlet-dyed transgressor.

These free offers are made without any prerequisites on our part of worth or merit. We are not to work out one part of our salvation and expect Christ to do the rest. He must save us wholly, or not at all. All that is required of us is, to feel our sinfulness and our need of a Saviour, and to take him as our alone Redeemer. He will work in and with us to do the rest. These free offers of grace are made in good faith on the part of God. He "is not a man that he should lie." He is not a deceiver, promising much and fulfilling little. "Hath he said it, and shall He not do it? Hath he spoken, and shall it not come to pass?" "Heaven and earth," he says, "shall pass away, but my word shall not pass away." So that we may rely with the most implicit trust in the free salvation offered to us by our Lord and Saviour Jesus Christ. These offers of grace are also as full as they are free. They cover all sins, for "the blood of Jesus Christ cleanseth from all sin;" they extend to all our spiritual needs, for Christ Jesus "is of God made unto us wisdom, and righteousness, and sanctification, and redemption;" they leave nothing to be supplied by human means or merit, for we "are complete" in Christ; and they open to us full and unending glories in the world to come, for, once there, we "shall go no more out for ever."

Secondly. We might suppose that offers of mercy thus free and full would be accepted with delight, and that sin-burdened men would hasten to embrace the salvation proffered "without money and without price;" but our experience teaches just the reverse, for it is at this point that the perverseness and depravity of the human mind manifest themselves, in making light of and declining these invitations. Of the great majority of those to whom the Gospel invitation come, may it be said, that they either "make light of it," or else "with one consent begin to make excuse." That which is the most pressing want of their souls for time and for eternity, that which involves the highest interests of their moral natures, is made to occupy a subordinate place, or, too often, no place at all; while the farm, the merchandise, the cares of the family, things fleeting in themselves and comparatively of small value, are permitted to take an absorbing precedence. This is virtually saying that God's estimate of the soul and sin and salvation is wrong, and ours right; and thus, acting according to the counsel of our own minds and the deceitfulness of our own hearts, we reject the overtures of grace, and continue on in sin and unbelief. Such a charge may shock the sensibilities of some, and they may deny that they are guilty of making light of the invitations of grace, or of excusing themselves from attendance on the Gospel feast.

It is true that you may not have made a mock of the truth, or openly scoffed at the ministers of God, or laughed at the ordinances of the Church; you may, on the contrary, regard the Bible with profound respect, and reverence His servants and His sanctuary with many kindly demonstrations. When the Sabbath bell rings out its call to prayer, you may bend your head in worship; when the organ peal fills the vaulted roof, you may lift up your voice in the swelling chant; when the ambassador for Jesus proclaims the truths of salvation, you may listen "as unto a very lovely song of one that hath a pleasant voice, and can play well upon an instrument;" so that throughout your external conduct there shall be visible no impropriety of word or deed; and yet, after all this, you may be fully obnoxious to the charge of the text. We can illustrate this proposition by a single supposable case:—You are sick; a physician has been called in, and after due examination of your symptoms, he has left certain prescriptions, which he assures you will relieve your disease. Your common sense, your experience, your judgment, confirm his words; but, in spite of all this, you refuse to follow his directions. You do not laugh at them, the matter is too serious; you do not scoff at them, for your reason tells you that they are proper remedials; but you do not take the required medicines. On repeating his visit, the physician finds you no better; and learning that you had refused to take his prescriptions, he tells you he is sorry that you "made light" of them. "Oh, no, sir," you reply, "I did not make light of them—I did not laugh at them or turn them into derision—I doubt not that they are very valuable." "But," interrupts the physician, "did you follow my directions?" "Why, no, sir, I did not." "And does not this simple refusal to do as I directed," he might say, "show that you make light of them—that you do not prize them? Is it not treating me with the most practical levity and slight?"

The Great Physician of Souls has come to you and found you languishing under the disease of sin. "The whole head is sick, and the whole heart faint." He comes to you with the Balm of Gilead, and tells you what will cure your dreadful malady. His prescriptions commend themselves to your reason, judgment, and conscience. You will die unless you conform to His directions; yet day after day you hesitate, you put off compliance, refusing to take that which will make you morally sound and healthful in the sight of God. Is not this making light of Christ in a manner insulting to Him and ruinous to your own soul? Nothing can be plainer than the proposition, that we make light of that which is worthy of being received, and which it is important for us to receive, when we do not receive it into good and honest hearts. What more worthy of our reception than the offers of grace in Christ Jesus? What more important to our eternal interests? Yet, not accepting them, not providing for our souls' highest needs, we are in very truth making light of them, to the peril of our souls. Should you, however, instead of silently neglecting Christ, attempt with much honeyed plausibility to excuse yourself from His service, pleading your daily cares and domestic duties in extenuation, your condition would not be much better. Excuse yourself! to whom? to God your Creator for not obeying Him! to Christ your Redeemer for not loving Him! to the Holy Ghost the Sanctifier for doing despite unto His proffered Grace! Excuse yourself! from what? from the service of God! from union with Christ! from the renewing of the Holy Spirit! from peace of mind! from joy ot heart! from hope of heaven! from eternal life! Excuse yourself! for what? for a few days' continuance in sin!

for the fear of sneering friends! for the dread of coming out from the world! for lack of moral courage to acknowledge yourself a sinner, needing salvation, and seeking it where only it can be found, at the foot of the cross! How will such conduct appear in a dying hour, when the vanities of the world are dissolving, and the realities of eternity rising into view? How will it appear at the judgment seat of Christ, before those open books, and that great white throne, and the once rejected Saviour, then sitting there in His divine glory? God inviting! man making light of the invitation! this is a wonder hitherto unheard of in the moral universe.

Thirdly, we notice the righteous vengeance which will overtake those who make light of the invitation, and excuse themselves from the feast.

In the parable of the Marriage of the King's Son, it is said, that when the king heard of the rejection of his invitation, "he was wroth, and he sent forth his armies, and destroyed those murderers, and burned up their city;" in evident allusion to the fate that befell Jerusalem, where these very things came to pass. In the parable of the Great Supper, the master of the feast declared, "None of those men that were bidden shall taste of my supper;" while he who neglected to put on the wedding garment was "cast into outer darkness." All these are figurative illustrations of God's wrath against the deliberate and wanton rejecters of the Lord Jesus; and they indicate the positive determination of the Most High, that He "will not in anywise clear the guilty." As a God of holiness, He must, by the very necessities of His nature, punish sin as long as sin exists. This punishment of sin must also be commensurate with the greatness of the sin; and though, in one sense, all sins are great, because committed against a great God, and because they are violations of a great law; yet there is a grade in transgressions, rising in degrees of guilt from the simplest thought of evil to the sin against the Holy Ghost, which, our Lord says, shall never be forgiven. We cannot classify our sins, because we do not know their real malignity or influence; yet we can easily see that transgressions such as are implied in making light of Christ, and refusing the overtures of grace, must be very grievous, and must evoke severe vengeance. And what we thus argue on principles of ordinary reason, the Bible declares, by setting forth in language of the most vivid and decided kind, the greatness and the woe of those who thus draw upon themselves swift destruction.

But we turn from the consideration of these mournful yet impressive truths, to listen for a moment to a voice which speaks to us in one of the parables, uttering the sweet invitation, "Come, for all things are now ready!" It is the voice of mercy, speaking from the very throne of God. It is a voice calling to each sin-stricken heart in tones of comfort, for it is full of promise, hope, and joy. It tells us that "all things are now ready" *on Earth*. The incarnation, crucifixion, resurrection, and ascension of Christ, by which atonement was made for sin, and death and the grave stripped of their victories, have taken place, and their blessed results are now ready to be applied to the hearts and consciences of men. The Church on earth is ready to embrace you; the earthly ministers of Christ are waiting to receive you; the ordinances of grace are ready for your participation; so that in every particular we can say, "all things" *on earth* "are ready; come unto the marriage."

This blessed voice also tells us, "Come, for all things are now ready" *in Heaven*. Christ has swung open to us its long-closed door; and, having gone before to prepare the way, has fitted up those mansions in His Father's house, destined for the occupation of believers. Everything is prepared in heaven; angels wait there to receive us; the spirits of the just watch for our coming; the gates of pearl are opened to admit us; the harp, and crown, and robe, and palm-branch are made ready for our use; the marriage supper is already spread out beneath the sunless sky of glory; so that, in every particular, we can say, "all things" *in heaven* "are ready, come unto the marriage."

And with this invitation there is also coupled the assurance, "and yet there is room." There is room in the Church for more disciples; there is room in the mercy of God for the very chief of sinners; there is room in the blood-filled Fountain of Salvation for multitudes more of the vile and the degraded; there is room in the grace of the Holy Ghost for all classes, ages, sexes, stations, climes, and kindred; there is room in Heaven; the number of its inhabitants is not yet completed; its "many mansions" are not yet all occupied; its wardrobe of wedding garments is not yet exhausted: and not only room in Heaven, but welcomes; and not only welcomes, but anthems of joy, as one after another shall come from the North and from the South, from the East and from the West, and sit down, with Abraham and Isaac and Jacob, to the marriage supper of the Lamb. If we perish now, after this full and free provision, the fault is all our own; for God still says to us in His holy Word, "Come, for all things are ready;" come, for "yet there is room."

THE END.

www.ingramcontent.com/pod-product-compliance
Lightning Source LLC
Chambersburg PA
CBHW030402230426
4364CB00007BB/711